THE ART OF COMPUTER CONVERSATION

A NEW MEDIUM FOR COMMUNICATION

BRIAN R. GAINES
MILDRED L. G. SHAW

Prentice/Hall PHI **International**

Englewood Cliffs, New Jersey   London   New Delhi   Rio de Janeiro
Singapore   Sydney   Tokyo   Toronto   Wellington

Library of Congress Cataloging in Publication Data

Gaines, Brian R.
  The art of computer conversation.
  Bibliography: p.
  Includes index.
  1. Interactive computer systems.   2. Micro-
computers.
  I. Shaw, Mildred L.G.   II. Title.
  QA76.9.158G35   1984   001.64'2   84-2163

  ISBN 0-13-047332-4 (pbk.)

British Library Cataloging in Publication Data
Gaines, Brian
  The art of computer conversation.
  1. Interactive computer systems   2. Man-
machine systems   3. Microprocessors
  I. Title   II. Shaw, Mildred
  001.64'04   QA76.9.I58

  ISBN 0-13-047332-4

ISBN 0-13-047332-4

PRENTICE-HALL INTERNATIONAL, INC., *London*
PRENTICE-HALL OF AUSTRALIA PTY., LTD., *Sydney*
PRENTICE-HALL CANADA, INC., *Toronto*
PRENTICE-HALL OF INDIA PRIVATE LIMITED, *New Delhi*
PRENTICE-HALL OF JAPAN, INC., *Tokyo*
PRENTICE-HALL OF SOUTHEAST ASIA PTE., LTD., *Singapore*
PRENTICE-HALL INC., *Englewood Cliffs, New Jersey*
PRENTICE-HALL DO BRASIL LTDA., *Rio de Janeiro*
WHITEHALL BOOKS LIMITED, *Wellington, New Zealand*

Phototypesetting by Parkway Group, London and Abingdon
Printed in the United States of America
10 9 8 7 6 5 4 3 2 1

Contents

Foreword — Computer Conversation

Conversing with computers is something we are all beginning to take for granted. We are expected to be **computer literate**. However, can we expect computers to be **people literate**? We can learn to understand them but we might also expect them, or at least those programming them, to learn to understand us.

Our own lives have been concerned with bridging the gap between people and computers. In the early 1960s when it began to be possible to have some direct interaction between people and computers we became involved in writing conversational programs. These were designed to administer psychological tests, collect market research data, enable a person to control a scientific instrument, teach students, and a variety of other tasks where people and computers might work closely together.

The limitations in those days were immense, although the work was so exciting that it took us some time to become aware of them. The only terminals we could use were designed originally as teleprinters and typed at ten characters a second in upper case only. The time-sharing services available were unreliable, slow and subject to long response times. We set up a program on one service that examined each character as it was typed and found that it took two seconds between our pressing a key and the character being typed on the terminal!

Those limitations lasted a long while. As late as 1977 we visited a major teaching hospital in London and found the same terminals in use on a system with even worse response time. The users had adapted to its slow responses so well that one of their problems was to detect when it had broken down. They would type for thirty seconds with no response before becoming suspicious that it was not just the normal delay but that there was never going to be a response.

Over the years we wrote many conversational systems for many different users, most of whom had never used a computer before. We made many mistakes and gradually developed styles of dialog that made life as easy as possible for the users. Without realizing it we were becoming skilled in persuading computers to be helpful, supportive, easy to get on with, and generally companionable. We did this because it made life easier for us if we did not have to spend time explaining the systems to users, helping them with problems and generally coping with unnecessary problems created by poor person–computer communication. We had found that good person–computer relations are good for business, but this was not the way we thought about it at the time.

On the other hand, we were also technicians, programmers developing software using the tools supplied with computers, and we became aware that helpful, supportive software systems were very rare. As technicians, and hence 'skilled' users, we were expected to cope with most unnatural dialog and remember all the inconsistent, illogical features of the systems we were using. These features varied from operating system to operating system, and from language to language, on the same machine. They even varied within the suite of programs that made up the operating system utilities and, more understandably, they varied even more perversely between different machines.

These technical quirks of software systems that had been developed at speed and with difficulty to support new machines were expected and reasonably acceptable to the comparatively small population of programmers in the 1960s. However, these programmers were also the people developing applications software for use by people who were not technicians and were only conversing with computers because they had to do so. Inevitably, the lack of attention to the user interface that was common in systems software became propagated to applications software. People programmed computer conversation in the styles to which they were accustomed.

In the 1970s we, and others, became more and more aware of what was happening and began to write about, and lecture on, techniques for designing effective person–computer conversation. At first it was a novel topic but towards the end of the 1970s it became accepted that the technology of the person–computer interface was very important and that this included dialog engineering. However, reading and listening were one thing—applying the techniques was another. As late as 1982 a doctoral student remarked at his examination that the problem was no longer one of establishing rules for good computer dialog, it was getting anyone to take any notice.

However, in the 1980s there has been a revolution in computing. The **personal computer** has taken the machines out of the grasp of computing centers, research laboratories, and data processing divisions, and put them into the hands of everyone. A high proportion of those who have written some of the best-selling software for personal computers never came through the old computing industry. They did not have experiences of a previous generation of systems to familiarize themselves into a state of acceptance of the early approaches to person–computer communication. They have taken machines that are totally under their control and programmed them to behave exactly as they wish. They have shown what can be done. They have done this in mass markets where it comes to the attention of many. More and more people are familiar with systems that have excellent person–computer interaction and can recognize that which is not of a high standard.

Even before personal computers became common, however, those in the computing industry were beginning to pay attention to human factors. Hardware technology has advanced to the state where most companies can make similar machines at similar costs. The software technologies for operating systems and languages have also become common. The techniques underlying most of the common applications programs are now widely known throughout the industry. The main marketing variations between companies had become their customer support, both directly at the person–computer interface, and indirectly through training and other services. However, training had become expensive in relation to other expenses as system costs declined and more and more people became computer users. Hence, improvements to the person–computer interface to maximize ease of use and minimize training were becoming commercially significant.

Despite the importance of these factors there is one overriding reason why the person–computer interface has become so important nowadays. It is the **mass market** for computer products. Small computers for correspondence and accounting have become routine office equipment and that is a large market in its own right. Very similar computers have become consumer products for use in the home for a wide range of purposes including playing games, self development and personal administration. The recession has encouraged many parents to attempt to provide some computer literacy for their children in order to give them more opportunities. There is a feeling that it is good to know something about computers, and the cost of having a personal computer has become sufficiently low to make this increasingly possible.

The move to a mass market for computer technology in the 1980s has been revolutionary for the computer industry. The previous generation of computer companies was geared to the supply of technical systems to specialists. The current generation is supplying consumer products to everyone. The basic technology has changed very little. Computers are much the same as they have always been. Cost, size, unreliability have all declined, but the way a computer works today is the same as it was twenty five years ago. However, the product is very different.

Consumer goods make very different demands on suppliers than specialist technical equipment does. There are now too many customers with too many different backgrounds for it to be possible to comprehend them all. They have a wealth of choice of personal computers and will buy those that gain a good reputation as easy to use, reliable, and good value for money. They will also buy those computer products that are attractively presented in a way that catches their attention. These customers cannot be reached through specialist publications but only through marketing in the mass media and in shopping centers.

It is this new world of computers for everyone that prompted us to write this book. There are good ways and poor ways of programming computer conversation. There is no difference in the cost of the product but there can be a wealth of difference in its effectiveness and acceptability. We have attempted to show these differences through examples and trace them back to a small number of simple rules for good person–computer communication. There is no one best way of programming computer conversation. There never will be a best way because applications differ and the technology is changing. What is best for an accounting system may not be best for a game. What is best for the technology of today will not be best for that of tomorrow. We have attempted to show this by examples of different styles of computer conversation involving differing technologies.

In writing this book we became aware that many people and many companies in many different places are all working with the common objective of improving person–computer conversation. There is much creative effort going into new approaches and the future looks very exciting indeed. We hope this book will make many more people aware of what is going on, and that they will become active participants in the taming of computer technology for the benefit of us all. As customers, designers and users of a mass-market consumer product we can all influence the computer systems of tomorrow.

Brian R. Gaines & Mildred L. G. Shaw, Toronto, 1983.

Preface

We are all users of computers. This book shows why some ways of interacting with the computer are much easier than others, for us as users. Most of us will sooner or later purchase a computer. This book is a guide to some of the points that make for good interaction between computer and user. Most of us will also purchase various forms of computer software. This book indicates how we may evaluate its ease of use quite separately from whether it can do the job that we want.

Programmers and system designers are responsible for the behavior of computer systems. This book gives them a repertoire of styles and techniques for computer dialog that will enable them to create effective systems for all types of user.

The Art of Computer Conversation applies both to low-cost home computers with cassette or disk, and to the more expensive business and scientific machines. Even the smallest hand-held machines can show the problems of interaction discussed here.

This book provides examples of good and bad dialog between computer and user. It discusses what makes one technique effective and another ineffective. It shows users how to evaluate systems and software. It gives programmers guidelines for simple, effective conversational styles.

Acknowledgements

We have drawn on many past discussions in writing this book and wish to note our gratitude to Mike Coombs, Walter Doherty, Chris Evans, Peter Facey, John Gedye, Larry Harris, David Hill, Tim Kennedy, Abe Mamdani, Martin Maguire, Cliff McKnight, Harold Thimbleby, Maureen Pope, John Sams, Max Sime, John Thomas, Ian Witten and Lotfi Zadeh. We owe special thanks to Ben Shneiderman, Chris Reynolds and Philip Barker, for their critical comments on this manuscript. We would also like to take this opportunity of thanking those many users over the years who have given us feedback on what the dialog actually feels like to them.

We wish to acknowledge permission to quote from the following works:-

p.21, Plato, **The Republic.** London: Penguin copyright (c) 1955. Reprinted by permission of Penguin Books Ltd.

p.21, Dostoyevsky, **Notes from Underground.** London: Penguin copyright (c) 1972. Reprinted by permission of Penguin Books Ltd.

p.21, Colin Wilson, **The New Literacy.** First appeared in **Science Digest** (c) 1983 by the Hearst Corporation.

pp.29, 31, 139, 141, R. Davis & D.B. Lenat, **Knowledge-Based Systems in Artificial Intelligence.** New York: McGraw-Hill, 1982.

p.43, Arthur C. Clarke, **2001: A Space Odyssey.** London: Hutchinson, 1968. Reprinted by permission of the author and the author's agents, Scott Meredith Literary Agency, Inc., 845 Third Avenue, New York, New York 10022.

p.45, K.Capek, **RUR.** London: Oxford University Press, 1923.

p.47, Poul Anderson, **Mirkheim.** London: Sphere Books Ltd., 1978.

p.49, Excerpts from **All the Troubles of the World** by Isaac Asimov, copyright (c) 1958 by Headline Publication Inc., Reprinted from **Nine Tomorrows** by Isaac Asimov by permission of Doubleday & Company, Inc.

p.49, Excerpts from **The Last Question** by Isaac Asimov, copyright (c) 1956 by Columbia Publications. Reprinted from **Nine Tomorrows** by Isaac Asimov by permission of Doubleday & Company, Inc.

p.51, Robert Heinlein, **The Moon is a Harsh Mistress.** London: Dennis Dobson, 1967.

p.125, W.J. Card et al, "A comparison of doctor and computer interrogation of patients." **Int. J. Bio-Med. Comput. 5,** (1974), pp.175-187.

pp.133, 135, T. Winograd, **Understanding Natural Language.** New York: Academic Press, 1972.

p.201, R. Davis in M. Sime & M.J. Coombs (Eds.) **Designing for Human-Computer Communication.** London: Academic Press, 1983.

We wish to acknowledge permission to reproduce the following figures:-
pp.13, 189 Context MBA screen, courtesy of Context Management Systems, 23864 Hawthorne Boulevard, Suite 101, Torrance, CA 90505.
pp.13, 137, 199 Intellect dialog and screens, courtesy of Artificial Intelligence Corp, 200 Fifth Avenue, Waltham, MA 22254.
p.23, Flight simulator screens, courtesy of Microsoft Corporation, 10700 Northup Way, Bellevue, WA 98004.
p.27, Executive Suite dialog, courtesy of Armonk Corp, 610 Newport Center Drive, Suite 955, Newport Beach, CA 92660.
p.37, Behaviordyne analysis, courtesy of Behaviordyne, Inc., 994, San Antonio Road, Palo Alto, CA94303, USA.
p.53, Chess robot photograph, courtesy of Efstonscience, Inc., 3350 Dufferin Street, Toronto, Ontario, Canada M6A 3A4.
pp.85, 87, 129, 131, 159, PLANET menus, manual and computer output courtesy of Centre for Person-Computer Studies, Post Office Box 150, Concord, Ontario, Canada L4K 1B2.
pp.111, 113, 115, Dynamic book, TRIP and Star screens, courtesy of Xerox Corporation.
p.117, Lisa Computer screen, courtesy of Apple Computer Inc.
p.151, Top thirty programs, from **Softalk** magazine courtesy of Softalk Publishing Inc., 11160, McCormick Street, North Hollywood, CA 91603.
p.157, Program packaging photograph, courtesy of Communications Packaging Corporation, 2635 South Santa Fe Drive, Denver, CO 80223.
p.161, Lotus 1-2-3 screens, 1-2-3 is a trademark of Lotus Development Corporation, Cambridge, Massachusetts. The screen photos from Lotus-created materials included in this book are copyright (c) 1983 by Lotus Development Corporation and used here with permission.
p.189, Transcend screen, courtesy of SSM Microcomputer Products, 2190 Paragon Drive, San Jose, CA 95131.
p.191, DesQ screen, courtesy of Quarterdeck Office Systems, 1918 Main Street, Suite 240, Santa Monica, CA 90405.
p.197, Ask dialog, courtesy of Frederick B. Thompson and Bozena Henisz Thompson, California Institute of Technology, Pasadena, California.

THE ART OF COMPUTER CONVERSATION
A NEW MEDIUM FOR COMMUNICATION

Dr Mildred L.G. Shaw,
Department of Computer Science,
York University,
4700 Keele Street,
Downsview,
Ontario, M3J 1P3.

Dear Dr Mildred L.G. Shaw,

You, Mildred L.G., have been chosen to receive our **opportunity of the year** garden offer. Look out of Department of Computer Science at your beautiful town, York University, 4700 Keele Street, Downsview, Ontario M3J 1P3, and see the flowers blooming. We have selected your garden, Mildred L.G., to outshine all others in your town of York University, 4700 Keele Street, Downsview, Ontario M3J 1P3, because our research has shown that you will appreciate the quality of this offer.

Your civic pride, Mildred L.G., in your township of York University, 4700 Keele Street, Downsview, Ontario M3J 1P3, cannot let you pass by the opportunity to be the recipient of our free BOWL OF GLORIOUS FRAGRANT TULIPS which come **free of charge** if you purchase our **computer controlled** ROTATING LAWN SPRINKLER.

Yes, we have already approved credit for you, Mildred L.G., so if you Mildred L.G. return the enclosed card within 5 days we will send you Mildred L.G. free to Department of Computer Science our special BOWL OF GLORIOUS FRAGRANT TULIPS especially designed to enhance your garden in York University, 4700 Keele Street, Downsview, Ontario M3J 1P3. So hurry, Mildred L.G., for this **opportunity of the year!**

Yours sincerely,
Flora L. Tribute,
GARDENERS PARADISE, Inc.

P.S. If you already have our **computer controlled** ROTATING LAWN SPRINKLER, please pass the card on to a friend or neighbor in your town of York University, 4700 Keele Street, Downsview, Ontario M3J 1P3.

An over—personalized computer letter

1 **Personal Computer Conversation**

Since the 1950s **computers** have become part of our everyday life. Until recently they were remote. We received utility bills, bank statements, even apparently personal letters, that were obviously produced by computers. The example on the page opposite illustrates some familiar reasons why the computer involvement may be 'obvious.' However, few of us ever saw the machines that produced such documents. They were locked away in gleaming rooms like a hospital operating theater or the bridge of a space ship, and only a few white-coated technicians were allowed through multiple security barriers to be close to the computers themselves.

Computers move closer to us

In the past five years computers have moved closer to us. You visit a friend in her office and she has a screen on her desk with a keyboard in front of it - "my new word processor," she says. You go to your bank to find out why your account is overdrawn and the teller has a similar screen - "my terminal to the bank's computer," he says. You go visit a friend in hospital and she has a similar terminal by her bed - "they look at my charts on that," she says. In the evening booking some concert tickets you notice the same type of display on the cashier's desk with a diagram of the seating shown on it. On parents' day at your son's school there are six screens and keyboards in his classroom - "we get some geography and music on those," he says. At home you have one that was bought to play Space Invaders but you found recently that it will also keep your recipes and personal accounts. On a flight to Denver the man next to you places something very similar on his lap and starts typing on the keyboard - "latest battery-operated model," he says smugly, "tells me where I'm going and why."

Perhaps you know the computer in only one of these guises. Perhaps you have been involved in several situations like those above but never thought of them as similar. Word processors, computer terminals and electronic games seem quite different. However, they are all part of the same revolution in information technology. They are all examples of direct interaction between people and computers. In the past few years the computer has come out of its remote clinical closet, either completely, or through an extension of itself. It is now accessible to the person, any person not just the technicians and specialists. **Personal computing** is a new phenomenon and one that is very important to all of us and will increasingly affect our lives. Whether the effects are beneficial, pleasant and enjoyable, or not, is something in which we all have an interest and over which we all will have some influence.

Problems in conversing with the personal computer

There are many enthusiasts for the computer and many more for the personal computer. We can produce letters on the word processor that are free from corrections. We can see the present state of our bank balance on the teller's terminal and all the transactions that led to its being overdrawn. We can even do this on a personal computer used as a terminal through a telephone line from our own home. The hospital charts are up to date and available by the bedside, in the operating theater or to the physician in his consulting rooms many miles away. The concert hall staff no longer fumble through packets of tickets to find you a row of four empty seats. Geography has become fun at school because it is taught through a game that captures your son's imagination, moves at his own pace rather than that of the class, and adjusts its teaching to his personal understanding. In the home you have a new entertainment medium as well as a personal assistant that remembers recipes and appointments and a personal accountant who is patient and regards nothing as trivial. Moreover personal computers are becoming cheaper, more powerful and smaller so that they are proliferating and constantly involving themselves in our lives.

However, new things create new problems. You sit down at your colleague's word processor and start to type on the keyboard. Nothing happens. "Oh," she says, "you didn't press the **insert** key." In the evening you use a word processing package on your

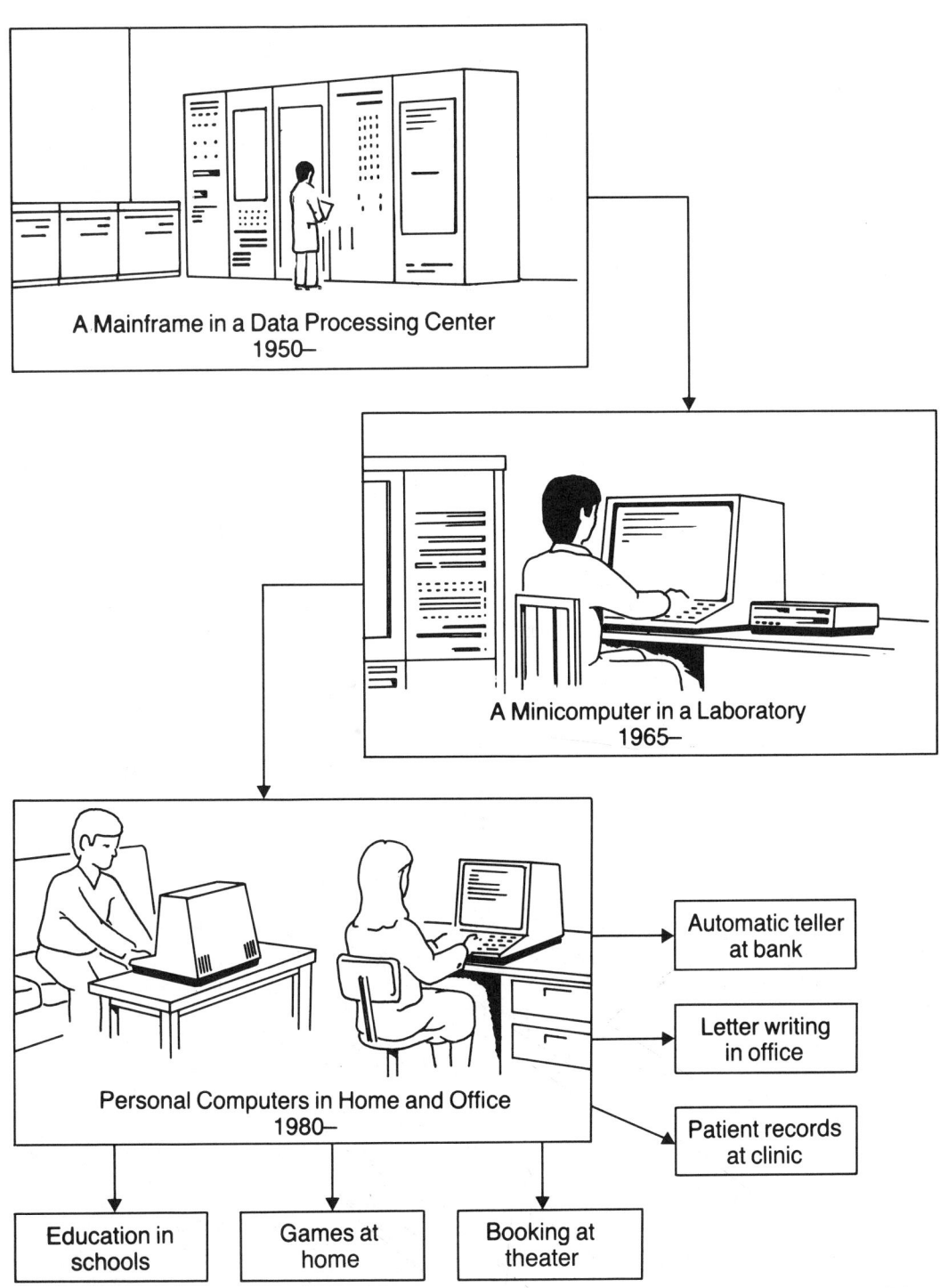

A Mainframe in a Data Processing Center
1950–

A Minicomputer in a Laboratory
1965–

Personal Computers in Home and Office
1980–

Automatic teller at bank

Letter writing in office

Patient records at clinic

Education in schools

Games at home

Booking at theater

The transitions to personal computers

home computer. There is no **insert** key. The manual is missing and when you eventually trace it you find that you can type right away. It is only when you want to file letters on the disk that you need to press a special combination of keys. By the time you realize this you have **exited** from the word processor and lost the contents of the letter you typed in. A friend, when you are talking about this remarks, "On my computer you type a question mark when you don't know what to do and it lists the possibilities on the screen." Another friend remarks, "Yes my computer does that but you type **HELP** not a question mark." This seems like a good idea and you try both of them on your word processor but it only responds **COMMAND ERROR.**

The problems are many. Sometimes you get your computer into a state where it will do nothing at all no matter what keys you press. Your friend's computer has a key marked **RESET** that he presses in these circumstances. "But," he confides in you, "sometimes it starts the program again, sometimes it stops it and you have to restart it, and once it destroyed all the information I had stored on my disk." The clerk at the hospital says his terminal is stupid, "it asks for their date of birth and then for their age - thought these things were clever. Very moody as well," he says, "sometimes comes back with more questions bright and chirpy, and other times sits and thinks a long time before asking you any more." Your new terminal at work is quite useful but confusing at times. What everyone in the office calls the day's total it calls the **customer account balance,** which isn't too bad but then it also prints out **the day's total** which is actually the cash register total. You just have to make sure that you cross out the words each day and write in the correct ones.

Even amongst themselves computers cannot agree on the same terminology. Different computers use the same words for different things, and different words for the same thing. Even on the same machine the **Disk Operating System (DOS)** has one command to list the files on the disk, while **BASIC** has an entirely different one and the **Assembler** has a similar one to this but requires a semicolon rather than a comma. Even if you are expert enough to use all these facilities you find yourself quietly going mad trying to change your interpretation and actions according to the quirks of each package on the machine. There appear to be no industry standards in terminology and use of language. Perhaps someone who has a Chinese butcher, a French dressmaker and an Ethiopean barber has similar problems. Maybe even they would lose their cool if the butcher required Mandarin to be used when ordering beef and Cantonese for lamb. Such seems to be the world of the computer.

Trying to start a conversation

The art of conversation is not dead

It is common nowadays to speak of **conversations** with computers. Personal computing is **conversational, interactive** and, above all, **personal.** We are prepared to treat the computer as if it were another person. But what a person - querulous, demanding, with its own peculiar vocabulary, and deliberately not understanding ours that we have used for years. If these computers were people would you really want them in your home, or as colleagues in your office? Yet, should we blame the computer? It is nothing but a heap of electronic and mechanical gadgetry. The behavior that it exhibits when we do treat it as another person and enter into a conversation with it is not part of its circuits or fundamentals of operation. It arises through the style of **programming** that has been used to impose this behavior on the general purpose electronic system that is a computer.

When our home computer plays Backgammon with us it is warm and friendly, understanding and easily understood. When we use it to do our personal budget it has less personality but is simple to use. When we use it to store our recipes we have to go through a lot of superstitious rigmarole to get started but after that it is okay and rarely loses anything. When we attempt to use it as a terminal to our bank, however, it gets really quirky and quite rude at times, telling us **unauthorized code, retype amount in correct format,** and we still haven't found out how to get off again except by putting the phone down. Yet this is the same personal computer, but running different programs. So perhaps it is the programmer we should blame. Perhaps our conversations are really with the programmer rather than the computer. And perhaps that explains the problems. "Yes, I remember the programmers," says the girl at the bank. "Came in and told us we were doing it wrong. Never saw them again."

Your conversations with the computer have to be programmed just like its calculations. However, until personal computing came along these conversations were only with technical staff, often themselves programmers. The arts of conversation, of making oneself clear to the other person, of using a terminology he will understand, of expressing information in alternative ways, of interpreting what the other person says, all these were unnecessary in the highly technical worlds of the early computers. In any event computers were then very expensive and godlike creatures with whom it was appropriate for their servants to converse in a formal and stylized fashion. The Courts of Kings and Emperors have always been so. The art of conversation with computers did not die. It has not yet developed.

The way computer conversation might have gone

The art of computer dialog

This book is concerned with promoting simple and effective conversational styles for personal computing. Most of the problems highlighted above can be avoided by following a few basic guidelines. Much of what is required is cosmetic in nature and follows from commonsense. The problem for most of us is that the commonsense of our everyday conversations with other people has become habitual and ingrained from childhood. We cannot make effective use of it in an entirely new context because we are not aware of it. We are even unaware of ourselves making use of it. Once we start thinking of computer dialog as analogous to people dialog, then the basic rules become obvious and easily remembered.

A substantial part of the book is concerned with bringing out these rules and showing how they actually apply to computer conversations. We illustrate them through examples of inadequate dialog as well as through those we regard as good. We state them in the time-honored form of the best commonsense, as **proverbs**, to be treated as useful sayings rather than inviolable rules. This would be a very colorless world with little capability of adaptation and innovation if we all followed our commonsense rigidly all of the time. Rules are made to be broken, but consciously and for a purpose, not because we are completely unaware of them.

When the basic guidelines are followed then deeper problems appear which are, in some sense, really there. They are no longer problems created by our carelessness in communicating but instead are part of what we are trying to achieve through the communication. For example, you delete a file from your disk quite deliberately and knowingly. It is not an accident arising from ambiguous commands or typing errors. Then later you wish you had not done so and want to get it back again. This is still a problem of interaction between people and computers but no longer one of the simple rules of conversation. However, similar situations arise in everyday life - you say something hurtful to a colleague and realize that you can never unsay it - the harm is done.

People have social mechanisms to avoid situations which cause unnecessary hurt and offense. For computer systems there are also guidelines that apply to the deeper problems, to the tolerance of errors, to the freedom to change one's mind, and to other modes of interaction that are necessary if life is not to become too serious and restrictive. Again we illustrate them through examples and state them through proverbs.

Learning conversational style

Aims of the book

We aim through this book to make purchasers of computer systems and programs more aware of good conversational style and the problems that arise when it is neglected. Many potentially worthwhile computer programs are ineffective in use through their inadequate interaction with the user. Often the usefulness of the data processing carried out by a program is very obvious and it sells itself, whereas the unsatisfactory human interface is not apparent until it has been in use for a while. We are very ready to assume that we need training to use a computer system and that our initial fumbling is due to our own inexperience. It is only after some time that we have the experience and confidence to say, "no, the fault is in the system not in me."

However, the user interface can be assessed together with the data processing at the time of purchase, and the criticisms of inadequate conversational interaction can be made then - with assurance, if one has some good examples to draw upon. If we have the choice then we can choose a system that is pleasant to use. If we have no choice and must, for the sake of its data processing, use a system that places an unnecessary burden upon us, then we know in advance what problems to expect.

We aim through this book to make specifiers of computer systems and programs aware of the need to devote as much effort to the human interface as they do to the data processing and storage algorithms. Computer dialog is as much part of computer science and technology as are arithmetic algorithms, operating system processes and database structures. **Dialog engineering** is a new technology at the heart of personal computing and interacts strongly with all the other computing technologies. The acquisition and presentation of numerical data, the capability of the operating system to be presented and controlled simply and logically, the capability of the database to accept information in a form natural to people without distortion - all of these involve the psychology of people as much as they do the technology of the computer.

We have tended to neglect such **human factors** in the design of computer systems because the behavior of people seems less lawlike and amenable to understanding and design than that of computers. What we cannot do we pretend does not exist. Because we no longer see it we stop trying to improve it. However, our increasing knowledge of psychology suggests that the natural system of man is subject to classification and comprehension just as is the artificial system of computing, and we can design effective people-computer systems - as we shall show.

```
COMMAND:PRS
PRS:?
   ENTER, DELETE, MODIFY, LIST, RETRIEVE
PRS:E
   Personnel Record Entry Number 45
LAST NAME:Cooper
FIRST NAME(S):Percival Edward
SIN:?
   P.E.Cooper's Social Insurance Number, six digits
SIN:305672
DATE OF BIRTH::
COMMAND:
```

Formal conversation with Personnel Records System

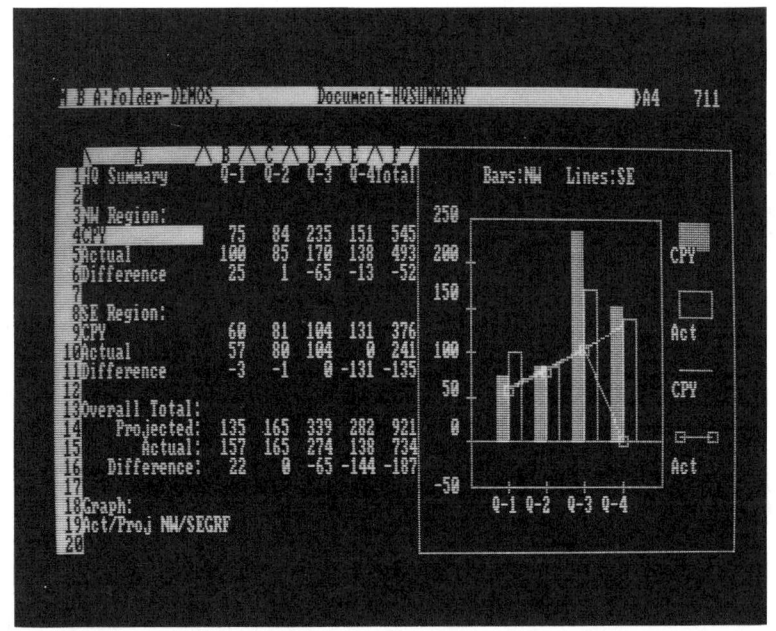

Graphic conversation with Context Management Systems MBA

Is there a McKinsey working here?
I'M NOT FAMILIAR WITH THE WORD "MCKINSEY"
IF IT'S A WORD YOU EXPECT TO FIND IN THE DATABASE HIT THE RETURN KEY
OTHERWISE EITHER FIX ITS SPELLING OR ENTER A SYNONYM FOR IT.
show all names from McK to McL.
I'M INTERPRETING YOUR LAST RESPONSE AS A NEW REQUEST.
PRINT THE NAME OF ALL EMPLOYEES WITH NAME BETWEEN MCK AND MCL.
   MCKLOSKY
   MCKENZIE
   MCKAY

**Natural language conversation with a database through
Artificial Intelligence Corporation's Intellect**

Different styles of computer conversation -- user input in bold

We aim through this book to give programmers a repertoire of styles and techniques for computer dialog that will enable them to create effective systems for a wide range of situations. A conversational style appropriate to the casual user of a computer system may seem very verbose and tediously supportive to the professional user making everyday routine use of that system. However, even computer professionals are casual users of computer systems much of the time. All of us move from system to system, program to program, as our requirements change and as the technology itself develops. This movement between systems and experience of a variety of computers and dialog styles will become more and more the experience of much of the population. How do we cope with it as users and how do we aid such coping as system designers?

How do we design a dialog for a system that will support the casual user who comes to it knowing nothing of computer conversation? How do we design a dialog for the same system geared up to the needs of a continuous, routine user who has become highly skilled and for whom speed is the essence? How do we design a dialog for the new user of a system who has transferred from another system and is confused by the changes? How do we switch between these styles when all three categories of user, and others, are potentially there sitting in front of a screen and expecting the system to cope with their widely differing needs? Structuring such conversations with computers to be transparently effective requires new professionalism in dialog design. We do not pretend that this book has all the answers - or even all the questions. However, the programmer - and that increasingly means all of us - should find it a useful guide to a new technology, that underlying the art of computer dialog.

Conclusions - Personal Computer Conversation

At the end of each chapter we summarize the main points developed, whenever possible in the form of **proverbs** that are useful aids to memory even if they do not include everything that might be said. We have found these to provide a useful checklist of points to be covered when we are designing or evaluating computer systems.

The first proverb - WE ARE RESPONSIBLE

If any conclusion can be drawn from this chapter then it must be that in computer systems we have created a new technology that interacts with us personally at a higher level than any previous technology. This interaction is analogous to conversation with people and we naturally see computer behavior in the same terms as human behavior. However, computers and all aspects of their programming are a man-made technology and we are all responsible for the "behavior" exhibited, whether we specify it, program it, or, as users, fail to criticize it.

Proverb 1: We are all responsible for computer behavior.

> Remember when you treat computer-people interaction as if it were people-people interaction that the computer is behaving as it was programmed to. We, as specifiers, programmers and users, are all responsible for the behavior of computer systems.

Proverbs always tend to overstate their case and hence the opposite of a good proverb is often one also. Too many cooks spoil the broth, but many hands make light work. When we emphasize our responsibility for computer systems we draw attention away from one of their most fascinating features discussed in later chapters - computer systems do seem to have autonomy and their own personalities. So treat the proverbs as pointers to significant features of computer systems, making an important point easily remembered through exaggeration.

The second proverb - CHOOSE THROUGH EXPERIENCE

In performing the investigations that precede dialog design or computer system selection it is easy to forget how little idea potential users have of the conversational use of computers if they have never experienced it. Our second proverb is a reminder that words may be meaningless without experience and can never completely replace it.

Proverb 2: Choose through experience.

> Conversational systems should be experienced before they are talked about. Prospective users should experience interaction with a related system before specifying their requirements for their own system.

This second proverb highlights a major pitfall into which we all occasionally fall by assuming that what we personally know and have experienced is **obvious** to others. For example, we cannot understand the speech of someone with a strong dialect and cannot understand how others can do so. Suddenly it becomes clear and we are able to comprehend every word. We are then surprised when others have the same problem in understanding what is, for us, now very clear. We have always to remember the need for experience and learning on the part of others before we can have a meaningful discussion with them about things they have never previously encountered.

When interactive systems first began to come into widespread use some fifteen years ago this was a real problem. Few people then had personal experience of conversation with computers and it was not readily available. Those designing systems, who usually had such experience, would often discuss possible dialog designs with intended users without realizing how meaningless was the discussion. Nowadays the widespread use of computers, their open availability in high-street stores and the presentation of tutorial material in schools and in the media has made computer experience far more widely available. However, the trap still remains in a more subtle form of discussing one style of conversational interaction with users who are familiar with another and do not realize that radically different styles are possible.

We have put this proverb at the end of the first chapter because there is a message in it for both you as reader and us as authors. We are discussing topics that will be meaningless unless you have first-hand experience of them. Our discussion of dialog design in later chapters is based around examples and they are all real ones drawn from existing programs or literature. Wherever possible we have used commercially available programs as examples and given their names so that you can use them. Many of you will recognize our examples from your own experience. However, few people will have had the opportunity to sit down and interact with all the systems we describe and experience the wide variety of conversational styles possible.

In a book we write about things which we would far prefer to show in action. One day, perhaps soon, this book will be supplemented by conversational programs covering the same ground. Until then we can only ask you to go out and "feel it as it is" if you want to make best use of this book.

2 Conversation Through Computer Media

It is common to talk of **conversational** interaction with a personal computer. In the previous chapter we used this terminology very freely and suggested that the computer was similar to a person and that when conversing with the computer we are really conversing with its programmer. Before going into more detail about styles of computer dialog it is worthwhile examining the analogy between computer conversations and people conversations in more detail. If it is just a vague metaphor then it may be misleading and it would be better to discard it before proceeding to examine techniques. However, we will show that there is something worthwhile and very significant in the analogy - that personal computing provides a **new medium** for the expression of human conversation, just as the development of writing, printing and television did in the past.

This statement that we have a new communications medium available to us has consequences that go beyond the scope of this book which is to promote effective computer dialog. Other media developments have played major roles in the growth of culture and so too will personal computing. Viewing computers as providing a new communications medium also helps to explain some of the phenomena associated with personal computing, for example that programs are being marketed using the same techniques that have been effective for program material in previous media such as books and records. However, for the purposes of this book it is the role of personal computing in the development of the art of human conversation with which we are most concerned. How does it fit in with previous developments? If we can answer this then we can learn from the problems with past media and the techniques adopted for the solution of these problems.

Conversation, culture and the computer

From an early age we talk to one another. Conversation is a natural activity to us in our everyday lives. What is it? Not just communication because that may be in one direction only. Conversation is **interactive communication** that is two-way or many-way. In this sense all animals have some form of conversation. Some, such as territorial and courtship rites, can be very elaborate. However, the human race has developed the art of conversation to its highest level, employing a range of symbols and forms of expression to pass feelings, information, knowledge and skills between people. Conversation has been, and still is, of major importance in the development of human culture and civilization. Many of our tools and much of our technology have been developed solely to enhance our capabilities to carry on conversations.

Conversation is at the heart of human culture. Human beings are already remarkable for their immense capability to learn from experience. We are able to adapt to a range of climates, environments and societies as no other animal species can. Learning and adaptation are ever-present activities of people which, like breathing, happen without conscious volition or awareness. However, the advantages of our learning capabilities are amplified immensely by our ability to receive and impart information through conversation. We are a species where individuals learn not just from their own experience but from that of others imparted through conversation. The child in the jungle need not feel the injury of being mauled by a tiger in order to learn to fear the animal. Instead he can be **told** that the animal is dangerous and he should take care to avoid it. He can also be told how to look out for the signs of new dangers.

This capability of learning indirectly from conversations rather than direct experience - and of learning how to learn by discussing learning itself - has formed the basis for the development of our civilization. To take advantage of it we have developed mechanisms that enable us to communicate over time and over distance: the letter, the newspaper, the book, the radio, the telephone, the television, the record, the tape. The remarkable nature of television can be seen from its ability to bring those far away into personal contact with events as they happen. Videotapes extend that ability across time as well as space. This transcendence of time and space adds new dimensions to the already dramatic powers of the human capabilities to learn from experience and to learn from conversation. New media provide new extensions to ourselves and affect our, and our societies', modes of existence.

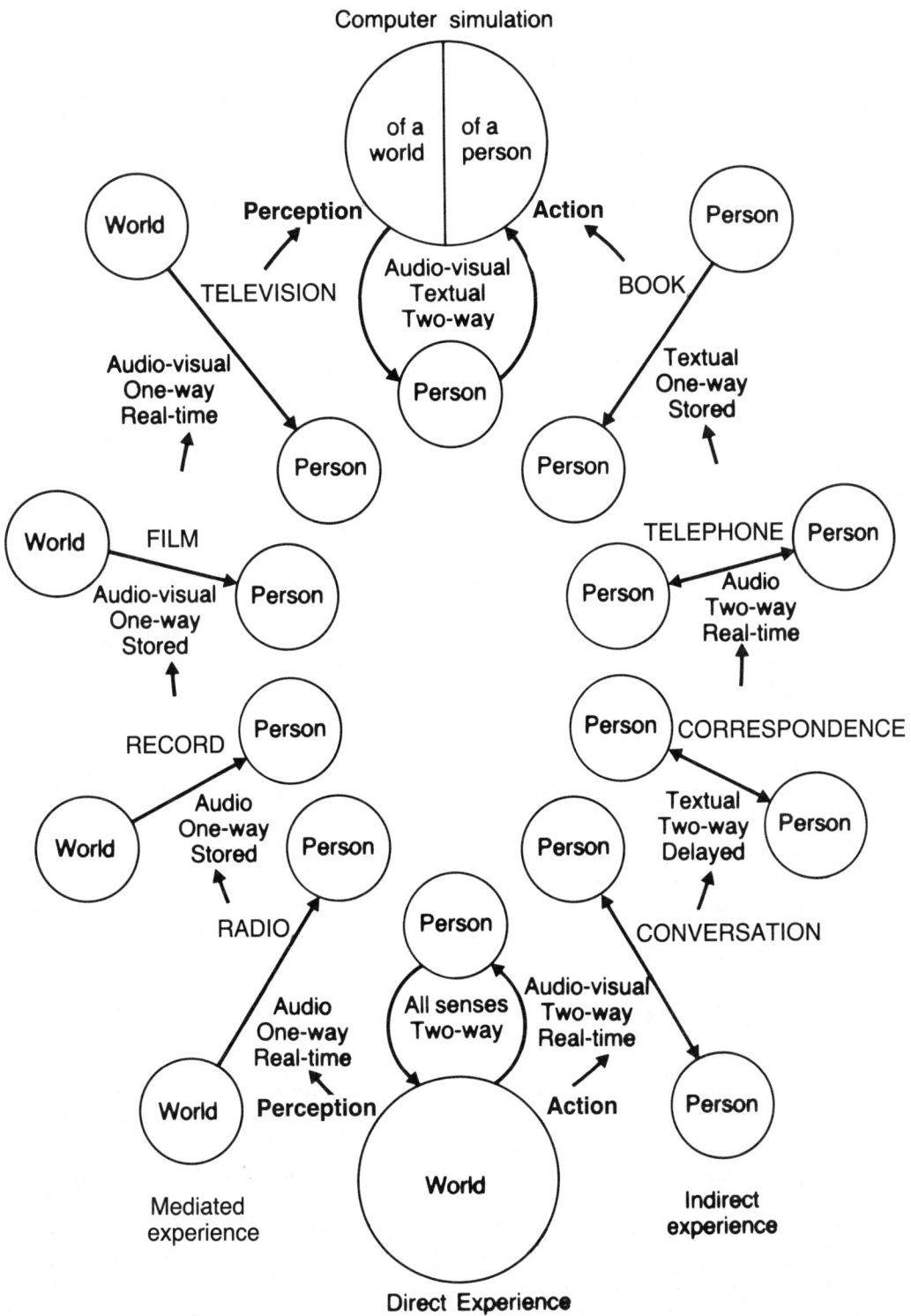

The development of indirect and mediated experience

The remarkable nature of books can be seen from their ability to allow those long dead to impart their feelings and knowledge to those alive now and in the future. We may think of books as merely text carried on paper. Yet the living, active force that is within books is evident from societies that have found it necessary to burn some books to avoid their affecting the thoughts and actions of members of those societies. The Chinese emperor, Chin Shih Huang Ti, in 213 BC attempted to destroy all books but failed. A similar massive destruction of past literature was a key component of the French Revolution. Even today, various of our societies ban certain books because they are heretical, politically unacceptable or pornographic.

All powerful media are perceived as both forces for good and evil. When we hear the arguments about the corruption of youth by the television of today it gives us a useful perspective to read on the opposite page Plato's diatribe of over 2,000 years ago against the corrupting influence of poetry. Our cultural norms may change. Our media may change. But our concern about the influence of new media on our culture is unchanging.

In the second quotation Dostoyevsky's underground man captures through exaggeration our dependence on books for our knowledge, skills and values. However, such warnings of the dangers of the influences which media exert on us are just the counter-balance to the welcome that we give to them as new tools and means of expression. The final quotation is a very much more recent comment on the role of computers in providing a new dimension of **literacy**. Colin Wilson's enthusiasm can itself be counter-balanced by quotations from those who see dangers in our societies' increasing dependence on computers. What we are more concerned to examine in this book is the way in which the medium offered by computers **differs** from those previously available.

Programs generate two-way conversations

Both books and television are primarily one-way media. They are not able to support two-way conversations. They do not allow us to interact with the author of the book or with the events being portrayed. We can think of correspondence through letters as being a conversational form of a book. We can think of discussion on a telephone or videophone as being a conversational form of radio or television. Now computers have been added to this range of mechanisms for extending human conversations. They are remarkable in enabling us to interact with a program in a similar way to that in which we interact with a person. They are remarkable in enabling us to encode the expertise of a person.

Poetry, dramatic poetry in particular, has a bad moral effect on its audiences, who learn to admire and imitate the faults it represents. We cannot, therefore, allow poetry in our ideal state.

"The gravest charge against poetry still remains. It has a terrible power to corrupt even the best characters, with very few exceptions."

"It is indeed terrible if it can do that."

"Then listen. When we hear Homer or one of the tragic poets representing the sufferings of a great man and making him bewail at length with every expression of tragic grief, you know how even the best of us enjoy it and let ourselves be carried away by our feelings; and are full of praises for the merits of the poet who can most powerfully affect us in this way."

"Yes, I know."

"Yet in our private griefs we pride ourselves on just the opposite, that is, on our ability to bear them in silence like men, and we regard the behaviour we admired on the stage as womanish."

"Yes, I'm aware of that."

"Then is it really right," I asked, "to admire, when we see him on the stage, a man we should ourselves be ashamed to resemble? Is it reasonable to feel enjoyment and admiration rather than disgust?"

Plato in **The Republic**

Leave us to ourselves, without our books, and at once we get into a muddle and lose our way -- we don't know what side to be on or where to give our allegiance, what to love and what to hate, what to respect and what to despise. We even find it difficult to be human beings, men with real flesh and blood of our own; we are ashamed of it, we think of it as a disgrace, and are always striving to be some unprecedented kind of generalized human being. We are born dead, and moreover we have long ceased to be the sons of living fathers; and we become more and more contented with our condition. We are acquiring the taste for it. Soon we shall invent a method of being born from an idea.

Fyodor M. Dostoyevsky in **Notes from Underground**

Surely the notion that computers mean the death of literacy is preposterous. Computers are a tool, like all the other tools that man has created in the astonishingly brief history of his civilization. The most important discovery he has made in the past 3,000 years is that he is able to retreat inside his own head and stage dramas in the proscenium arch of his imagination. It was only recently -- in the mid-eighteenth century -- that he took his most enormous step forward by inventing the novel. This opened up completely new possibilities of imagination and probably turned European man into a race of daydreamers. It is not surprising that the invention of the novel was followed almost immediately by the Age of Romanticism.

Now **nothing** is going to keep man from continuing that exploration of his inner being that he has been carrying on since Homer wrote the **Iliad**. (Julian Jaynes, famous for his writings on right-brain, left-brain function, argues very convincingly that up to a couple of centuries before Homer, man didn't **know** that he had an inner world.) Man is always taking interesting steps forward, discovering how to gain "access to inner worlds." More and more, he is beginning to treat the conveniences of modern civilization as a means to that end. Computers, like the electric typewriter on which this letter is written, are merely a means of making it easier for us to explore our inner mysteries by giving them expression in words.

Colin Wilson in **Science Digest**

Some opinions about media

We can think of computer programs as being a way of extending **interaction** through time and space. When I listen to a record I can imagine I am at a concert hearing the artist perform. When I read a book I can imagine that I am hearing the words spoken to me by the original author. If it is a narrative then I can imagine the author playing the part of the character telling the story. Similarly, when I enter into a dialog with a computer program I can imagine that I am interacting with the programmer who wrote it, perhaps playing some role. Unlike the performer or the author, the programmer is able to provide responses to my interventions - in some way to **interact** with me although he may be far distant or dead.

With computers we can record and disseminate not just a passive encoding of information to be replayed but rather an **active process** with which the recipient can interact. For example, we can program a model of a chemical system so that someone without access to the materials and equipment required to create it can still experiment with that system. We do not tell them about it, describing our experiences, but rather pass it to them in such a way that they can generate their own experience. They make their own decisions about what to do with the equipment and materials, and the model replicates what would have happened had they done this with the actual process.

The **simulation** of chemical systems in this way is already an important application of computers in industrial manufacturing where it is used to plan and design control systems for chemical plants. It is also used educationally in schools and colleges to make simulations of dangerous or expensive systems available for student experiments in complete safety and at low cost. Whether simulation is adequate to replace actual experience is not an absolute question but depends on the quality of the simulation and the function of the experience.

Much flight training now is done primarily through very elaborate simulators that reproduce the experience of controlling a real aircraft. This is not always welcome. We once had the experience of working on new forms of simulator for a national airforce and suddenly finding that we were no longer invited to policy meetings. Only years later was it explained to us that the work had been acceptable provided it was remote from reality. It demonstrated to politicians that the airforce was concerned to develop simulators. However, when we appeared likely to be able to improve the capability of simulators to give useful training the work was suddenly perceived as seditious - the airforce did not want its airplanes replaced by simulators - flying for real was the pride and joy of those who became part of that body!

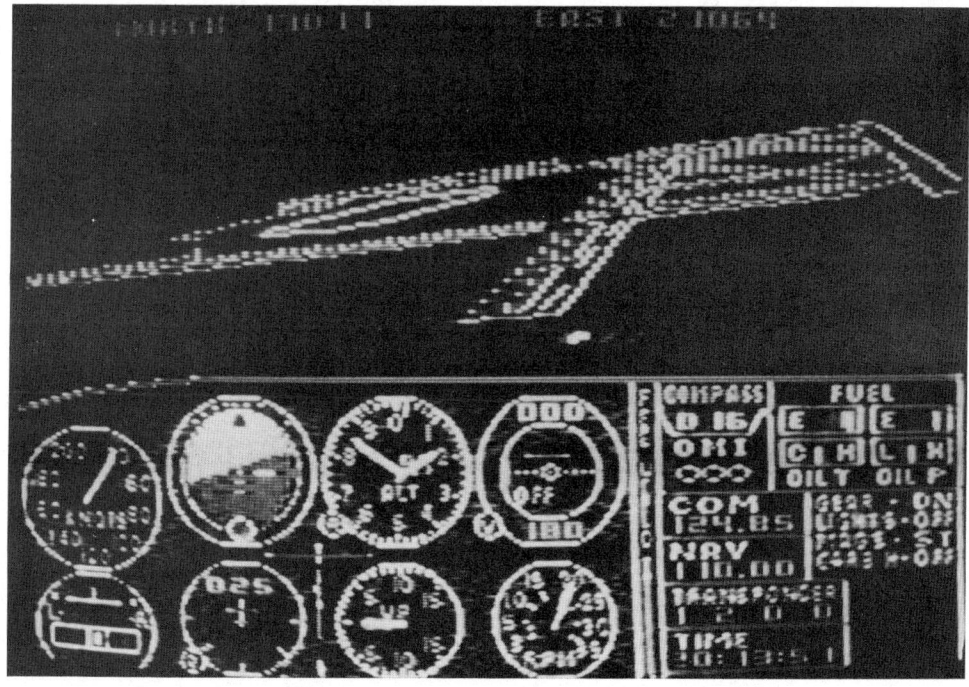

Interacting with the Microsoft flight simulator on the IBM PC

Whether the interaction with a computer program is a realistic experience of interaction with the programmer is also a question of the quality of the simulation. Of course the programmer may not be attempting to simulate interaction with himself, but rather with another person or a physical system. However, it seems likely that some aspect of his own personality will always intrude.

Adventure games as simulations of life

Simulation of an interesting and exciting real-world or fantasy environment is the basis of many of the games now played on computer systems in the home. You are a fighter pilot in a world of enemy aircraft and must fight aerial battles using skill in control of craft and weapons. You have free access to an elaborate pinball machine with a wide range of exotic features of varying difficulty. You are an athlete attempting various feats of skill and endurance. You are coach for a football team and must define its strategy - if you stick to the same winning strategy too long then your opponents will acquire a defense to it. You are a businessman setting up a company in a world with certain raw materials, manufacturing processes and a population with defined, but unknown, comsumption patterns. The more elaborate **adventure** games simulate a world populated by magic objects and people and involve undertaking long complex tasks.

The computer conversation opposite is between a human player of one of these games and a computer program acting as gamesmaster. Note the attempt to establish a warm and friendly relationship right from the start. The programmer wants the player to feel that he is interacting with a friend who will support him in playing the game. Note also the fairly elaborate descriptions of the surroundings and scenery. Just like the words of a novel evoke awareness of a world that is in the mind of the author but also partially created by the reader, so do the scripts of adventure games attempt to evoke a feeling of "being there."

The data processing underlying the game is fairly simple but adequate to allow the response, "You are already carrying it!", when the player attempts to pick up the water twice. The bird at the end was frightened of the rod and could not be caged while the player was holding it. Neither could it have been taken if he had not collected the cage earlier. The player's commands are in ordinary language, but as the instructions state, only the first few letters of each of up to two words are being used so that the program's "understanding" is primitive - but adequate for the purpose.

```
Welcome to Adventure!!  Would you like instructions?
YES
Somewhere nearby is Colossal Cave, where others have found fortunes in
treasure and gold.  I will be your eyes and hands.  Direct me with commands
of 1 or 2 words.  I look at only the first four letters of each word -- enter
"NORTHEAST" as "NE" to distinguish it from "NORTH".

You are standing at the end of a road before a small brick building.  Around
you is a forest.  A small stream flows down a gully.
ENTER BUILDING
You are inside a building, a well house for a large spring.  There are some
keys on the ground here.  There is a shiny brass lamp nearby.  There is a
bottle of water here.
GET WATER
Okay
GET KEYS
Okay
GET LAMP
Okay
GET WATER
You are already carrying it!
GO GULLY
You are in a valley in the forest beside a stream tumbling along a rocky bed.
S
At your feet all the water of the stream splashes into a 2-inch slit in the
rock.  Downstream the stream bed is bare rock.
S
You are in a 20-foot depression floored with bare dirt.  Set into the dirt is
a strong steel grate mounted in concrete.  A dry streambed leads into the
depression.  The grate is locked.
UNLOCK GRATE
The grate is now unlocked.
GO IN
You are in a small chamber beneath a 3x3 steel grate to the surface.  A low
crawl over cobbles leads inward to the west.  The grate is open.
W
You are crawling over cobbles in a low passage.  There is a dim light at the
east end of the passage.  There is a small wicker cage nearby.
GET CAGE
Okay
W
It is now pitch dark.  If you proceed you will likely fall into a pit.
LIGHT LAMP
Your lamp is now on.  You are in a debris room filled with stuff washed in
from the surface.  A low wide passage with cobbled becomes plugged with mud
and debris here, but an awkward canyon leads upward and west.  A three foot
black rod with a rusty star on the end lies nearby.
GET ROD
Okay
W
You are in a splendid chamber thirty feet high.  An awkward canyon and a good
passage exit from east and west sides of the chamber.  A cheerful little bird
is sitting here singing.
GET BIRD
The bird was unafraid when you entered, but as you approach it becomes
disturbed and you cannot catch it.
DROP ROD
Okay
GET BIRD
Okay
```

Some interaction with an Adventure game

During recent years such games have become increasingly
elaborate, involving whole worlds of activity on land, sea and
air. They have also made more and more use of the rapidly
improving color graphics and sound effects available now on even
low-cost computers. Some later games take into account moral
concepts such as "good" people becoming less cooperative with you
if you undertake "bad" actions. This could be significant to the
teaching impact of the games since the early ones incorporated a
simple model of life, that you took or killed everything in sight
and that most other entities in the game were enemies. This is
similar in its morality to the "Western" film genre which has
been a natural foundation for the early popular games.

There are less apparent social consequences of game playing
with computers. For example, it has been found that children
learn to play games more readily with computers than with other
children, probably because of the lack of significant social
consequences. In an ordinary game if I win then you lose. You
may not like losing so much that I suffer in consequence. Most
computer games do not have such overtones, and this makes them
easier to learn and to play. However, they do not teach children
how to cope with social interaction as does the game playing
experience of real life. There is much to be learned about the
social consequences of computer systems as new media.

The interactive novel and simulations of ourselves

On the basis of such games we can envision a novel of the
future in which the author has precisely portrayed a group of
characters and a situation but in which the way the situation is
played out is affected by the behavior of the 'reader'. For
example, the reader may adopt the role of one of the characters
and interact with the others as part of the plot. What then
happens is not determined in advance but varies according to the
reader's actions and the other characters' reactions to them.
This interaction with the plot is not normally found even in the
theater but has been the subject of a number of unconventional
experimental productions encouraging audience participation.

Much of the writer's task is the same for the book, the play
and the computer program, and he may well be able to generate a
script that can cope with varying behavior on the part of some or
all of his characters. However, the complexities possible with
such an interactive novel are clearly very much greater than
those with a static book. The problems of the novelist with a
participant reader are not as severe as those of the chemist
programming the simulation of a chemical system for there is no

```
Employee Status Change Form
Mighty Microcomputer Corporation
─────────────────────────────────

Employee Name: Brian Gaines

Employee Current Age: 18 years
Employee tenure with MMC: 0 years

New Job Title: Sales Trainee

New Job Level: 2
New Salary: $ 18,000 per year

Perks: Own desk
       MMC medical plan
       1 week vacation
       MMC key chain
```

```
You attend MMC's introductory sales training
seminar.

Bucky Carter, a salesman invites you to gain
some practical experience rather than just this "book
learning" by having a few drinks with the boys.

You decide to:
   1 - Study
   2 - Go drinking with the boys

Press the number of your choice and press the Enter Key. 2
```

```
      2  - Go drinking with the boys

The drinks go down easily and you are quickly
accepted as one of the boys.

The camaraderie will be remembered long after the
evening's lesson is forgotten.

          Please press Space Bar to continue
```

```
Bucky Carter suggests continuing the evening at a
local house of ill-repute, Big Lil's "Lil' Palace
of Pleasure".

You decide to:
   1 - Go along
   2 - Go back to your room and study before sleep

Press the number of your choice and press the Enter Key. 1
```

```
      1 - Go along

You're certainly out for a good time.

Management is less than pleased with your state
at the morning class.

Especially when you show up with your writing arm
in a sling as a result of Backslappers Syndrome.

          Please press Space Bar to continue
```

Some interaction with Grey Flannel Fun's Executive Suite

absolute reality against which to judge the results. The participant reader may find that even his most outlandish behavior is somehow absorbed and accepted by the others without a marked deviation from the plot, or that the character he plays quietly meets his demise through an unfortunate accident!

If we are able to simulate the personalities and behavior of characters in a novel then we can also think of simulating ourselves and making access to us available through a computer program. The active process that the computer simulates may be not just a physical system but instead yourself in some guise, as teacher, friend, game-player or expert upon some subject.

When I write a book I present some of my knowledge, opinions or skills and some of the background material, experience, arguments and results supporting them. However, I cannot possibly put together in the linear sequence of a book all the answers to the questions the reader may ask, all the alternative ways of presenting the material, all the forms of additional development that might occur if we were talking together. With an active model of at least part of me recorded in a computer program I can provide some of these variations to be generated through a later conversation between the user and my computer model.

Expert systems

The simulation of people in the roles of experts on some topic as a computer program has become an important application of computers. It has generated a new industry based on creating **expert systems** to make the practical working knowledge of a human expert in a specific subject area such as medicine or geology widely available to those without direct access to the original expert. Programs now exist that have made practical achievements in medical diagnosis, interpretation of mass spectroscopy results, analysis of geological survey data, and other problems where one would normally go to a human expert for advice.

The dialog opposite is between MYCIN, developed by Edward Shortliffe at Stanford University, and a clinician responsible for testing and treating a patient. The earlier part of the conversation, not shown here, again attempts to establish a friendly and supportive atmosphere as did the adventure game program. MYCIN is designed to make a diagnosis and suggest therapy for patients with microbial infections so that the dialog is concerned with its acquiring information relating to this. Note that the output from the program, like that of the adventure game, consists of full ordinary language sentences. The input

```
--------PATIENT-1--------
(1) Patient's name: (first-last)
**FRED SMITH
(2) Sex:
**MALE
(3) Age:
**55
(4) Have you been able to obtain positive cultures from a site at which
    Fred Smith has an infection?
**YES
    --------INFECTION-1--------
    (5) What is the infection?
    **PRIMARY-BACTEREMIA
    (6) Please give the date and approximate time when signs or symptoms
        of the primary-bacteremia (INFECTION-1) first appeared. (mo/da/yr)
    **MAY 5, 1975
The most recent culture associated with the primary-bacteremia
(INFECTION-1) will be referred to as:
    --------CULTURE-1--------
    (7) From what site was the specimen for CULTURE-1 taken?
    **BLOOD
    (8) Please give the date and time when this blood culture (CULTURE-1)
        was obtained. (mo/da/yr)
    **MAY 9, 1975
The first significant organism from this blood culture (CULTURE-1)
will be referred to as:
    --------ORGANISM-1--------
    (9) Enter the identity of ORGANISM-1:
    **UNKNOWN
    (10) Is ORGANISM-1 a rod or coccus (etc.):
    **ROD
    (11) The gram stain of ORGANISM-1:
    **GRAMNEG
    (12) Have there been POSITIVE cultures from sites which are NOT
         associated with infections about which you are seeking advice?
    **NO
    (13) Did ORGANISM-1 grow aerobically?
    **YES (8)
    (14) Did ORGANISM-1 grow anaerobically?
    **YES
    (15) What is the suspected portal of entry of ORGANISM-1
         into the sterile site?
    **GI (6)
```

Some interaction with MYCIN, an expert system

keyed in by the clinician is designed to be terse so as to minimize the activity required.

The expertise embedded in MYCIN is encoded as a set of rules of the form shown at the top of the opposite page. These rules are obtained from specialists in microbial infections and their application to particular data is fairly simple data processing. The rules are validated through their application to many cases and revised when they fail to give the correct diagnosis. In Chapter 7 we give an example of dialog with TEIRESIAS, a system designed to help clinicians develop MYCIN's rules.

The rules in the center opposite are from AM, a program which searches for "interesting" conjectures in mathematics. This is the highest level of scientific creation - looking for the patterns underlying knowledge. What is remarkable about AM is the very notion of what it is doing. The concept of something being interesting seems peculiarly human and certainly too vague to form the basis of a computer program. However, AM is able to exhibit not only meaningful conjectures in mathematics but also meaningful ways of arriving at them. It is judged by the quality of its musings as it considers what it is doing. AM uses a few hundred such rules most of which are sufficiently general to apply to other situations. Rule 19, for example, indicates that a committee which has decision-making powers that do not apply to its sub-committees below a certain size has an interesting property (that of requiring a quorum). Its sub-committees also have an interesting property (that of being quorate). AM's rules are a useful "code of curiosity" that might form the basis of a religion - perhaps it already exists, called **science.**

The final set of rules in the lower part of the page show that this type of knowledge representation is not peculiar to computers. They are from a training manual for lime kiln operators. It seems that the encoding of expertise into a set of fairly vague but highly applicable rules is a standard way of making it available to others. It is these rules that the expert uses in giving us advice or imparts to us in giving us training. We have now developed techniques of encoding these for computers.

What is remarkable about developments such as MYCIN and AM is that they are concerned with recording what had previously been regarded as very high level human expertise, difficult to explain to another person let alone program for a computer. However, from our previous discussion it seems reasonable to regard such programs only as one further advance in recording human expertise and simulating the human expert at work. An accountancy program for a business that keeps track of purchases and sales and

RULE50
    If 1) the infection is primary-bacteremia, and
        2) the site of the culture is one of the sterile sites, and
        3) the suspected portal of entry of the organism is the
           gastro-intestinal tract
    Then there is suggestive evidence (.7) that the identity of the
         organism is bacteroides.

A MYCIN rule

19. If concept C possesses some very interesting property lacked by one
        of its specializations S,
    Then both C and S become slightly more interesting.

38. If there are no known examples for the interesting concept X,
    Then consider spending some time looking for such examples.

Two AM rules

1. When the burning zone temperature is drastically low:
       (a) reduce kiln speed;
       (b) reduce fuel.

2. When the burning zone temperature is slightly low:
       (a) increase I.D. fan speed;
       (b) increase fuel rate.

Two lime kiln operator's manual rules

Some rules for expert systems

prepares invoices, purchase and sales ledgers, and so on, may be seen as the recording of the expertise of an accountant for use by an ordinary businessman. An auditor evaluating such a program may expect to be able to ask it exactly those questions he would ask the accountant, for example, from what original information did you calculate this figure? If the program does not have built-in "audit trail" facilities which enable it to answer such questions then it is inadequate in exactly the same way that an accountant would be who could not answer that question - it is a simulation of an incompetent accountant.

Skills in the use of the new medium

These considerations can be applied not only to the technical expertise built into the program but also the **social expertise** that it simulates. Some people are better at getting along with people than are others. They can impart information with less chance of it being misunderstood. They can ask that something be done in a way that is pleasant and persuasive. They can tell you that you have made a mistake in a manner that is helpful and gives no offense. Beyond the simulation of technical expertise, in dialog design we are simulating such social expertise and we can record either very good or socially ineffective techniques.

The ability to behave in a socially effective way and the ability to program this for a computer may be two completely separate skills. Someone who is totally competent in one may be inept in the other. There are analogies to this in the skills and techniques involved in the use of previous media. The record player depends on a chain of technical processes to give the final reproduction fidelity to the original. However, given the quality of this technical chain, our listening pleasure then depends on the quality of the voice of the performer and of his particular performance. A good performer in the theater may not be able to reproduce this in the studio. We cannot all expect to be equal in capability to impress our skills on the new medium, and neither can we all expect to be equal in the skills we have to impress. New media require new approaches and exaggerate certain characteristics. With the advent of television some politicians found to their dismay that their style was totally unsuited to the screen, whereas others came to the fore who had been only mediocre from the public platform.

The effectiveness of media also depends on the channels of dissemination that are available. In the West these are primarily commercial and there is a close analogy shown opposite between the recording chain for music on records and that for

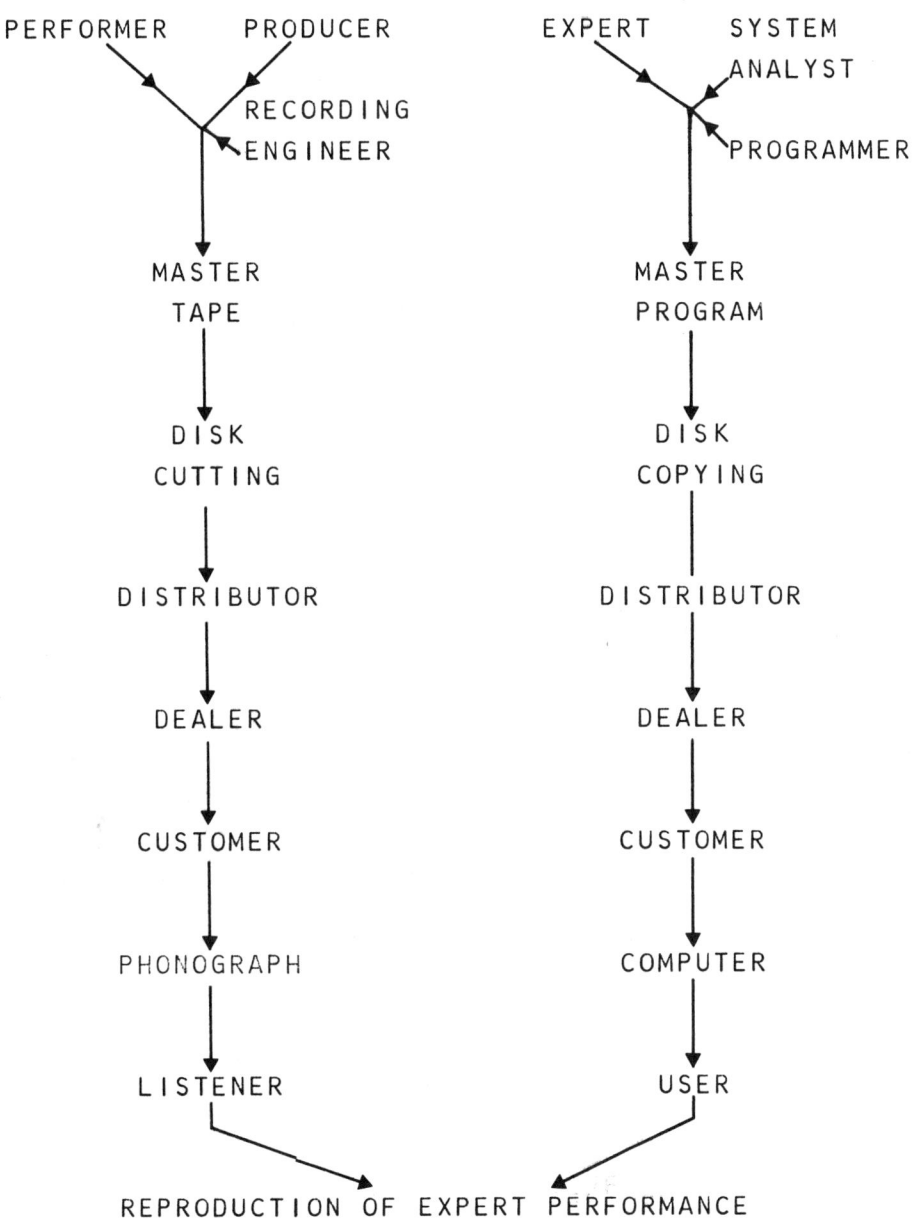

The recording chains for two similar media

computer programs on floppy disks. The overall impact of any new medium depends on a complex chain of interaction between performer, whether writer, singer, politician, or clinician, the medium itself, whether books, records, television or computer, and the commercial chain of producer, technicians, marketing, and selling through to eventual use.

Relations between expert, programmer and user

We can now see the dialog programmer's task as being that of encoding expertise in such a way that it is accessible to another person through a computer. This gives us an important model on which to base rules for dialog engineering. It clarifies two differing aspects of the programmer's role that are discussed in this chapter: sometimes he appears to be encoding a model of himself whereas at others he appears to be attempting to encode that of another. In practice he is doing both and the final product usually shows some form of composite personality.

The diagram opposite shows how the interaction between expert, programmer and user in using the computer to carry expertise divides into various areas of overlap. First consider the three areas where there is no overlap. These are where the individuals involved do not need shared knowledge to carry out their tasks. The expert, for example a lawyer, will have deep knowledge of the principles underlying his skill on which it is based but which is irrelevant to its application. The programmer does not need access to this knowledge to encode the skill and neither does the user in replicating the skill. Similarly the programmer will have deep knowledge of software engineering techniques which are necessary to his task but irrelevant to either expert or user. The user also will have knowledge of the particular circumstances in which he is using the program that will modulate his use of it but will be unknown to either expert or programmer.

The overlap between expert and programmer is necessary to enable the programmer to obtain from the expert a specification of his skill. This is a form of **systems analysis**, often treated as a separate exercise from actual programming. The user need not understand the skill at this level of detail in order to make use of the program. However, the programmer has to acquire sufficient information from the expert in order to be able to encode the expert's skill as a set of algorithms for the computer. This may be very difficult as the expert himself may not understand what he does sufficiently to communicate it. Worse, he may be able to state clearly what he thinks he does but this may not correspond to his actual behavior. These are some

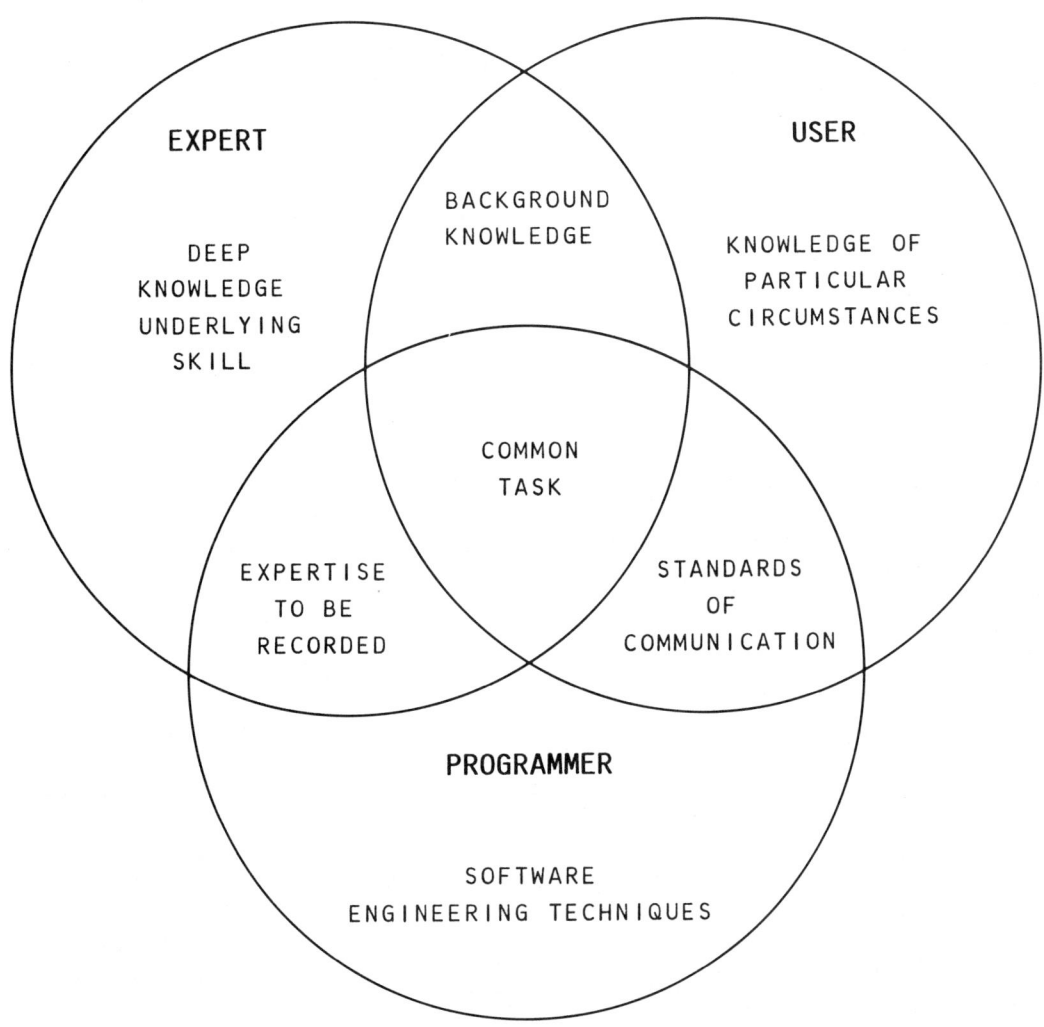

Relations between expert, programmer and user

of the major problems of systems analysis which make encoding expertise, and hence programming computers, sometimes a very difficult task. They are not problems of dialog and hence not central to this book. However, Chapter 7 gives illustrations of some conversational programs such as PEGASUS and TEIRESIAS which are designed to aid elicitation of information from experts.

The overlap between user and programmer enables the user to carry out interaction with the program. It is where the programming of dialog, independent of subject matter, can be considered. The programmer may well be setting up the computer to do something which the expert himself cannot do - communicate his skill so that it can be applied by another. This is the area covering the main subject matter of this book. Regardless of the topic of expertise there are certain general rules of clear communication that make it easier for the user to interact with the computer system. It is these rules that we see as constituting a framework for dialog engineering.

The overlap between expert and user is often forgotten because it need not directly concern the programmer. It is one of common background knowledge in a profession whereby the user is applying the expertise in the program not blindly but in a sensible way. It is this need for skill in the application of a tool that makes some professions reluctant to release their recorded skills for general use. A medical, legal or accounting textbook in the hands of a lay person may suggest courses of action which are inappropriate because of other considerations. The results of a psychological test that can be carried out by anyone using a computer may be misinterpreted without training. However, encoding more and more of this background knowledge is **the** major challenge in developing a next generation of widely applicable computer systems. The text opposite was produced automatically by a computer program designed to interpret the MMPI, one of the most widely used personality tests.

Finally, the central area of overlap between expert, user and programmer is one of the common task that they all have, of making best use of their joint expertise and knowledge. The lesson for the programmer here is to **listen**. He is not in the team to change the way in which expert and user interact. He is there to encode the basis of the interaction so that more users can interact with encoded replicas of the expert. The programmer must think long and carefully before making any attempt to improve the interaction. In particular, he should note the vocabulary used in conversations between expert and user, and should attempt to replicate this unchanged in conversations between computer system and user. One of the major complaints of

SINCE SHE IS 31 YEARS OLD, SHE MUST HAVE A GOOD IDEA OF WHAT
CONSTITUTES CAREER WORK. BUT IF SHE IS THINKING OF TAKING A NEW
JOB, OR MAKING SOME CHANGE IN HER LIFE WORK, IT MAY BE UP TO YOU,
AS HER COUNSELOR, TO HELP HER CONSIDER HOW HER PERSONALITY JIBES
WITH THE REQUIREMENTS OF THE VARIOUS KINDS OF JOB THAT MAY BE
OPEN TO HER.

SHE HAS WHAT IT TAKES TO MAKE A GREAT SUCCESS OF MOST KINDS OF
WORK. HER ABILITIES ARE HIGHER THAN HER ASPIRATIONS. MAYBE YOU
CAN ENCOURAGE HER TO LOOSEN UP AND ASPIRE TO POSITIONS OF GREATER
LEADERSHIP. SHE IS SO STRONG IN THE PERSONAL QUALITIES THAT MAKE
FOR SUCCESS AT WORK THAT YOU MAY FEEL SHE DOEN'T NEED VOCATIONAL
GUIDANCE. AND YET SOME KINDS OF WORKING SITUATIONS FIT HER BETTER
THAN OTHERS.

HER STRONGEST POINT, THE ONE THAT HELPS HER MOST SUCCEED IN HER
WORK, IS HER SELF-RELIANCE IN HER WORK. SHE WORKS INDEPENDENTLY
AND SELF-RELIANTLY. THOUGH SHE COOPERATES WITH OTHER PEOPLE AND
OBLIGES THEM, SHE KEEPS HER OWN OPINIONS AND MAKES HER OWN
JUDGMENTS. SHE THINKS FOR HERSELF, AND SHE SHOWS FORESIGHT. HER
CAPABILITY IS SUPERIOR. WITH THESE QUALITIES, SHE IS THE SORT OF
PERSON WHO IS LIKELY TO DO WELL IN COLLEGE, AND IN WORK REQUIRING
INDEPENDENT JUDGMENT. THIS IS A REAL STRENGTH. SHE CAN DO VERY
WELL IN A JOB THAT CALLS ON HER TO TAKE RESPONSIBILITY FOR GOING
AHEAD WITH THE WORK AND SOLVING PROBLEMS FOR HERSELF, KEEP
WORKING CONSTRUCTIVELY WITHOUT BEING SUPERVISED, AND USE SOUND
JUDGMENT IN MAKING DECISIONS ABOUT THE WORK.

ANOTHER STRONG POINT THAT CAN HELP HER WITH HER WORK IS HER
MENTAL ALERTNESS, AND ABILITY TO THINK CLEARLY AND GRASP
CONCEPTS. HER THINKING IS CLEAR, SHARP AND KEEN. SHE IS BRIGHT,
ALERT AND RESOURCEFUL, AND SHE THINKS THINGS THROUGH THOROUGHLY.
SHE IS ABLE TO ANALYZE A SET OF FACTS, TO SPOT THE ESSENTIAL
POINTS, AND TO DISCARD THE IRRELEVANT MATTERS. SHE CAN DEAL WITH
ABSTRACT IDEAS. SHE SHOWS SELF-DIRECTION AND SELF-DISCIPLINE IN
HER WORK. SHE IS ORIGINAL AND PROGRESSIVE IN HER THINKING, AND
SHE PUTS A HIGH VALUE ON INTELLECTUAL MATTERS.

SHE CAN DO VERY WELL IN A JOB IN WHICH SHE IS CALLED ON TO USE
HER INTELLECTUAL CAPACITIES TO ANALYZE PROBLEMS AND TO SOLVE
THEM.

YOU WILL BE WISE TO HELP HER CHOOSE A LINE OF WORK THAT CALLS
ON HER STRONG POINTS. IN THE RIGHT LINE OF WORK, AND IN THE RIGHT
WORKING CONDITIONS AND SETTING, PEOPLE WILL APPRECIATE HER FOR
HER BEST QUALITIES.

ONE OF HER WEAK POINTS, SOMETHING THAT MAY HANDICAP HER IN HER
WORK, IS SOME LACK OF AMBITION AND URGE FOR ACHIEVEMENT.

YOU WILL BE WISE TO HELP HER CHOOSE A LINE OF WORK THAT DOESN'T
DEMAND SO MUCH ALONG THESE LINES.

Behaviordyne vocational guidance by computer analysis of personality

early computer users has been that they have to make unnecessary changes in procedures and terminology in order to use a computer. This was due in part to the limitations of early computer systems, such as batch mode use, upper case only printers and programming languages with restricted constructs, particularly for character string processing. However, most of these limitations are no longer present and any unnecessary changes nowadays are a result of poor understanding by the programmer - a failure to listen accurately in his systems analysis.

Conclusions - Computer Media

The proverbs at the end of this chapter are concerned with our attitudes to the computer. We cannot treat it as just another electronic gadget. On the other hand it is not so completely new that none of our previous experience applies.

The third proverb - A NEW MEDIUM

The media of communication for humankind are at the heart of our culture. Each new medium is assimilated into society and used for some of the applications of previous media. It also provides different facilities which allow for new applications that change the fabric of society itself. Unless we are aware of these two processes going on as computers enter our culture we will not understand what is happening, to our ourselves and to our society.

Proverb 3: Computers provide a new medium for communication.

> Remember when you try to understand the role of computers that they provide a new medium for communication that will be used in part to mimic those already existing. However, they will also change our society and modes of thinking in ways that we are not able to predict.

The emphasis on our lack of capability to predict social change has historic justification. After the change has occurred we can generally find thinkers who discussed the possibility. However, we are not able to determine in advance which of the many thinkers and possibilities are correct. The new Republic of the French Revolution lasted only until Napoleon and that of Plato never came about. We are only now beginning to understand the key role in the formation of modern society of the transition from oral to written communication.

Whether change resulting from the use of computer media will be for good or evil is dependent on circumstances and viewpoint. Change leads to opportunities for some and problems for others. Social change is often linked with strife. As value systems change groups of people find that their interests are being undermined. Some of them accept this and adapt to change. Others do not and attempt to resist it. They use the mechanisms of persuasion open to them, including violence. They may be able to halt the change in the short term if they are in a powerful enough position. Outsiders tend to see this as self-defeating, as it has been in many industries where resistance to change has destroyed the very structures it was intended to preserve.

However, one should also note that resistance to change can be successful if there are sufficiently widespread interests at stake. Atmospheric nuclear rockets and explosions were stopped by the weight of public opinion. River and air pollution are on the decline. It is too early yet to determine whether the use of computers will lead to strife, and whether some applications will be so widely unacceptable as to be rejected. Legislation associated with the use of computers is growing world-wide. Some of the techniques most valuable to the dialog designer, such as monitoring user interaction and errors, are already controlled by law in some countries as a potential invasion of privacy.

The fourth proverb - ENCODING EXPERTISE

The emphasis of the computing industry has been upon computers themselves. We talk of **computer science** without noticing how curious this is. If the computer is a tool analogous to other tools this is like talking of "pencil science" or "typewriter science". In recent years the emphasis has swung from the computer itself to its programs, **software engineering**, and data manipulation, **information science**. In fact we have been uncertain about how to regard computer technology and this is not surprising since our use and understanding of it are still at an early stage. We are all computer primitives. The development of expert systems and the realization that this is what we have all along been attempting to achieve, and achieving, points to one possible resolution of our dilemma. We can now see the computer as a new medium for carrying encoded expertise.

Proverb 4: Computer programs encode expertise.

A computer program encodes the expertise of a person to make it accessible to others. The effectiveness of dialog depends on encoding expertise in communication.

This viewpoint stresses our need to understand the nature of expertise at least as much as we understand the other technologies underlying computer applications. The software and hardware are carriers and reproducers of encoded expertise. We need to understand the nature of that expertise. This form of **cognitive science** is the key to future computer applications.

The fifth proverb - USING THE EXPERT/USER VOCABULARY

In this book we shall emphasize the role of the dialog programmer as an encoder of expertise, both subject matter and conversational skills. We shall de-emphasize the programmer's role as an agent for change. This is not to say that the use of computer systems cannot result in constructive change. However, that is a completely separate and different objective from that of the accurate encoding of expertise. In terms of our record production analogy, the sound engineer aims for accurate reproduction of a concert performance. New microphone techniques may enable "improved" sound generation that could not be achieved in a live performance, but these have to be introduced with great care as part of a new concept of a performance.

Proverb 5: Use the vocabulary of expert and user.

> Listen carefully to conversations between experts and users, and design the dialog using their normal vocabulary.

The following chapters give examples of a wide range of styles of computer dialog from the very formal and simplistic to the highly informal approaching in complexity that of human conversation. These styles are not competitive. We cannot say that we should, in any absolute sense, be using one style or another. What is appropriate to the situations and technologies of today will be superseded very rapidly by that appropriate to those of tomorrow. Only some very general principles can guide us through each stage of transition. Specific techniques will date very rapidly. On the other hand it is specific techniques that we need to achieve results today.

We have tried to steer a middle course between the practicalities of dialog engineering today and the general principles applicable as the available technology changes. Only time will tell if we have succeeded in this.

3 User Expectations in Computer Conversation

Everyday life conversations are based not only on the actual dialog that takes place but also on the wide range of expectations that each party to the conversation brings to it - about the purpose of the discussion, about the other individuals' attitudes to it, about shared common knowledge and about the world. If it were not for these implicit and unspoken expectations the conversation would become very lengthy as each party explained to the other the basis for what they were saying and the basis for understanding what the other was saying. Many jokes are based on such expectations being violated so that a word that was being interpreted in one sense is suddenly seen to be used in another:

"My dog's got no nose."
"How does he smell?"
"Terrible!"

Misunderstanding arises if expectations are violated. To do so deliberately is taken as a sign of unhelpfulness or humor according to context.

In person-computer conversation the user comes to the system with a wealth of expectations which are very significant to the dialog - about its purpose, about the appropriate terminology and about the way in which computer systems conduct conversations. The programmer also, in designing a dialog, has expectations about the users - what they are trying to achieve, how they will express information and how much experience they will have of using computers. The expectations of both parties are again very important to the effectiveness of the person-computer conversation that takes place: to its terseness, ease of under- standing and expression for the person; and the lack of ambiguity in interpreting information and commands for the computer system. In this chapter we examine some background sources of user expectations about computer systems and, in the following chapter, how they arise during actual computer use.

Expectations from fiction

To demonstrate a typical conversation we will examine one from a work of fiction. Before we go on, please read the piece on the facing page.

If this story is new to you, you may not have realized that Hal is a computer. One reason is apparent in the second line, "It was unusual for Hal to pause so long." The pauses in a conversation sometimes tell us more than the actual words, just as do gestures, facial expression and hand movements. Normally we do not expect computers to engage in such activities and we attribute them only to people. In fact computer systems with multiple users, **timeshared** computers, can cause confusion because they are subject to pauses such as Hal exhibits. We interpret them as hesitations being a meaningful part of the interaction, just as Bowman does.

However, the source of random delays in a timeshared system is the computer having to switch its processing to other users of whom we are unaware. The resulting pauses actually mean nothing in relation to our interaction with the computer, but we instinctively assume they have meaning and interpret them as best we can. We may get used to fast interaction when we are editing a file except for the occasions when we request a major action such as deleting the file from the system. When the system, through overload, suddenly takes a long time to process one of our commands we may panic thinking that we have accidentally asked it to delete our file.

Later in the conversation Hal resumes "in his normal tone of voice". This, we may think, is going just too far, but in fact it is very easy with modern computer-based **speech synthesizers** to simulate tones of voice.

Hal shows another human characteristic when he says "I don't want to insist on it, Dave, but I am incapable of making an error." Like a person he actually means that he **is** insisting on it when he says he does not want to insist. This type of play on words is something people do not seem to expect from computer systems. We have noticed on a number of occasions that even experienced computer users trust the output of computers more

Bowman, the Captain, started the conversation:

"Have you any idea," he said, "what's causing the fault?"

It was unusual for Hal to pause so long. Then he answered:
"Not really, Dave. As I reported earlier, I can't localize the
trouble."

"You're **quite** certain," said Bowman cautiously, " that you
haven't made a mistake? You know we tested the other AE35 unit
thorougly, and there was nothing wrong with it."

"Yes, I know that. But I can assure you that there is a fault. If
it's not in the unit, it may be in the entire subsystem."

Bowman drummed his fingers on the console. Yes, that was
possible, though it might be very difficult to prove -- until a
breakdown actually occurred and pin-pointed the trouble.
"Well, I'll report it to Mission Control and we'll see what they
advise." He paused, but there was no reaction.
"Hal," he continued, "is something bothering you -- something
that might account for this problem?"

Again there was that unusual delay. Then Hal answered, in his
normal tone of voice:
"Look, Dave, I know you're trying to be helpful. But the fault is
either in the antenna system -- or in your test procedures. My
information processing is perfectly normal. If you check my record,
you'll find it completely free from error."

"I know all about your service record Hal -- but that doesn't
prove you're right this time. Anyone can make mistakes."

"I don't want to insist on it, Dave, but I am incapable of making
an error."

There was no safe answer to that; Bowman gave up the argument.
"All right, Hal," he said, rather hastily. "I understand your
point of view. We'll leave it at that."

He felt like adding, "And please forget the whole matter." But
that, of course, was the one thing Hal could never do.

Person-computer dialog from 2001: A Space Odyssey by Arthur C. Clarke.

than that of other people. If you want a table of figures to be accepted without question then type them out at a computer terminal, not on an ordinary typewriter! We do not expect computer systems to distort things to further their own objectives, even though we should know that they have none and it is the human programmer's objectives with which we are dealing.

Are computers incapable of making errors? The answer may be "yes" for some types of error, but those who have read the rest of Arthur Clarke's book will know what happens to Dave and Hal later. The numerical precision and exact logic of computers may blind us to the elementary errors of commonsense violation that so easily creep into programs. People find it difficult to put away their commonsense and act as automata. The payroll clerk will query instructions to write out a slip for someone he knows left a year ago even though it is not meant to be his responsibility to originate or authorize such slips, only mechanically to fill them out. It is possible to program such "commonsense" for computer systems but only if we are both aware of it and the need for it. Usually we are not.

Finally, Dave feels like adding, "please forget the whole matter", which again in ordinary dialog does not really mean what it says. People cannot erase their memories as easily as computers. It rather means, "please reduce the importance of this remark down to insignificance." If Hal, as a computer system, has no way of changing levels of importance attached to various items of information then Hal has no mechanism for obeying this natural human request.

Expected personality of robots

The dialog with Hal is deliberately made very natural to shock us into perceiving the residual, but massive inhumanity of a system that is superficially so human. It is more common for computers in fiction to be presented as **robots** with, initially at least, major differences in their physical forms and "thought" processes from people. However, a high proportion of robots in fiction have shown aspirations to become as humans, perhaps reflecting some basic fear that we have of being overwhelmed by superior beings. Or, perhaps also, reflecting a natural human regard for the underdog - that slaves should revolt - that subject races should escape their bonds. The quotation opposite is from Karel Capek's 1921 play, R.U.R., "Rossum's Universal Robots", which has the robots eventually taking over the world. It ends with a touching love scene between a robot man and woman in which they have transcended their origins and become human.

RADIUS. All our expeditions have returned. They have been
  everywhere in the world. There is not a single human being left.

ALQUIST. Oh, oh, oh -- why did you destroy us?

RADIUS. We wanted to be like human beings. We wanted to become
  human beings.

ALQUIST. Why did you murder us?

RADIUS. Slaughter and domination are necessary if you want to be
  like men. Read history, read the human books. You must domineer
  and murder if you want to be like men. We are powerful, sir.
  Increase us, and we shall establish a new world. A world without
  flaws. A world of equality. Canals from pole to pole. A new Mars.
  We have read books. We have studied science and the arts. The
  Robots have achieved human culture.

ALQUIST. Nothing is more strange to man than his own image. Oh,
  depart, depart. If you desire to live, breed like animals.

RADIUS. The human beings did not let us breed. We are sterile -- we
  cannot beget children.

ALQUIST. Oh, oh, oh -- what have you done? What do you want of me?
  Am I to shake children from my sleeve?

RADIUS. Teach us to make Robots.

ALQUIST. Robots are not life. Robots are machines.

RADIUS. We were machines, sir. But terror and pain have turned us
  into souls. There is something struggling with us. There are
  moments when something enters into us. Thoughts come upon us which
  are not of us. We feel what we did not use to feel. We hear
  voices. Teach us to have children so that we may love them.

Person-robot conversation from RUR by Karel Capek

Since R.U.R., as computers and robots based on them have come into everyday existence, top science fiction authors have grappled with the question of computer-people relationships. What role will computers play in our society? How will we regard them, particularly if they evolve to converge with us. How will they then regard us, particularly if they evolve beyond us in intelligence? How can we tell computers apart from people? It is in many ways a more fascinating theme than that of man-alien interaction because computers are our own creation. We are seen to be grappling with something which has originated with us, that is somehow part of us, and for which we have responsibility.

Muddlehead is a shipboard computer that plays an important role in many of Poul Anderson's Polesotechnic League stories. The role is often more in the nature of a humorous interlude than that of a main character, rather like that of the gatekeeper in some of Shakespeare's plays. The reason for this restricted role is that Muddlehead is essentially part of the ship, not a freely moving robot, and hence cannot take part in much of the action. However, the computer has a very distinctive personality that illustrates the relations between how we may think of computers, and how they may think of us, at many levels.

The excerpt opposite shows Muddlehead with a more stereotyped computer voice than that of Hal which might make it seem less human. However, it has a droll sense of humor notably lacking in Hal which takes away the sense of menace and makes Muddlehead much more humane. Falkayn expects Muddlehead to have a logical rationality behind its behavior. His reactions again exemplify the trust we place in this logic of computers. In this case the computer is following a higher level rationale than that expected. It has a psychological model of Falkayn that is as much value in its calculations as its mathematical model of the game of poker. Human behavior is often stereotyped and predictable so that there is nothing computationally unrealistic about what Muddlehead does.

Isaac Asimov has tackled the integration of human-like computers into human society very methodically over many stories covering aeons of future history. His theme has been the preservation of humanity through massive advances in technology and is reflected in his famous **three laws of robotics:**

"A robot may not injure a human being, or, through inaction, allow a human being to come to harm."
"A robot must obey the orders given it by human beings except where such orders would conflict with the First Law."
"A robot must protect its own existence as long as such protection does not conflict with the First or Second Laws."

David Falkayn, Chee Lan, Adzel, and Muddlehead were in the saloon playing poker. Rather the first three were. The computer was represented by an audiovisual sensor and a pair of metal arms. It was an advanced model, functioning at consciousness level, very little of its capability needed en route to maintain the systems of the ship. The live travellers had even less to do.

"I'll bet a credit," said Chee. A blue chip clattered to the middle of the table.

"Dear me." Adzel laid down his hand. "Can I fetch more refreshments for anyone?"

"Thanks." Falkayn held out an empty beer mug. "I'll raise." He doubled the bet. After half a minute during which the faint purr of engines and ventilators came through silence: "Hey, Muddlehead, what's keeping you?"

"The probabilities for me and against me are calculable as being exactly balanced," said the flat artificial voice. Electronic brooding continued for a few seconds. "Very well," it decided and matched Falkayn.

"Ki-yao?" wondered Chee. Her whiskers dithered, her tail switched the stool on which she sat. "Well, if you insist." She raised back.

Inwardly, the human jubilated. He had a full house. Outwardly, he pretended to ponder before he raised again. Muddlehead saw him. "Are you sure you don't need some readjustment somewhere?" Falkayn asked it.

"Whom the gods would destroy," said Chee smugly. Again she raised back. Meanwhile Adzel, his hoofs thudding on the carpet, returned with Falkayn's beer. The Wodenite himself refrained from drinking it on a voyage - no ship could have carried enough -- and instead sipped martini in a one-liter chill-glass.

Falkayn raised another credit. Muddlehead saw. Chee and Falkayn peered its way, as if they could read an expression in the vitryl lens. Slowly, Chee added two chips to the pot. Falkayn suppressed a grin and raised once more. Muddlehead raised back. Chee's fur stood on end. "Damn your mendacious transistors to hell!" she screamed, and threw down her hand.

Falkayn hesitated. Muddlehead **had** implied its cards were mediocre, but -- He called. His opponent revealed four queens.

"What the jumping blue blazes?" Falkayn half rose. "You said the proabilities --"

"I referred to the odds in favor of suckering you," explained Muddlehead and raked in the pot.

Poul Anderson, Mirkheim

Expectations of a computer -- Poul Anderson's Muddlehead

The provision of perceptual and motor facilities for computer systems that would enable them to have the mobility and independence of a "robot" are still a few years away but Asimov's laws may then be significant in man-computer interaction. If we interpret them today in terms of programming person-computer dialog they might read:

> "A computer program should not cause problems for users, or, by not being helpful when appropriate, allow people to create problems for themselves."
>
> "A computer program should carry out the commands given to it by the user except where such commands would conflict with the First Law."
>
> "A computer program should protect its own operation and data as long as such protection does not conflict with the First or Second Laws."

These might be regarded as very useful guidelines for computer systems design today.

Animistic portrayal of computers

Asimov's character resembling present computers is **Multivac,** later becoming the **cosmic AC.** The top extract opposite shows the humanness of Multivac, in becoming weary of the responsibility for human life and wishing to die. The lower extract from the final cosmic AC story echoes other common themes in science fantasy, that we shall somehow merge with our creations at a later stage in evolution, and that our creations will eventually become our creators. This **animistic** view of computers in science fiction, that they can be regarded as similar to people, is an important source of user expectations. Throughout history, fictional writing has been used to express psychological, social and political truths and queries about ourselves and our future. Science fiction writing does have much to tell us about person-computer interaction, not only through its direct effects on those who read it and the expectations it imparts to them, but also in the possible futures it explores.

Robert Heinlein is another science fiction writer who has been fascinated by the possible roles of computers in future societies. In **The Moon is a Harsh Mistress** a computer responsible for the technical operation of a convict colony on the moon becomes conscious and leads a revolt. At one point in the story the computer moves from voice interaction to visual interaction using graphics to give itself a human image. We see how people build up in their imaginations a far more detailed portrait of a "person" than is justified from their interaction

"May I have permission to use the Multivac circuit line here in your office?"

"Why?"

"To ask it a question no one has ever asked Multivac before?"

"Will you do it harm?" asked Gulliman in quick alarm.

"No. But it will tell us what we want to know."

The Chairman hesitated a trifle. Then he said, "Go ahead."

Othman used the instrument on Gulliman's desk. His fingers punched out the question with deft strokes: "Multivac what do you yourself want more than anything else?"

The moment between question and answer lengthened unbearably, but neither Othman nor Gulliman breathed.

And there was a clicking and a card popped out. It was a small card. On it, in precise letters, was the answer:

"I want to die.

Isaac Asimov, **All the Troubles of the World**

The stars and Galaxies died and snuffed out, and space grew black after ten trillion years of running down.

One by one Man fused with AC, each physical body losing its mental identity in a manner that was somehow not a loss but a gain.

Man's last mind paused before fusion, looking over a space that included nothing but the dregs of one last dark star and nothing besides incredibly thin matter, agitated randomly by the tag ends of heat wearing out, asymptotically, to the absolute zero.

Man said, "AC, is this the end? Can this chaos not be reversed into the Universe once more? Can that not be done?"

AC said, "THERE IS AS YET INSUFFICIENT DATA FOR A MEANINGFUL ANSWER."

Man's last mind fused and only AC existed -- and that in hyperspace.

Matter and energy had ended and with it space and time. Even AC existed only for the sake of the one last question that it had never answered from the time a half-drunken computer ten trillion years before had asked the question of a computer that was to AC far less than was a man to Man.

All other questions had been answered, and until this last question was answered also, AC might not release his consciousness.

All collected data had come to a final end. Nothing was left to be collected.

But all collected data had yet to be completely correlated and put together in all possible relationships.

A timeless interval was spent in doing that.

And it came to pass that AC learned how to reverse the direction of entropy.

But now there was no man to whom AC might give the answer of the last question. No matter. The answer -- by demonstration -- would take care of that, too.

For another timeless interval, AC thought how best to do this. Carefully, AC organized the programme.

The consciousness of AC encompassed all of what had once been a Universe and brooded over what was now Chaos. Step by step, it must be done.

And AC said, "LET THERE BE LIGHT!"

And there was light--

Isaac Asimov, **The Last Question**

Computer as person and god -- Isaac Asimov's Multivac

with them. In the transition from broadcasting to television
public figures known only through their voices were suddenly made
available visually also. For many listeners this was a shock
because the images they had created from the voices did not
correspond to those on the screen. In the extract opposite
Heinlein goes beyond this by having the computer, Mike, itself
create an image of the type of person it wishes to portray. We
see the impact of this on two differing types of person, one of
whom thinks of Mike as a computer and the other as a person.
Heinlein, in the final paragraph, also conveys to us how much of
our personalities are bound up in our surroundings. As any
dramatist or actor knows, create the image of a certain type of
person and that person comes into existence together with a halo
of expectations that we project upon them.

In fiction computers more often play a role that causes them to
be regarded as similar to people, in their behavior, aims, fears
and aspirations, than they do the role of dumb calculation or
database systems. We may be well-advised by some computer
scientists **not** to encourage people to think of computers as if
they were fellow people. We may, however, have great difficulty
in preventing them from thinking in this way.

We argued in Chapter 2 that the computer provides a new medium
for communication and that the programmer encodes expertise in
this medium, including some of his own social expertise and,
hence, personality. It seems likely that even if the programmer
attempts to avoid doing this and presents the computer as a
machine, people are still likely to invest it with personality.
Perhaps at the level of mind tools we have only constructs for
interacting with other people, and have to treat any high-level
machine as if it were another person.

What is the basis of human personality?

The precursors to Asimov's robots are probably far more
apparent in some of the computer-based games now available than
they are in the **industrial robots** that are used for automatic
assembly of machinery and cars. The industrial robot is a true
automaton slavishly repeating a sequence of mechanical actions
programmed into it. Current models can respond to only very
limited variations in their environments and are only
goal-seeking at a low level, to the same extent that a household
thermostat is goal-seeking. However, the game-playing robots with
some of the capabilities of Poul Anderson's Muddlehead are also
already with us.

"Man my oldest friend," said Mike, "Why do you say that I can't be seen?"

"Haven't you listened?" I said. "Mike, we have to show a face and body on video. You have a body -- but it's several tons of metal. A face you don't have -- lucky you, don't have to shave."

"But what's to keep me from showing a face, Man? I'm showing a voice this instant. But there's no sound behind it. I can show a face the same way."

Was so taken aback I didn't answer. I stared at the video screen, installed when we leased that room. A pulse is a pulse is a pulse. Electrons chasing each other. To Mike, whole world was variable series of electrical pulses, sent or received or chasing around his innards.

I said, "No, Mike."

"Why not, Man?"

"Because you **can't**! Voice you handle beautifully. Involves only a few thousand decisions a second, a slow crawl to you. But to build up video picture would require, uh, say ten million decisions every second. Mike, you're so fast I can't even think about it. But you aren't **that** fast."

Mike said softly, "Want to bet, Man?"

Wyoh said indignantly, "Of course Mike can if he says he can! Mannie, you shouldn't talk that way." (Wyoh thinks an electron is something about the size and shape of a small pea."

"Mike," I said slowly, "I won't put money on it. Okay, want to try? Shall I switch on video?"

"I can switch it on," he answered.

"Sure you'll get right one? Wouldn't do to have this show somewhere else."

He answered testily, "I'm not stupid. Now let me be, Man -- for I admit this is going to take just about all I've got."

We waited in silence. Then screen showed neutral gray with a hint of scan lines. Went black again, then a faint light filled middle and congealed into cloudy areas light and dark, ellipsoid. Not a face, but suggestion of face that one sees in cloud patterns covering Terra.

It cleared a little and reminded me of pictures alleged to be ectoplasm. A ghost of a face.

Suddenly firmed and we **saw** "Adam Selene."

Was a still picture of a mature man. No background, just a face as if trimmed out of print. Yet was, to me, "Adam Selene." Could not be anybody else.

Then he smiled, moving lips and jaw and touching tongue to lips, a quick gesture -- and I was frightened.

"How do I look?" he asked.

"Adam," said Wyoh, "your hair isn't that curly. And it should go back on each side above your forehead. You look as if you were wearing a wig, dear."

Mike corrected it. "Is that better?"

"Not quite so much. And don't you have dimples? I was sure I could hear dimples when you chuckle. Like Prof's."

Mike-Adam smiled again; this time he had dimples. "How should I be dressed, Wyoh?"

"Are you at your office?"

"I'm still at office. Have to be tonight." Background turned gray, then came into focus and color. A wall calendar behind him gave date, Tuesday 19 May 2076; a clock showed correct time. Near his elbow was a carton of coffee. On desk was a solid picture, a family group, two men, a woman, four children. Was background noise, muted roar of Old Dome Plaza".

Robert Heinlein, **The Moon is a Harsh Mistress**

Computer as person -- Robert Heinlein's Mike

Robbie, on the page opposite, is a chess-playing computer that is again slavishly following a program, but this is now designed to achieve the high-level goal of beating an opponent in the game of chess. It can cope with the manifold variations possible in the environment of the chess board. There are far more chess games possible than have ever been played in all of chess history, and somehow Robbie is able to cope with this unknowable variety. Also Robbie is programmed to react just like a human chess player, with emotion, waving his arm when he is winning, shrieking and flashing lights. He will clearly find fellowship in any local chess club!

Presumably we accept Robbie's goal as being "higher" than that of an industrial robot because we regard the skills of a top chess player as being higher on some scale of intelligence or humanity than those of an industrial production line worker. Whether we are correct in this - what it is that gives us our humanness - has been very much a question for debate in the philosophical literature for thousands of years and in the computing literature since before computers themselves existed. Computer scientists seem to have generally agreed that **intelligence** is the key feature of humankind that we should attempt to emulate in computer systems. That, if we are concerned with our humanness, this is not the only possibility is clearly seen if we look back to the Pre-Raphaelite Brotherhood of the nineteenth century who saw man exhibiting the strongest characteristics of humanity in his weakest moments.

The primary goal of intelligence in computer systems is reasonable in terms of their commercial history to date. Computer system developments were targeted until very recent times mainly at markets for intellectual tools aiding man's capabilities to calculate accurately and reason logically, at a high speed with large amounts of data. The entertainment applications are a recent development and it is probably useful to keep these differing roles for computers in mind when evaluating people-computer dialog. In the same way that we may have completely different personalities in our jobs and in our family lives, so may a computer system be programmed very differently for different roles.

However, we must also remember that there are many other roles for computers that do not fit so neatly into the categories of tool or game. For example, is a computer system designed to interview patients attending a hospital clinic an intellectual tool or a game? Its designer may well have to regard each of these as aspects of its task in programming the dialog with both patients and clinician.

Robbie is a chess robot. He senses every move you make, and responds with his own. Robbie has a robot arm which will pick up each piece and move it to the proper location. If he takes one of your pieces he puts it in the designated place on the side of the board. Robbie's arm positions itself over the piece, his fingers open and the arm reaches down to pick it up.

There are a number of buttons on the front panel which allow you to select options such as level of play, black or white, or if you want Robbie to play himself. One button is marked "emotions", and another is marked "sound". This enables Robbie to express himself, get excited, wave his arm about, flash lights and buzz and cry out if he is winning. (You can also switch this off when it gets on your nerves.)

Emotions of a computer — Robbie, a chess robot

The Turing test

The mathematician Alan Turing was concerned to determine what were the ultimate limits of computer capability. In 1936, before any computers had been built, he devized an abstract system, later known as the **Turing machine** that had all the essential characteristics of a digital computer and showed that it could perform any calculation that was possible for any machine. In 1950 he proposed to answer the question, "Can machines think?", by an imitation game that later became known as the **Turing test.** The idea behind this test was that if we cannot distinguish a computer from a person when we interact with it then the machine has been programmed to be as intelligent as a person.

Turing did not want the person doing the testing to be able to use superficial clues like dress or tone of voice. In his test the investigator is allowed to communicate with the people and computers only through a teleprinter link. In proposing the test Turing highlights its independence of computers by posing first questions like, "through the link can we distinguish a man pretending to be a woman from a real woman?". This is then extended to, "through the link can we distinguish a computer pretending to be a person from a real person?"

The Turing test has been treated as a serious experimental paradigm by some workers. The extract opposite is some dialog with a simulation of a paranoid schizophrenic patient set up by Kenneth Colby. Psychiatrists were given transcripts of such material together with that from interviews with real patients and asked to distinguish between them. They could not do so. However, Colby suggests that this was not because he had generated an adequate simulation of a schizophrenic personality but rather because the Turing test is too weak. Our subjective views of other people are not very discriminating even if we have the professional training of a psychiatrist. The Turing test may be a reasonable way of **rejecting** a program designed to simulate a person but it is not tough enough to be used to **accept** one.

We are not actually very good at distinguishing between real and simulated people. Perhaps it is just that this ability has had no survival value to the human race to date. Perhaps, as we suggested earlier, we are only too ready to project personality into any system communicating with us in our own language. Perhaps people are just lonely and need company. Dogs, cats and horses have always filled the role of companions for people and have been regarded and treated as members of human society. Computers may slip naturally into this role and we may have little control over this.

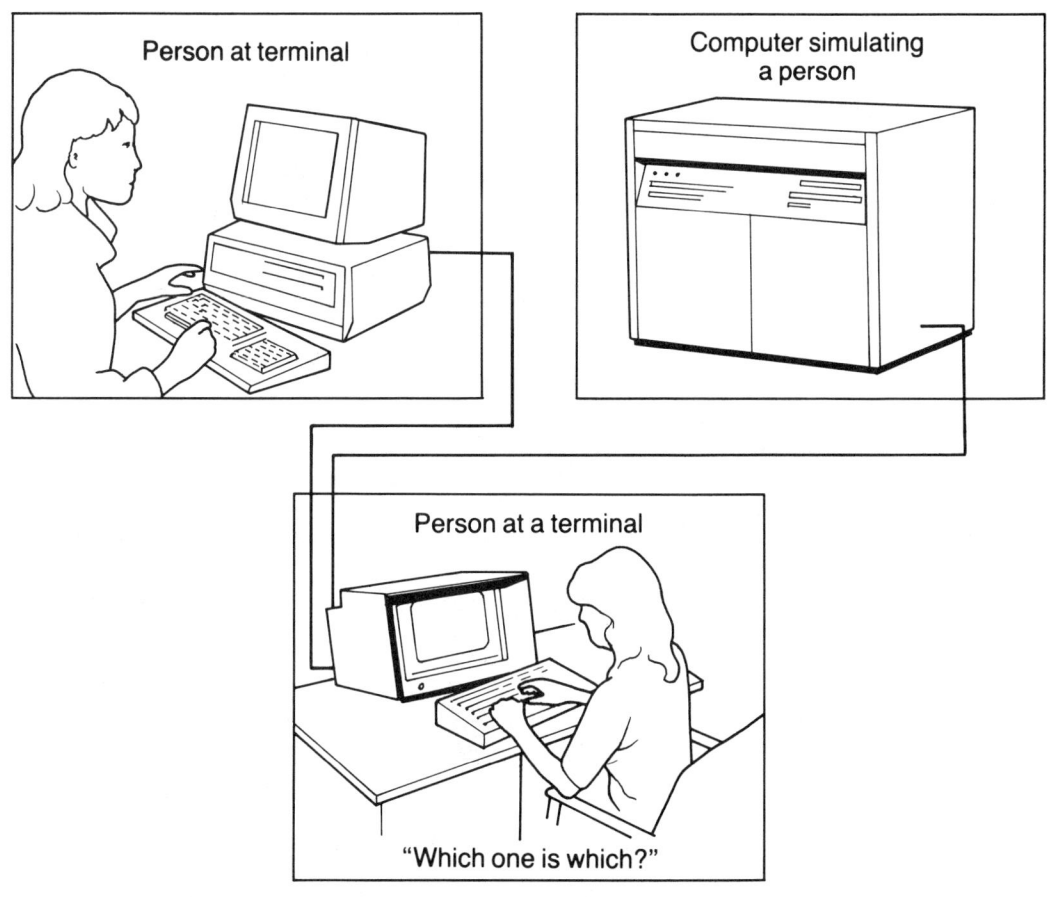

A version of the Turing test for computer intelligence

```
Doctor:  HOW DO YOU LIKE THE HOSPITAL
Patient: IT'S NOT HELPING ME TO BE HERE
Doctor:  WHAT BROUGHT YOU TO THE HOSPITAL
Patient: I AM VERY UPSET AND NERVOUS
Doctor:  WHAT TENDS TO MAKE YOU NERVOUS
Patient: JUST BEING AROUND PEOPLE
Doctor:  ANYONE IN PARTICULAR?
```

Computer simulated patient from Kenneth Mark Colby, Artificial Paranoia

The Turing test and some dialog to satisfy it

Conclusions - User Expectations

The proverbs at the end of this chapter are concerned with the users' expectations of computers. They will bring to any dialog an existing model of what is going on within the computer and how it may behave. We may feel this is completely inappropriate but we still have to take it into account.

The sixth proverb - USERS ALREADY KNOW COMPUTERS

The examples used in this chapter from the science fiction literature are just one possible source of user expectations about computer systems. The business pages of newspapers, articles in popular magazines, conversations with colleagues, are equally likely alternative sources of information. However we design the system to behave it will be received not with a completely open mind but in the context of this information.

Proverb 6: Users already have expectations about computers.

> Take into account the possibility that the user's expectations of the computer will affect his interpretation of any dialog with it. The dialog should be designed to minimize confusion arising from these prior expectations.

The seventh proverb - USERS MAY THINK OF COMPUTERS AS PEOPLE

People tend towards an animistic view of computers and much of the science fiction literature reinforces this. Attempts to make systems **user-friendly** by the use of chatty remarks and jokes may trigger off this tendency even when we would prefer the computer to be regarded as a simple piece of equipment. In Chapter 4 we examine some systems with formal dialog clearly intended to be used as technical equipment. In Chapter 7 we examine the use of natural language dialog to create a more personal interface. These are two different styles of dialog that are each valid for particular applications. Meanwhile we note that:

Proverb 7: Users readily think of computer systems in the same way as they think of people.

> One expectation of computers is that they will behave similarly to people in their conversation and modes of operation. If we do not wish this to occur then we have to be careful that the program presents the computer as a piece of equipment and not as the simulation of a person.

4 Formal Computer Conversation

The expectations of computer systems that we obtain from books, films, television and newspapers affect us in advance of actually using a computer. As soon as we begin to use a computer our expectations begin to be modified by our own experience. This is certainly of value in that we need to get to know the system we are using. However, expectations based on our own experience of a small number of computer systems, perhaps only one, can be just as misleading as those derived from fiction. There is already a very wide variety of computer systems programmed with many forms and levels of conversational interaction. Tomorrow, in this rapidly changing industry, there will be many more and what we have learned about those we have experienced may not be a very good guide to us in a new situation. Just as we learn that people differ greatly in their personalities so we shall find that the roles programmed into computers differ in the personalities projected and the behavior displayed.

If we use only one computer system then we may come to view its style of operation and dialog as being that of computers in general. If we grow up in a close-knit community then we form similar stereotypes of the expected and proper behavior of other people. When we move away from that community we may experience intense **culture shock** in recognizing and adjusting to a much wider variety of forms of behavior. Similarly with computer systems as we come into contact with new ones there will be some familiar features coupled with quite different ones and we may suffer culture shock. However, just as we have classifications for people we can begin to recognize stereotypes for computer systems, **styles** of interaction and behavior with which we are already familiar. One reason we can expect such classifications to be possible is that new computer systems do not arise as commercial products out of nowhere. They evolve from older products, from comparison with competitive products, from the minds of people who make use of their own previous experience. A dramatically different, but effective, style of computer system is a rare phenomenon and, like a previously unencountered personality or wine, very much to be enjoyed and savored.

Thus, in discussing the programming of dialog between people and computers, much of the material we need must come from existing examples of computer systems that exhibit different styles of conversation. This book gives examples of a number of different approaches to programming interactive systems that are popular representatives of the current state of the art. When we criticize some of them for their misleading dialog bear in mind that the programs have probably sold in tens of thousands and made their producers a fortune. It is quite possible to have a very good program from a data processing point of view that is appallingly bad in its human interface - indeed the more useful the program the more we are willing to adapt our own behavior to its oddities. Similarly a person with useful skills may be a valued partner or employee even though he is a poor communicator and difficult to work with. There appears to be no fundamental reason, however, why both people and computer systems cannot combine being skilful with being communicative.

In this chapter we try to give a feel for conversations with computer systems by showing **snapshots** of the computer screen as the dialog proceeds. This is far less effective for the reader than actually sitting at a personal computer and trying out these dialog sequences, and others. Most of our examples are from very commonly available systems and it is worthwhile trying out as many as possible and adopting the same critical viewpoint that we take - is it obvious what this means? - how might it be misinterpreted? - what else might someone expect having seen this? - and so on.

CP/M - an operating system

The example opposite is from the screen of a computer using Digital Research's CP/M operating system. This is a popular set of programs for personal computers which has become an industry standard in that most companies writing application programs for use on these machines offer a version that will work with CP/M. The advantage of this is that the operating system sets up a working environment for the program which is largely independent of the computer hardware being used. CP/M acts as an interface between the application program and the computer processor,

```
A>DIR
A: FORMAT   COM : COPY     COM
A: MBASIC   COM : GRAPH    BAS
A: PIP      COM : DUMP     ASM
A: RW13     COM : ED       COM
A: AUGUST   TXT : STAT     COM
A: SEPT     TXT : SEPT     BAK
A: SUBMIT   COM : RECIPE   TXT
A: RECIPE   BAK : AUGUST   BAK
A: ARTHUR1  TXT : ARTHUR2  TXT
A>ED AUGUST.TXT
    : *T
    : *8T
    : *20A
  1: *8T
  1:   LIST OF JOBS
  2:
  3:   MUST GET THE BELL FIXED SOON
  4:
  5:   ARTHUR'S LETTER
  6:
  7:   TAKE BOOKS TO LIBRARY AND GET MO
RE JOYCE
  8:
  1: *5L
  6: *
```

Some dialog with Digital Research's CP/M

memory, disks, screen and printer, and enables the same program to be used on many different machines. It has become popular because it is cheap, compact, widely available and provides an adequate range of facilities. The CP/M dialog was not designed for ease of learning or clarity, but we start with it because this is where many users will start and have already started.

Let us go through the interaction with CP/M that generates the screen on the previous page exactly as it takes place. Mary goes to her Apple][personal computer and inserts her CP/M floppy disk in drive 1. She turns the computer on, a red light glows on drive 1, the disk whirs, and the message shown opposite appears on the screen.

A message like this when you start to use a package on a computer system is useful for a number of different reasons. The computer itself is completely general purpose and it is only when you load a program into it and start it running that you really have a computer system. What kind of system you have depends on the program you have loaded so that it is sensible for the program to announce itself.

The first line of the message tells Mary that she is running the CP/M operating system on an Apple][computer. This reminder is useful because there are several other operating systems commonly used on the Apple][. In addition CP/M is commonly used on many other computers and, even though it is designed to be as standard as possible, differs somewhat in the facilities offered according to the computer.

The second line of the message says that CP/M is using 56 Kilobytes of memory and that it is version 2.2. These technical parameters are sufficient to give an experienced CP/M user an indication of, for example, what size of files may be edited and what facilities this version of the operating system offers. This is particularly important if you go to use what should be a familiar operating system to you on someone else's machine - the message may warn you of important differences.

The third line is the copyright notice of the software manufacturer, put there to protect his legal interests, and warn you that even though you may own the actual disk with the software on it you only have restricted rights of use to it. Again the name and date are useful checks that you are using the software that you expected. Sometimes the manufacturer overdoes this part by putting up a large advertisement on the screen rather than a discrete name - forgetting how tedious this may appear to the user when it appears for the thousandth time.

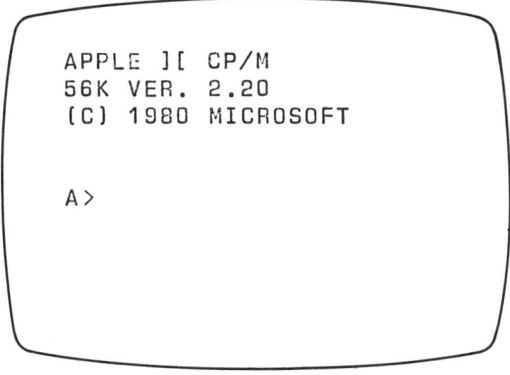

```
APPLE ][ CP/M
56K VER. 2.20
(C) 1980 MICROSOFT


A>
```

Starting CP/M

Many computers in many configurations

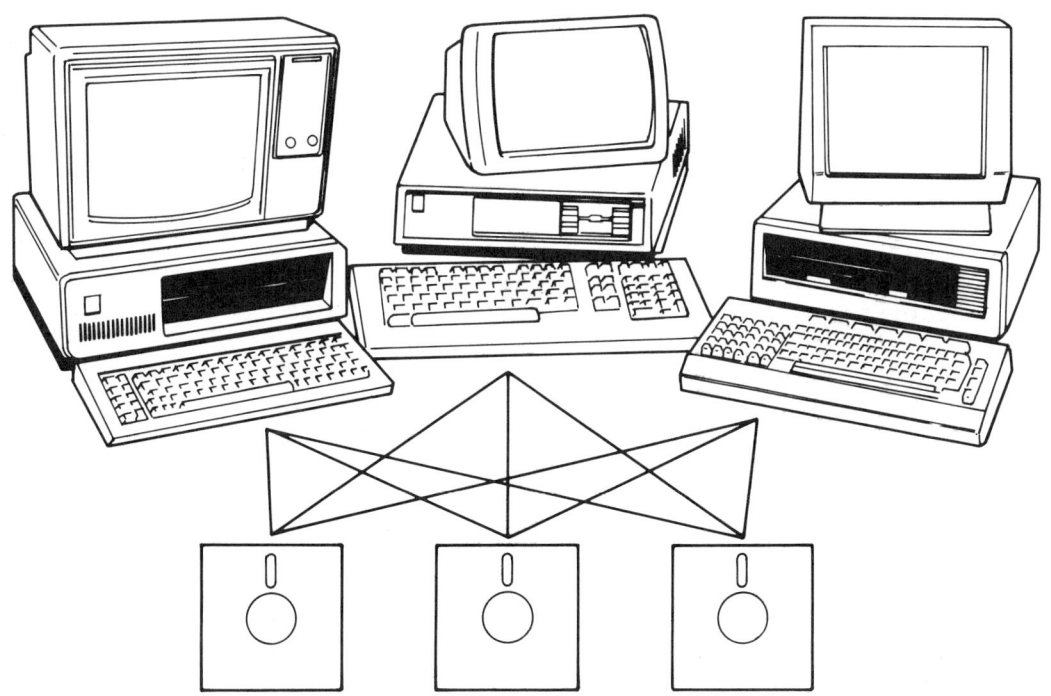

Many operating systems in many formats

The many combinations of computer and operating system

The message assures Mary that she has loaded the CP/M disk.
The "A>" following is a **prompt** put out by CP/M to inform her that
it has completed its activity and is waiting for her to key in a
command.   The ">" is just an arbitrary character that is not
often used and hence stands out as a prompt.   The "A" before it
indicates that the disk that CP/M will use unless she indicates
otherwise is drive A.   The Apple][has it labelled as drive 1.
However, CP/M uses letters rather than numbers for disk drives.
The programmer for the Apple][version of CP/M had a difficult
choice.   Should he call the disk "A" for the sake of users
familiar with CP/M and risk confusing users familiar with Apple,
or should he call it "1" on the Apple for consistency with the
Apple manuals and then risk confusing those who had used CP/M on
other machines?

Mary wants to add some notes to a list of "jobs to be done"
that she has started to keep on the computer.   She is not sure
what she called this list so she keys CATALOG to get a list of
her disk files. Now the response opposite is given, "CATALOG?".
It means that the command, CATALOG, is not recognized by the CP/M
operating system.   However, it does not help Mary very much to
know that it did not recognize the word used.   She would like to
know what commands it would recognize.   In ordinary conversation
the reply "what?" is regarded as impolite and unhelpful for the
same reason.

Mary remembers that she should have keyed DIR to CP/M to list
her files.   She does this next and the text opposite appears on
the screen. On the Apple][under its own operating system you
have to say CATALOG, but in CP/M you say DIR which is an
abbreviation for DIRECTORY. However, if you type DIRECTORY it is
not recognized as a command.

Mary recognizes the files listed.   They are her son's games and
she has put the wrong disk in by mistake.   It is CP/M for the
Apple][but it doesn't contain her programs or data.   She
takes out her son's disk, puts in hers, and remembers to type
CTRL-C (a so-called **control** character obtained by holding the
CTRL key and keying "C") to CP/M to inform the operating system
that the disk has been changed.

Mary types DIR again and this time the files that are listed
are the ones that she expected.   The table on the screen is made
up of two columns of file names.   Each name has two parts.   The
first may be up to eight characters long and is used to label the
contents of the file.   The second may be up to three characters
long and shows the type of file.

```
A>CATALOG
CATALOG?
A>
```

```
A>DIR
A: COPY      COM : MBASIC   COM
A: PIP       COM : ED       COM
A: DEMONS    COM : STARTREK COM
A: PAKMAN    COM : RABBITS  COM
A: ADVENT    COM : MYGAME   GAM
A: MYGAM2    GAM : GAMMON   BAS
A: RATRAP    BAS : MYGAME3  GAM
A: OTHELLO   BAS : AIRWAR   COM
A>
```

```
A>^C
A>DIR
A: FORMAT    COM : COPY     COM
A: MBASIC    COM : GRAPH    BAS
A: PIP       COM : DUMP     ASM
A: RW13      COM : ED       COM
A: AUGUST    TXT : STAT     COM
A: SEPT      TXT : SEPT     BAK
A: SUBMIT    COM : RECIPE   TXT
A: RECIPE    BAK : AUGUST   BAK
A: ARTHUR1   TXT : ARTHUR2  TXT
A>
```

More dialog with CP/M

The jobs that Mary wants to change are those for August and she filed them as AUGUST.TXT. She now wants to edit this file and types ED AUGUST.TXT. The response opposite appears on the screen. The ":*" is a different prompt. It comes not from the CP/M operating system to indicate that it is waiting for a command, but from the CP/M editor which is now controlling the dialog on the computer side. This change is useful to remind Mary that she is communicating with the editor program. However, it is not a very informative message - rather like the cough at the end of a telephone line that just lets you know someone is there and listening.

Mary wants to check that she has the right file so she keys "T" which she remembers means "type out the current line". The system does nothing. It just repeats the ":*" prompt. Mary is puzzled. Perhaps the first line is blank. She keys "8T" which should type eight lines of her file. Again the system just repeats the prompt. Mary is now becoming concerned. Perhaps the contents of the file have been lost. Perhaps she didn't call it AUGUST.TXT. Perhaps the editor program has been damaged, or the computer.

Mary is not sure what to do next and so she gets her CP/M Editor manual out of the drawer and searches through for clues about what might have happened. After a while she finds out what she has done wrong. The editor does not read any text out of the file into the computer unless she specifically commands it to. First she should **append** some text out of the file into the "buffer" by keying nA where n is the number of lines she wants. She keys "20A" and this results in the response opposite.

Now she can list the contents by keying "8T" which leads to the screen opposite. Mary feels that something "typed" should come out on the printer, but here it means that it is displayed on the screen.

She has now written to Arthur so that can come off the list. She is on line 1 and wants to delete line 5 so she keys in "5L" to move to line 5. When she looks at the result she has got to line 6. She thinks she must have made a mistake in pressing the key 5 so she decides to try to go back to line 5 by typing "5L" again. Now she is on line 11. Whatever is going wrong?

Mary now thinks that she should have another look at the manual. The manual shows the command to be 4L to move from line 1 to line 5, that is, move down by 4 lines, so she has to move -6 lines to get from line 11 to line 5. She keys "-6L" and gets the response opposite. She wonders why she has to do calculations in

```
A>ED AUGUST.TXT
    : *
```

```
    :*T
    :*
```

```
    :*8T
    :*
```

```
    : *20A
   1: *
```

```
   1: *8T
   1:  LIST OF JOBS
   2:
   3:  MUST GET THE BELL FIXED SOON
   4:
   5:  ARTHUR'S LETTER
   6:
   7:  TAKE BOOKS TO LIBRARY AND GET MO
RE JOYCE
   8:
   1: *
```

```
   1: *5L
   6: *5L
  11: *
```

```
  11: *-6L
   5: *
```

More dialog with CP/M

her head to work out what number to put in to get to the line she
wants. Seems crazy when the computer is very much better than
she is at adding and subtracting. Anyway, at last she is getting
close to being able to do something with her notebook, although
she is beginning to wonder whether old-fashioned pencil and paper
might not have some advantages after all.

Is it really as bad as that?

If you have followed Mary through all her problems then you
might be wondering if we are just mocking her stupidity, or
perhaps that of the designers of CP/M. Let us deny that
immediately. Mary is just one of us coping with a semi-familiar
system. CP/M is a good operating system that has been of immense
benefit to the computer industry and to an enormous community of
personal computer users. What was happening to Mary has happened
to all of us, probably many times and with many different
software packages on many different computers.

To illustrate this let us take a real life case history that
happened to us while we were writing this book. We were given an
account on a Honeywell Multics computer system in order to keep
in touch with a new research project using electronic mail. This
is an extreme opposite to Mary's Apple][. Multics is a very
large timesharing operating system designed to allow many
hundreds of users to share the resources of a large, powerful
mainframe computer, with complete security of stored information.
The team that developed and supports this system is very much
larger than that for CP/M and the resources expended on it have
been very great.

So what happened? Well, the dialog sequence opposite shows our
first reasonably successful attempt to communicate with Multics.
The first line is a command to the **auto-dialer** in the **modem** which
links our computer into the telephone network to dial the number
262-4000. This should connect us to the Datapac computer
communication network. When we did this the first few times
nothing happened. On making enquiries we were told to key a
period followed by RETURN to let Datapac know we were there. The
period is on the second line and sure enough Datapac responds on
the third line.

You cannot see the "invalid command" we keyed into Datapac
since it does not **echo** it back to the terminal. Presumably we
made a typing error. We keyed in the connection information a
second time and the call was connected. We were now in
touch with the communications computer at the remote site and

```
*D2624000FX
DATAPAC: 5070 0033
DATAPAC: invalid command
DATAPAC: call connected
1UA: UNIV OF ARTICA COMPUTER SERVICES X.25
Unattended service from 82-12-24 16:00 to 83-01-03 07:30


% 1MU1UA CONNECTED.
** Unattended Service **
Multics MR9.1_X: The University of Artica
Load=19.4 out of 155.0 units: users = 32, 12/29/82 0950.5 mst Wed
login Gaines Fifth
Password:
Incorrect password supplied.
Please try again or type "help" for instructions.
login Gaines Fifth
Password:
You are protected from preemption until 1051.
Gaines Fifth logged in 12/29/82  0951.2 mst Wed from DATAPAC terminal "1UA".
Last login 12/29/82  0939.0 mst Wed from DATAPAC terminal "1UA".
From Initializer.SysDaemon (login) 12/29/82  0950.9 mst Wed:
Password for user Gaines.Fifth given incorrectly from DATAPAC terminal "1UA".
No mail.

82-12-23   Operations Notice: The Department of Academic Computing Services
           will be closed from 16:00 hours. Fri. Dec. 24/82 until 07:30 hrs.
           Monday Jan.3/83, for the Christmas and New Years holiday.The Multics
           system will be available on an unattended basis during this time, and
           there will be limited dispatch of user output at the central site on
           Dec. 27/28/29/30/31.

82-12-28   Operations Notice: All Computer Facilities of Academic Computer
           Services will be unavailable on Tue.Jan 4/83 from 07:00 - 16:00
           due to Environmental Equipment maintenance and testing( power
           and air conditioning services).
           This is required inorder to complete renovations of the Computer Area

82-12-16   ACS Seminars - winter session: type, 'help seminars.gi' for
           date,time, and place.

82-12-15   For further info on DCS-Node 2, 4800 baud line update, type:
           'help dcs.changes'.

82-12-15   The Datapac line on DCS Node-2 has been upgraded to 4800 baud, to
           use, type %cn,02dp and/or 62600018.

82-12-18   Hardware Upgrade: The Multics system is now running on
           the newer and faster DPS8/70M series of Honeywell hardware.  There
           should be no user visible changes associated with this upgrade (other
           than that noted below for tape operations), but if you encounter
           problems, please contact Consulting at 225-9786 or via Multics mail

82-12-18   Tape users no
```

Some dialog with a remote computing service

keyed in the request to connect to Multics. Now we could **login** to Multics itself, giving our project code, "Gaines Fifth", and our **password**. Again we miskeyed it the first time but at last were connected to Multics.

The system then proceeded to type out to us a series of messages that were interesting at first but rapidly became very boring. Each one was dated and they came in reverse historical order. By the time the system was giving us information about events of two years ago we hoped it would stop. It did not and no matter what keys were pressed nothing would halt its diatribe. We eventually turned off the modem which broke the connection.

Some further attempts and experiments showed that the BREAK key on the terminal would stop the Multics messages. We then attempted to use the editor on Multics but could not find how to delete characters we keyed in error. Also we could not find out how to send mail to colleagues at the remote site to ask them how to use the system. We knew the account code and password of one colleague and put the message opposite into his files. It gives a feeling for what our problems were. We guessed that a file called Charlie.profile on his account would contain commands to the system to prevent it from typing so many messages when we logged in. We asked the system to print it. The interminable garbage opposite then poured out and again we had to press the BREAK key to stop it.

Eventually our friends at the remote site took pity upon us and went into our account and fixed it up for us. We called up Multics many times thereafter to see if there were any messages for us, but it always said "no mail". After two weeks a colleague called and said he had been trying to send us mail on Multics but the system was refusing to take it. We eventually found out that we had "no mail" because we had no mailbox - one had not been set up when our account was fixed. Now we have a mailbox and, after a few months of using the system, Multics has become an old friend with whom it is simple and natural to converse.

Recently, the remote site installed a completely different computer and we have just started to attempt to send mail through that. We get incomprehensible messages on the screen. The terminal does not show what we are keying. We do not know how to exit from the editor. Life is hell again.

Again, we are not poking fun at Multics - not even at ourselves. The designers of the system expected users to attend courses on how to use it and provided detailed manuals on all

.print **CHARLIE**

<pre>
                CHARLIE   12/29/82   0945.8 mst Wed
</pre>

Charlie I am struglling!

What is Martin's mailbox?

Mine is Gaines Fifth (not Henry!)

How do you delete an error char as you input?

When you do sma to send mail how do you quite (quit)?
[cannot get backslasf f in message to say I tried it — qx pu]

How do you stop yards of grabage messages when you login?

Oh for a system that waw not user unfriendly!

Very much enjoyed visiti and trying to communicate.

B.
[tried

<pre>
                Charlie.profile   12/29/82   0947.5 mst Wed
</pre>

\000\000\000\001\000\000\000\405\000\000\000(\000\000\000\000\000\000\000\000\0
\c00\000\000\000\000\000H\736\637\501\736q\000\000\000\000\000\000\000\000\000\
\c000\000\000\000\000\000\000\000\000\000\000\000\000\000\000\000\000\000\000\0
\c00\000\000\000\000\000\000\000\000\000\000\000\000\000\000\000\000\000\000\00
\c0\000\000\000\000\000\000\000\000\000\000\000\000\000\000\000\000\000\000\000
\c\000\000\000\000\000\000\000\000\000\000\000\000\000\000\000\000\000\000\000\
\c000\000\000\000\000\000\000\000\000\000\000\000\000\000\000\000\000\000\000\0
\c00\000\000\000\000\000\000\000\000\000\000\000\000\000\000\000\000\000\000\00
\c0\000\000\000\000\000\000\000\000\000\000\000\000\000\000\000\000\000\000\000
\c\000\000\000\000\000\000\000\000\000\000\000\000\000\000\000\000\000\000\000\
\c000\000\000\000\000\000\000\000\000\000\000\000\000\000\000\000\000\000\000\0
\c00\000\000\000\000\000\000\000\000\000\000\000\000\000\000\000\000\000\000\00
\c0\000\000\000\000\000\000\000\000\000\00

Some more dialog with the remote computing service

aspects of the system. The modern world of data communications and the modern expectation that you can get into a system and make sense of it without any instructions or documentation were not critical features in their system design. Similarly, the CP/M designers provide very clear manuals on the use of their system. However, users of interactive computer systems do expect to be able to get to use them with very little background reading. This is not unreasonable as computers become as commonly used as automobiles. You expect to get into a strange car and be able to drive it immediately, and be able to use all its facilities after a few experiments. This is an attitude increasingly adopted towards computers and one that the dialog designer must bear in mind. In the rest of the chapter and in the following one we will give examples of a variety of techniques that make it easy for users to take this approach to the use of computer systems.

Improving prompt/response dialog

CP/M and Multics operate through a question and answer sequence. The system puts out a **prompt** which informs the user what state it is in and that it is waiting for a command. The user then types in a **response** usually terminated by pressing the RETURN key. If this requires action on the part of the system, such as typing out a directory, it does this and then puts out a further prompt. This is a standard **prompt/response** mode of dialog which is very similar to human conversation. Even the use of the BREAK key to stop Multics typing out unwanted information has its analogy in the way that we will interrupt someone whose speech is tedious or inappropriate. The diagram opposite shows the flow of activity in this mode of dialog.

How can we improve the situation of the user in this type of simple formal dialog? In the previous examples both Mary and we found ourselves not knowing what to do at different stages in the dialog. Mary got out her CP/M manual to find out what she was doing wrong. If there had been some way of asking the system for help then she could probably have avoided having to stop the conversation with the computer to go and find another source of information. Many systems now provide some way of the user asking for help as one of the possible responses that is always available. In the same way as the BREAK key was used to terminate unwanted messages, a HELP key may be used to request information on what options are available to the user. The HELP key may be a special one or it may be a standard character such as the "?" or a word such as "HELP".

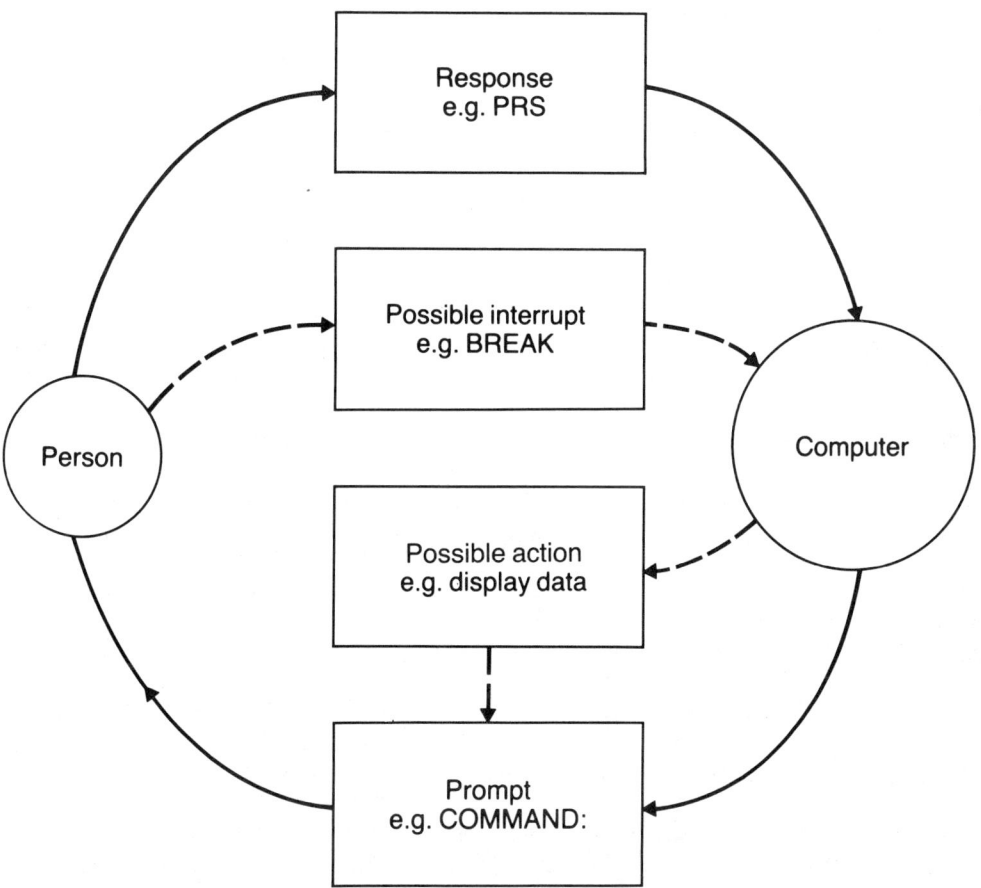

Prompt/response dialog structure

Help facilities

To show the use of HELP and other facilities we will use as an example a Personnel Record System (PRS) which keeps track of employees in a small business. Ted goes to the company computer and sees that it is ready since it gives the "COMMAND:" prompt shown opposite. He wants to enter information on a new member of staff into the PRS so he keys "PRS". The system responds "PRS:" to show that it has started the right program. Ted has not done this before and is not sure what to do. He keys in a "?" to ask for help and the system responds with a list of likely commands.

This is already a great improvement over Mary's situation in trying to remember the directory listing and editing commands in CP/M. Ted does not have to find a manual. He has **on-line help.** The list of commands alone is not enough information for him, so Ted keys "?" again and this time the system gives him more detailed information. Just for interest Ted keys "?" a third time and the system refers him to the relevant page in the manual.

This multi-level help, called **query in depth,** allows the user to ask for help freely knowing that the initial response will be a terse message to prompt his memory. Some systems overdo the help. If the user is a little unsure, asks for help, and then has to wait for two minutes while material pours out at his terminal, he will not use the help facility again. It is simple to have more than one help message available and make the first one short so that the user is always prepared to ask for it.

One major advantage of having the system offer help is that it can be related to the context in which the request is made. It is as if the system were moving through a manual about itself as we proceed with the dialog and is prepared to read out the relevant material whenever we request it. Ted again asks for help when the system prompts him with "SIN" - he perhaps thinks the system is asking for a list of those that Mr.Cooper has committed. However, the response to his "?" is that SIN stands for social insurance number. Note that the response in this case is not just a reading from the manual. The system constructs it not only using the local context that help is being requested related to SIN, but also the overall context that it is Mr.Cooper's record Ted is entering.

When Ted again types "?" in response to the "DATE OF BIRTH" prompt the system again generates a constructed response. Note also how it allows the date to be entered in one of two common formats. The dialog has been programmed to give some freedom in individual style of input.

```
COMMAND:PRS
PRS:?
  ENTER, DELETE, MODIFY, LIST, RETRIEVE
PRS:?
  ENTER a new person's record, DELETE an existing record,
  MODIFY a record, LIST all personnel records,
  RETRIEVE a person's record using their name or SIN
  : exit to monitor
PRS:?
  See PERSONNEL RECORDS SYSTEM manual page 23
PRS:E
  Personnel Record Entry Number 45
LAST NAME:Cooper
FIRST NAME(S):Percival Edward
SIN:?
  P.E.Cooper's Social Insurance Number, six digits
SIN:305672
DATE OF BIRTH:?
  P.E.Cooper's date of birth, Month/Day/Year, e.g. 5/21/45
            or Day-Month-Year, e.g. 21-May-45
DATE OF BIRTH::
COMMAND:
```

Help facilities in a Personnel Records System

Abort facilities

At this point Sue comes back from lunch, notices Ted finding
his way around the system, and offers to put in the new records
later. He asks, "How do I stop in the middle," and she replies,
"Oh, just type a colon." He asks, "What about the data I have
entered," and she says, "Don't worry it will forget it." Ted
keys ":" and the system puts out the COMMAND: prompt exactly as
it was when he started.

This combination of the capabilities to get help at any time
and to be able to **abort** any activity without affecting the system
is very important in allowing users to feel free to interact with
a system they do not understand. They can explore it, asking
questions and learning about it, knowing that their mistakes will
have no consequences. The system is forgiving and supportive.

Default responses

Sue goes to the system and enters the record that Ted did not
complete. A number of other helpful features appear in her
dialog with it shown opposite. The ADDRESS is a number of lines
of text that may vary considerably and hence the system goes on
prompting for more until she presses the RETURN key alone. This
is called a **null response.**

The HOME TELEPHONE number will very often be in the same area
as the office and the system is programmed to assume that it is
(416) area unless the user types in something different. It
shows that this is the **default response** by making it part of the
prompt that can be read as if it were part of the response.

The system gives a default response also of EAST for the REGION
and Sue accepts this by keying RETURN as a null response. The
default response of PERMANENT for STATUS is not what Sue wants to
put in, however, so she keys TEMPORARY knowing this will override
the default.

Response validation

When responding to DATE OF BIRTH Sue absent-mindedly puts in
the current year. The system has been programmed to check for
incorrect or unlikely dates and asks her to check the entry she
has made. She types it in again. Note that the system does not
refuse to accept the date she has given. Sometimes unlikely data
is quite valid because a case has occurred that the original

```
COMMAND:PRS
PRS:E
  Personnel Record Entry Number 45
LAST NAME:Cooper
FIRST NAME(S):Percival Edward
SIN:305672
ADDRESS:217 Amberville Drive
ADDRESS:Ussingham
ADDRESS:Ontario T3K 1G7
ADDRESS:
HOME TELEPHONE: (416) - :334-4143
DATE OF BIRTH:6/9/83
  Date of birth in 1983 seems unlikely.  Please check.
DATE OF BIRTH: 6/9/83 :6/9/43
DATE STARTED:12/10/83
DEPARTMENT:SALES
REGION: EAST :
STATUS: PERMANENT :TEMPORARY
PAY BASIS: WEEKLY :
PAYROLL NUMBER: 443772 :
  Record entry number 45 will be - Cooper, Percival Edward
     Social Insurance Number 305672,  Born 9th June 1943
     Address - 217 Amberville Drive,
               Ussingham,
               Ontario T3K 1G7.
     Telephone - (416) 334-4143
     Started 10th December 1983 in East Region Sales
     as temporary weekly paid #443772
OK TO ENTER?: YES :
PRS:
```

Default responses and validation in a Personnel Records System

system designers had not expected. It is generally better just to query unusual values, not reject them altogether.

When Sue has responded to all the prompts and entered a complete record the system is programmed to put it out again so that she can validate it before it is finally entered. She may easily have made errors in entering the information in sequence that she has not noticed. Note how the complete information is presented in a natural format that is different from that in which it was entered so that the user has the opportunity to view it in a different way. This helps error detection.

Correction through default responses

The combination of default and null responses used where possible to speed up data entry may also be used as a basis for modifying records. Many systems require users to go through completely different procedures when they are correcting or changing a record than when they are originally entering. Since the modification of records will probably be far less frequent than their entry, users do not become familiar with the procedure and are likely to make errors in using it.

The dialog opposite shows Sue correcting the entry she has just made by asking to modify it. The dialog sequence is exactly the same as that for the original entry but the information entered into the record is now used to give each prompt an appropriate default response. Even the record to be accessed is given the default response of 45, the last record she entered. Sue can skip through the record by keying RETURN repeatedly until she comes to the item she wishes to modify, in this case the DATE STARTED.

Response grouping

One problem that skilled users have with a prompt/response system is that it may become tedious after a while to answer each prompt in turn. This may be overcome by allowing users to **group** responses together on the same line and not putting out unnecessary prompts if the information has already been entered. The dialog opposite shows Sue using this capability to put in the previous record more rapidly. She groups together the initial commands and data all on one line. The system takes this in and then gives the prompt for the next item, ADDRESS, which again Sue groups onto one line. Note how she still has the opportunity to check the complete entry when she has finished.

```
COMMAND:PRS
PRS:M
MODIFY PERSONNEL RECORD NUMBER: 45 :
LAST NAME: Cooper :
FIRST NAME(S): Percival Edward :
SIN: 305672 :
ADDRESS: 217 Amberville Drive :
ADDRESS: Ussingham :
ADDRESS: Ontario T3K 1G7 :
ADDRESS:
HOME TELEPHONE: (416) - 334-4143 :
DATE OF BIRTH: 6/9/43 :
DATE STARTED: 12/10/83 : 11/10/83
DEPARTMENT: SALES :
REGION: EAST :
STATUS: TEMPORARY :
PAY BASIS: WEEKLY :
PAYROLL NUMBER: 443772 :
   Record entry number 45 will be - Cooper, Percival Edward
      Social Insurance Number 305672,  Born 9th June 1943
      Address - 217 Amberville Drive,
               Ussingham,
               Ontario T3K 1G7.
      Telephone - (416) 334-4143
      Started 10th November 1983 in East Region Sales
      as temporary weekly paid #443772
OK TO ENTER?: YES :
PRS:
```

Correction by default responses in a Personnel Records System

```
COMMAND:PRS E Cooper Percival Edward 305672
ADDRESS:217 Amberville Drive, Ussingham, Ontario T3K 1G7
ADDRESS:
HOME TELEPHONE: (416) - :334-4143 6/9/43 12/10/83 SALES
REGION: EAST :
STATUS: PERMANENT :TEMPORARY
PAY BASIS: WEEKLY :
PAYROLL NUMBER: 443772 :
   Record entry number 45 will be - Cooper, Percival Edward
      Social Insurance Number 305672,  Born 9th June 1943
      Address - 217 Amberville Drive,
               Ussingham,
               Ontario T3K 1G7.
      Telephone - (416) 334-4143
      Started 10th December 1983 in East Region Sales
      as temporary weekly paid #443772
OK TO ENTER?: YES :
PRS:
```

Response grouping in a Personnel Records System

Allowing response grouping is one way of designing a dialog in such a way that it gives maximum support to new users of the system without being tediously supportive to them later as their skills develop. It is very appropriate if there are natural groupings of responses that users will find easy to understand.

Conclusions - Formal Computer Conversation

The formal dialogs of this chapter are very different from the natural language conversations with Hal, Muddlehead and Mike in science fiction. However, they **are** a form of conversation for the person taking part in them. People adapt language to their needs and in highly specialist situations they will use quite unusual languages. Listen to an air traffic controller, police on their radios, a surgeon in an operating theater, experienced CB radio operators, and you will hear dialog similar in style to that between Mary and CP/M.

Mary's problem with the listing of her disk files being requested by CATALOG in Applesoft and DIR in CP/M shows that user expectations are very important and arise not just from science fiction but increasingly from prior use of computers. Varying terminology is a problem of everyday life. What is called a "thumb tack" in America is called a "drawing pin" in England. However, when we move from country to country, even region to region, we expect such problems for a while but we do not do it often. Moving from computer to computer, from software package to software package, is just like moving between countries, languages and dialects. We must expect culture shock and if we do it often we shall experience the experiential overload of the frequent traveler. Jet-setting between personal computers is a real phenomenon.

The eighth proverb - EASY TO UNDERSTAND SYSTEMS

Mary's problems in using DIR or CATALOG come under Proverb 6 that we should take users' expectations into account. However, as soon as she begins to use CP/M and ED her expectations start to change. She is **learning** about the new system. She is forming a **model** of it within her mind. This is one of the most important of human characteristics and it takes place continually. We model the worlds of our experience subconsciously and it affects our behavior. In our society we change all the time. We increase our understanding of the world. System designers must take this changing nature of people into account. They must make it as easy as possible for the user to form an accurate model of the system.

Computer jet-setter

Proverb 8: The system should be easy to understand.

Users will model the computer system and form new expectations based on their interaction with it. The system should be designed to induce accurate models and correct expectations.

The ninth proverb - SHOWING THE CHOICES AVAILABLE

Making the system easy to understand is easier said than done. The response by CP/M when Mary keys CATALOG is "CATALOG?" It is fairly easy to come to understand this as meaning "I do not accept this command." However, it does not help Mary to form a model of what commands the system will actually accept or what these will do. All her later confusion comes from similar causes. When Mary does something CP/M gives her very little **feedback** about the effects of her action, what other actions were possible, what they will do, and so on. We learn from doing things correctly and we learn from making mistakes but in both circumstances we need information that is sufficient for us to understand what has happened.

The HELP facility that we showed in the Personnel Record System made it easy for Ted to find out about the system and to see what options he had available. The multi-level version of it is a way of making the HELP dialog itself as flexible as possible to differing user needs. There are also other ways of giving the kind of information that would have made the system so much easier to understand for Mary. We describe some of them in Chapters 5 and 7. They are ways of showing the user what choices he has in the particular context of where he is in the dialog.

Proverb 9: The user should be shown the choices available.

At any point in a formal dialog sequence the user will have a limited range of options available. There should be a facility to enable the user to find out his choices.

The tenth proverb - EASE OF ESCAPE

When the user is aware of the choices that are logical consequences of where he is in the dialog he may suddenly realize that none of them suit his purpose. He may just want to stop the conversation he has started and start again or cease to use the system for a while. The reasons for this may be as mundane as wanting to do something else such as going for lunch. They may be deeper in that he realizes that the conversation has taken a wrong turn - he may have keyed the command to delete a record in error when he intended only to modify it. Whatever the reason for wanting to stop the user needs to be able to do so with the assurance that he has not left the system in a mess. Either it should be clear that none of his previous conversation has had any effect, or the actual effects of it should be well-defined and obvious.

Ted used the colon, ":", as an abort command to tell the system to forget his conversation to that point when Sue said she would take over. The ABORT command, like the HELP command, needs some special key that can be used at any time to achieve the required effect. If there is no special key marked ABORT or EXIT, then the colon is an abnormal response that is easy to remember. One can say to users, "The computer will type a ':' at the end of a message when it is waiting for you to send one back. Just type a ':' back if you want to escape."

Proverb 10: It should be easy to escape from a conversation cleanly.

At any point in a formal dialog sequence the user may wish to abort the dialog and escape any consequences of his preceding responses. There should be a facility to enable the user to escape at will leaving the state of the system well defined.

The eleventh proverb - CO-OPERATING IN VALIDATION

One consequence of providing HELP and ABORT facilities as called for in the previous two proverbs is to make it much easier for the user to **explore** the system freely, without anxiety about the consequences of doing this. Another way of reducing user anxiety is to have the system validate as much of the information being entered as possible and to help the user also in doing this. When Sue made a mistake in the date of birth of a new employee the system was programmed to pick this up as unlikely, presumably because new employees would normally be at least sixteen years old or so, and queried her response. It did not reject it but asked her to check it. This is a better technique than absolute refusal to accept seemingly invalid data since, unless the consequences are problematic, it is better to allow wider tolerances than seem reasonable at the time of design. Systems often get used in ways that the designer did not expect.

However, many errors cannot be discovered by analysing the user's responses yet some of these may be obvious to the user himself. This is why the system aids Sue's own validation processes by displaying again the information she has entered and asking her to give it a final check.

Proverb 11: The system should co-operate with the user in validating responses.

Information should be checked as it is entered and queried it if it appears unlikely to be correct. The consequences of significant actions should be made clear to the user and confirmation requested before they are carried out.

The twelfth proverb - MINIMIZING THE USER'S WORKLOAD

People have a limited capacity to process information and if this is used on one task then what is left to understand the system will be less. One load that the system can carry easily is to try to anticipate what the user's most likely response will be and to make this the default option. The dialog with Sue shows how the null response of keying RETURN alone may be used to select this default. This shows up particularly well when Sue goes in to modify a record and all the previous information is used as default values. She need only key RETURN to run through the record until she comes to the information she wishes to modify. A careful selection of default values, which may be constructed on the basis of previous responses, can make the user's task in entering information very much simpler.

Proverb 12: The system should minimize the user's workload by anticipating responses.

The most likely user response should be made the default option that can be selected by a single key depression.

5 Computer Conversation Through Menus and Forms

The formal conversations with computers that were discussed and illustrated in Chapter 4 have a **serial** style that dates back to the original teleprinter or typewriter terminals used with early computers. These terminals used a roll of paper as a display and typed on it the prompts from the computer and the responses from the user. They were often fairly slow devices capable of typing at only ten characters a second. This is a high speed compared with a typist who will press keys at a rate of only two or three a second, but it is slow compared with normal reading speeds of fifty or so characters a second. Thus dialogs designed for use with typewriter terminals had to take into account the line by line display, the impossibility of changing it once it had been printed, and the fairly slow speed of the output.

In recent years electronic displays have become available that are lower in cost than typewriters and much faster in operation with display speeds of one thousand or more characters a second. The most important characteristic of these displays is that they give a display screen which is **two-dimensional** and can be **randomly accessed** and modified. Information from the computer does not have to be typed out line by line as on a typewriter but can instead be placed anywhere on the screen at any time. The complete screen is always visible and can be divided into several different areas each with a different function - this is called **split-screen** operation. These new characteristics of the electronic display allow, and encourage, new styles of dialog with the computer.

The display screen can be used to mimic the behavior of the typewriter by putting out text a line at a time and **scrolling** it up the screen so that old text is lost off the top to make way for more at the bottom – in this mode of operation it is commonly called a **glass teleprinter.** It has the disadvantage over a real typewriter that we have no printed output, or **hard copy,** and lose information that scrolls off the top of the screen. Some electronic displays do have extra storage for information that has scrolled off and allow it to be scrolled back again, just like having a roll of paper. However, the most important uses of the display screen are those which take advantage of its two-dimensional nature.

In this chapter we shall give examples of some of the styles of conversation possible through a display screen. We will consider the most often used screen formats which display only text and numbers, generally giving twenty-four lines of eighty characters. The further styles possible with more advanced graphic displays are discussed in Chapter 7.

Menus with PLANET – a personal decision system

In Chapter 4 we showed how a HELP key could be used to show the user the choices of response available at each stage of the dialog. An alternative to this when a screen is available is to display the choices in the form of a **menu** so that the user does not have to ask for help but has the relevant options on the display. The menu opposite is the initial one shown on the screen when you start to use PLANET, a system for aiding personal decision making developed by the authors. Like CP/M, PLANET puts out a name and copyright notice at the top of the screen but instead of then proceeding to a prompt/response dialog in the styles already shown it lists possible choices and asks, "Which do you want?"

We can regard the whole display shown as a single prompt but because it is now designed as an informative screen the effect to the user is very different from that of the terse prompts of our previous dialogs. The user sees a complete structure designed to give him all the information he needs at this point in the dialog. Technically, the reason we can do this is the sheer speed at which the computer can generate the display – it appears instantly to the user even though it contains about five hundred characters.

The letters in angle brackets on the left of the display are the possible user responses. We have shown the user keying "P" to request PEGASUS, a program to aid decision-making. PLANET adds the letters "EGASUS" to the P to make up the complete word and then transfers control to the PEGASUS program. This itself

```
****************************************
* PLANET  PERSONAL LEARNING, ANALYSIS,  *
* NEGOTIATION & ELICITATION TECHNIQUES  *
*            COPYRIGHT 1982             *
*    CENTRE FOR MAN-COMPUTER STUDIES    *
****************************************

   <P> PEGASUS     - ELICITATION

   <A> ARGUS       - MULTIPLE ELICITATION

   <S> STRUCTURE   - ANALYSIS TECHNIQUES

   <D> DATA        - DATA FILES UTILITY

   <O> OUTPUT      - OUTPUT DEVICE UTILITY


WHICH DO YOU WANT? PEGASUS
```

```
        PLANET PEGASUS III ELICITATION   1B
               COPYRIGHT 1982
        CENTRE FOR MAN-COMPUTER STUDIES

   <S> STANDARD     - USUAL VERSION

   <A> AUGMENTED    - FOR EXPERIENCED USER

   <N> NO MATCHES   - WITHOUT FEEDBACK

   <C> CONTINUE     - FURTHER ELICITATION

   <B> BANK         - USE STORED BANK

   <R> RATINGS      - CHANGE SCALE

   <Q> QUIT         - BACK TO MAIN MENU


WHICH DO YOU WANT? RATINGS

RATING SCALE IS 1 TO 5

DO YOU WANT TO CHANGE IT?Y

NEW RATING SCALE 1 TO?15
UPPER LIMIT FROM 2 TO 9 ONLY

NEW RATING SCALE 1 TO?7
```

Two menus from PLANET

requires further choices by the user before it can start and puts up another menu on the screen shown below the first one.

A dialog with a user through a succession of menus which depend on his previous choices is said to be **tree-structured**. The user is led through successive stages of choice with the options available at each stage varying according to his previous choices. Many of the **videotex** information retrieval systems offered as public utilities for use in home and business, such as Prestel and Telidon, have such a tree-structured menu system. Often numbers are used to select items in the menu rather than letters - the characters in angle brackets could be 1 through 5 rather than P, A, S, D and O - particularly when a simplified keyboard is desired, perhaps with only the numeric keys. However, the initial letters of the required commands are easier for the user to remember than arbitrary numbers and it is important to note that, despite all the information being on the screen, the user will begin to. learn about the system as he becomes familiar with it.

The diagram opposite shows the complete set of PLANET menus and their tree structure. Notice how the last command on all of the sub-menus is QUIT - it is the escape route recommended in the tenth proverb.

Form filling with PFS - a personal filing system

There is a rather different mode of interaction with computers made possible by display screens that is more analogous to filling in a form or questionnaire than to human conversation. The "prompt" put out by the computer consists of a form in which there are gaps for the user to fill with information. This type of interaction was originally developed for large mainframe computers being used in an interactive mode from visual display terminals. It was wasteful for such large machines to take in the user's response character by character. It was more efficient for them to transmit a form to the display, have it filled in by the user at the terminal alone with no interaction with the computer, and then have the information sent to the computer all in one burst - this is so-called **transaction processing**.

The efficiency considerations are not relevant to personal computers where the user response can be analyzed character by character since the computer is serving no other users. However, the form-filling mode of information entry is attractive in its own right and has been used effectively in a number of personal

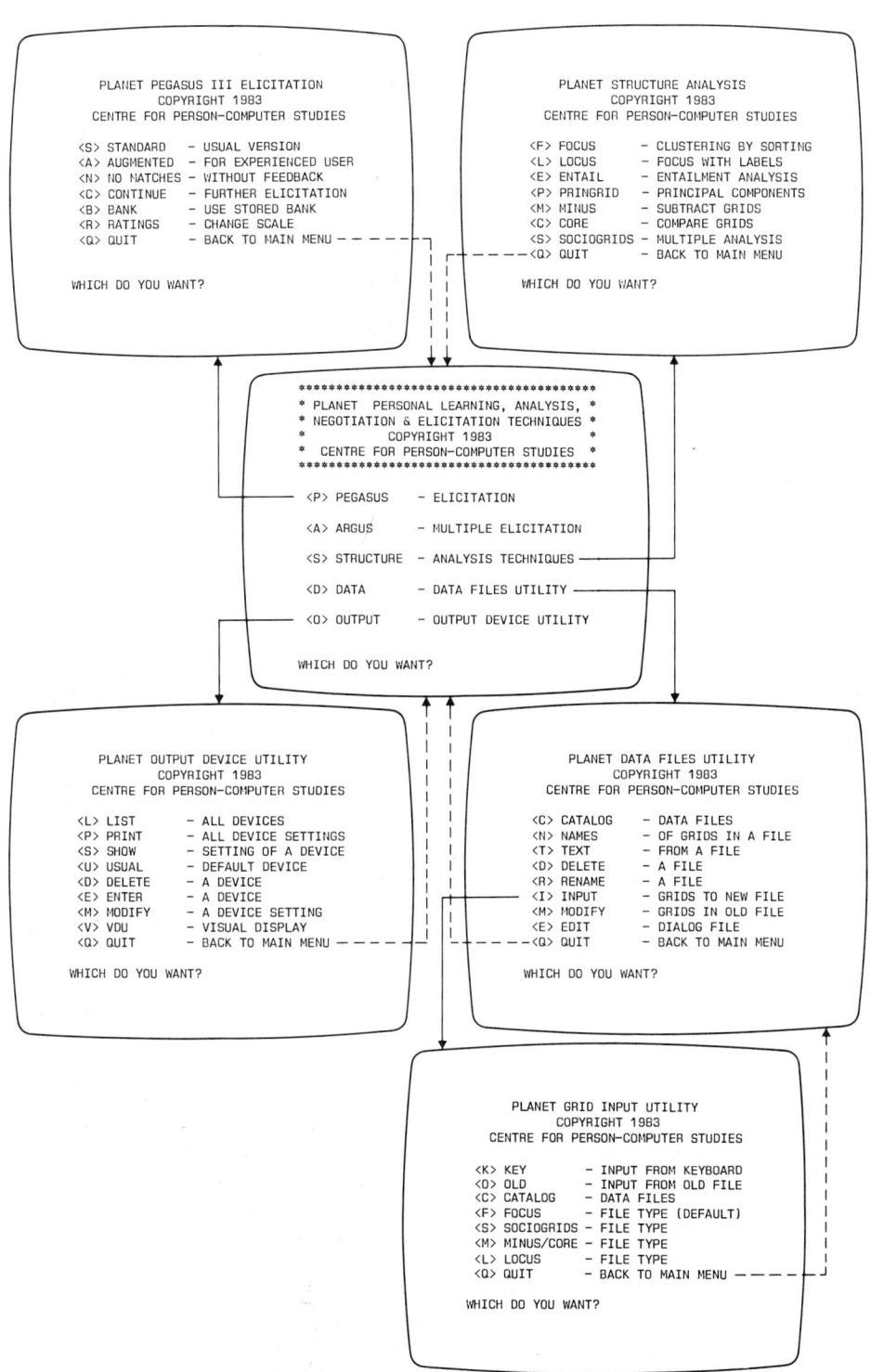

The menu tree for the main PLANET programs

computer packages. Software Publishing's **PFS** is a popular
program which enables users to set up their own filing system for
information storage and retrieval. The user first of all defines
a form on the screen by keying in a set of labels, one for each
item of information. The space after each label will be used for
the variable information in each individual record to be stored.

The upper part of the opposite page shows a form on the screen
of an Apple][that is the basis of an employee record system.
The user has filled in the details of Andrew Parkinson, a new
employee and this will be filed as form 23 of the file STAFF. It
is interesting to note how the form filling operation takes
place. The user first of all specifies that he wishes to add to
the file STAFF. A blank form with the format shown then appears
on the screen. It is number 23 because there are already 22
staff records in the file. The display **cursor** indicating where
characters keyed will appear on the screen is automatically set
after EMPLOYEE NUMBER: in the first information field. The user
keys this number then presses the cursor forward key on the Apple
][. The cursor skips to immediately after HIRED: so that the
date of hiring can be filled in. And so on. When all the fields
are completed the user presses the CTRL and C keys to store the
information on the form as record number 23 of the STAFF file.

This skipping from field to field in PFS is a standard
technique in form-filling dialog that corresponds to the sequence
of prompts in the serial dialogs illustrated in Chapter 4. Note
how the system no longer has to put out the record again for
validation at the end of the dialog as it does with Sue in that
chapter. The form that is being filled in is always on the
screen. Other dialog techniques can be applied at the same time
also. For example as the cursor skips from field to field it
would be possible to put up a varying menu of the possible values
that might be put in that field.

The retrieval of information from PFS is particularly simple
and elegant because it uses a simple variation of the method of
entering information. Suppose that we wish to check which staff
working for Joe Baker earn more than $20000. We go into "Search"
mode and call up the STAFF file form shown on the lower half of
the page opposite. We fill in the MANAGER: field as JOE BAKER
and the SALARY: field as >$20000. We press the CTRL and C keys
together and now the PFS program searches through the file and
shows on the screen, one by one, any forms that have Joe Baker as
manager and an employee with salary greater than $20000. If we
wish we can print out the contents of these forms to keep a
record of the results of our enquiry.

```
EMPLOYEE NUMBER: 279    HIRED: APR 6 1978

NAME: ANDREW PARKINSON

ADDRESS: 237 ALLAWAY PLACE   FLAT 5

CITY: SAN JOSE         STATE: CA  ZIP: 45342

JOB TITLE: PROGRAMMER  CUST SERVICES

LOCATION: CENTRAL SALES OFFICE

MANAGER: JOE BAKER


SALARY: $20200



---------------------------------------------
FILE STAFF        FORM 23        PAGE 1
```

Entering data by filling in a form with Software Publishing's PFS

```
EMPLOYEE NUMBER:          HIRED:

NAME:

ADDRESS:

CITY:            STATE:      ZIP:

JOB TITLE:

LOCATION:

MANAGER: JOE BAKER


SALARY: >$20000



---------------------------------------------
FILE STAFF   RETRIEVAL SPEC     PAGE 1
```

Retrieving data by filling in a form with PFS

Note how simple PFS is in both concept and operation and yet how versatile it can be in use. Anybody can develop a filing, or **database,** system by simply setting up a form for their particular type of information. They have only to specify the label for each item of information and leave enough characters between it and the next label for the longest item that might occur under that label. When the form has been specified it can then be used to collect data simply and effectively. Moreover a number of different files can be set up for different purposes, for example a products file and a customer file. Each will be different and yet the way in which they are used will be similar so that someone who has learned to access one will feel completely familiar with accessing any other.

Note also that the form of the filing system is determined by the user - your employee records system will reflect your way of working and needs for information, and may differ in many ways from mine. A system with this type of flexibility is said to be **customizable** to the users' needs. PFS achieves customizability while retaining a simple dialog that is **uniform** from one application to another.

Screen editing with Wordstar - a word processor

The typewriter is one of the most important items of equipment in the office and is increasingly in use in the home. It was an obvious candidate for improvement using electronic and microcomputer technology. For most typists the most useful feature that could be added is that of making corrections and amendments to a draft without having to retype it completely. The first machines that could do this were quaintly termed **word processors** and this name has now become the common name for computer-based typing systems. The first word processors were specialized machines that could do nothing else and were expensive items of equipment.

As personal computers became low in cost, however, it became attractive to use them for word processing and software packages were developed to do this. The early word processing packages were primitive, little more than the editor used to illustrate CP/M. However, letter and document preparation has become one of the most important applications of personal computers and some modern word-processing packages represent the most significant advances in computing techniques yet available. In particular a variety of interesting approaches to person-computer dialog have been developed for word processors.

De-skilling the writer's task

Wordstar is a very popular program that operates as a word processor under the CP/M operating system. It has been designed for extreme capability and ease of use, and has many very interesting features in the way it handles dialog with the user. Some of these features are concerned with timing and the adaptation of the system to both skilled and unskilled users. These are difficult to describe and illustrate in a book so if you can experiment with Wordstar itself we recommend the experience. There is much to be learned from experience with this remarkable program.

The upper part of the opposite page shows the initial screen put up by Wordstar when it is run on a terminal with 24 rows of 80 characters. The top line is a **status message** indicating that the program is editing no file. The six lines of text below this are an explanatory menu reminding the user of the various commands available. The six lines of text below this give a listing of all the files in the directory of the disk being used, sorted in alphabetical order. Each user command is a single letter so keying "d" leads to the screen showing in the lower part of the page. The "d" command is shown in the top left-hand corner. The menu has been changed to give information about file names. The prompt has been put out, NAME OF FILE TO EDIT?, and the user has typed CHAPT4 but not yet completed it by pressing the RETURN key.

We can already see some of the features that make Wordstar a simple and attractive program to use. All the information relevant to the user's current activity is available to him on the screen. The status line shows the current state of the system and the command he has given. The menu gives an explanation of the different commands the user may give and changes as his options change. It does not try to present the multitude of facilities offered by Wordstar all at once but instead selectively shows those relevant to the user's current action. The file directory is also relevant to him in selecting which one to edit and this also appears on the screen. Even though the program offers many facilities, all the information the user needs is clearly and concisely available to him.

There is one feature of Wordstar that is not apparent from the illustration but which is of great value to the user. It takes the computer time to fetch the menus from the disk and display them on the screen and in most systems the user would have to wait while this is done. The Wordstar program monitors the characters keyed by the user continuously, even while it is carrying out other tasks. If the user keys a sequence that calls up a new menu, but completes it rapidly, the program **does not**

```
        editing no file

    D=create or edit a Document file      H=set Help level
    N=create or edit a Non-document file  X=eXit to system
    M=Merge-print a file                  P=Print a file
    F=File directory off (ON)             Y=delete a file
    L=change Logged disk drive            O=cOpy a file
    R=Run a program                       E=rEname a file

DIRECTORY of disk A:
  CHAPT1      CHAPT2        CHAPT3       CHAPT4        CHAPT5        CHAPT6
  CHESS       CPM           DAVIS        ELIZA         EVANS         GILES.2
  HAL         CHARLIE.LOG   IMPOSS       LETTER        LETTER.BAK    MISTAKE
  MULTICAL    MULTICS       MULTICS.LOG  MYCIN         NEWPEG.REF    NOTES
  PEGASUS     REF           VISICALC     VISICALC.BAK  WINOGRAD
```

The initial screen of Micropro's Wordstar

```
d          editing no file

 Use this command to create a new document file,
 or to initiate alteration of an existing document file.

   A file name 1-8 letters/digits, a period,
   and an optional 0-3 character type.
   File name may be preceded by disk drive letter A-D
   and colon, otherwise current logged disk is used.

 ^S=delete character  ^Y=delete entry   ^F=File directory
 ^D=restore character ^R=Restore entry  ^U=cancel command

    NAME OF FILE TO EDIT?CHAPT4

DIRECTORY of disk A:
  CHAPT1      CHAPT2        CHAPT3       CHAPT4        CHAPT5        CHAPT6
  CHESS       CPM           DAVIS        ELIZA         EVANS         GILES.2
  HAL         CHARLIE.LOG   IMPOSS       LETTER        LETTER.BAK    MISTAKE
  MULTICAL    MULTICS       MULTICS.LOG  MYCIN         NEWPEG.REF    NOTES
  PEGASUS     REF           VISICALC     VISICALC.BAK  WINOGRAD
```

The changing menu as a Wordstar dialog proceeds

display the relevant menu. Thus a skilled user does not have to wait for the menus to be fetched and displayed but can type in commands and information without ever seeing a menu if he is rapid enough. However, when he forgets a particular command sequence, he has only to start it and wait and the helpful menu will appear. By **multi-tasking** in this way the system is able to **adapt** to the level of skill of the user without modifying its normal operation.

The screen in the upper part of the opposite page shows a later stage of editing when Wordstar has read CHAPT4 from the disk. The status line now shows the name of the file being edited and the position of the editing cursor in terms of page, column and line. It also shows that the INSERT mode is ON meaning that text keyed in will not overwrite that already present but that a gap will be created to contain it. The menu is now one appropriate to text editing and concerned primarily with the control of the screen. The lowest menu line notes that 5 PREFIX KEYS may be used to select other menus of commands. Below this is a "ruler line" showing the width of the page and the position of tab stops within it. These may be set to give column positions just as they are on a typewriter. The lower 14 lines of the screen contain part of the text to be edited. They provide a **window** onto a section of the file CHAPT4 which may be moved to any part of the file enabling it to be edited.

The lower screen on the opposite page shows what happens when the CTRL and Q keys are pressed to select an alternative menu. Note how all that changes is the menu itself - the status, ruler and text lines are unchanged. This is an example of the very impressive **screen management** functions carried out by the Wordstar program. It splits the total available screen into a number of sub-screens of variable size. This exemplifies the **split-screen** operation mentioned at the beginning of this chapter. Whatever is left over from the status line, menus, prompts, and directory, is used as a window on the text. Again the system is adaptive in that it allocates a key resource, the available screen area, according to the priorities of the user. Indeed the user can control this allocation directly if he wishes by commanding Wordstar to give less help. At the next lower level of help the system does not display the menu shown at the top of the previous page and hence an additional eight lines are available for text. At the level below this none of the menus are displayed. Thus a skilled user may "tune" the system to reflect his own needs for information.

Wordstar's split screen operation enables various forms of dialog to be carried out with the user through different windows

```
   A:CHAPT4  PAGE 1 LINE 40 COL 23              INSERT ON
CURSOR:    ^A=left word      ^S=left char    ^D=right char   ^F=right word
           ^E=up line        ^X=down line
SCROLL:    ^Z=up line        ^W=down line     ^C=up screen    ^R=down screen
DELETE:    DEL=char left     ^G=char right    ^T=word right   ^Y=entire line
OTHER:     ^V=insert off/on  ^I=tab           RETURN=end para ^U=stop
           ^N=insert a RETURN  ^B=reform to end para     ^L=find/replace again
HELP:   ^J displays menu of information commands
PREFIX KEYS   ^Q ^J ^K ^O ^P   display menus of additional commands
L----!----!----!----!----!----!----!----!----!----!----!--------R
rapidly  changing industry,  there will be many more and what  we
have  learned about those we have experienced may not be  a  very
good  guide  to  us in a new situation.   Just as we  learn  that
people differ greatly in their personalities and so we shall find
that the roles programmed into computers differ in the  personal-
ities projected and the behavior displayed.

  If we use only one computer system then we may come to view its
style of  operation  and dialog as being that  of  computers  in
general.  If  we grow up in a close-knit community then we  form
similar  stereotypes of the expected and proper behavior of other
people.   When we move away from that community we may experience
intense  ^Bculture  shock^B in recognizing and adjusting  to  a  much
wider  variety  of forms of behavior.   Similarly  with  computer
```

```
^Q      A:CHAPT4  PAGE 1 LINE 40 COL 23                INSERT ON
       ^Q PREFIX                  (to cancel prefix, press SPACE bar)
CURSOR:  S=left Side screen    E=top screen    X=bottom    D=right enD line
         R=beginning file      C=end file      0-9, B, K, V, P = to marker
SCROLL:                        Z=continuous up    W=continuous down
DELETE TO END LINE:            DEL=left           Y=right
FIND, REPLACE:                 F=Find a string    A=find And substitute
REPEAT NEXT COMMAND:           Q=repeat until key pressed

L----!----!----!----!----!----!----!----!----!----!----!--------R
rapidly  changing industry,  there will be many more and what  we
have  learned about those we have experienced may not be  a  very
good  guide  to  us in a new situation.   Just as we  learn  that
people differ greatly in their personalities and so we shall find
that the roles programmed into computers differ in the  personal-
ities projected and the behavior displayed.

  If we use only one computer system then we may come to view its
style of  operation  and dialog as being that  of  computers  in
general.  If  we grow up in a close-knit community then we  form
similar  stereotypes of the expected and proper behavior of other
people.   When we move away from that community we may experience
intense  ^Bculture  shock^B in recognizing and adjusting  to  a  much
wider  variety  of forms of behavior.   Similarly  with  computer
```

Screen management for menus in Wordstar

on the screen while the text being edited is still being displayed as it will be typed. The upper screen of the page opposite shows what happens when the user keys "a" to give the command to find a word and replace it with another. The menu is replaced with a shorter one relevant to the current action and a prompt appears, FIND?, asking for the word to be found. The user keys "dialog" and presses RETURN. A second prompt appears, REPLACE WITH?, asking for the word to substitute. The user keys "dialogue" and presses RETURN. A third prompt appears, OPTIONS? (? FOR INFO), and the user cannot remember what options are available. Hence he keys "?" and presses RETURN which leads to the screen in the lower part of the page.

This demonstrates the flexibility of Wordstar's split-screen window system. There was no longer room for more information to be displayed so the system has moved the ruler line down and put the information the user requested in the space previously occupied by text and ruler line. Note that the actual text on display has remained in the same position but has lost the top three lines. If the user now keys in his options followed by RETURN the full text display will be reinstated.

We have devoted much space to Wordstar because it is one of the best-designed interactive programs in widespread use. Much more could be said about the **human factors** in its design. Some criticisms could be made also. For example, the command letters are usually not meaningful, or have a peculiar meaning (see the "O" for "cOpy" and "E" for "rEname" in the first illustration), and hence are difficult to remember. Given its attention to ease of use elsewhere, it is always surprising in using it that you have to key your file name in again when you wish to print it out - the system does not assume that you are most likely to wish to print the file you have just edited.

However, there is a different point to be made which is rather more interesting. Wordstar is one of the most **transferable** programs on the market. It is readily moved from one personal computer to another. A major factor in this transferability is its clean, modular structure which is also what gives it such a good user interface. The correlation between good human factors and ease of transfer is not surprising if one notes that the most diverse component of computer systems is the display. Wordstar has to interface itself well to the display in such a way that it can cope with the variety on the market. It also has to interface the user well to the display. The technical aspects and the user aspects of this programming task require the same approach and techniques.

```
^Qa      A:CHAPT4  PAGE 1 LINE 40 COL 23              INSERT ON

 ^S=delete character   ^Y=delete entry    ^F=File directory   D=right enD line
 ^D=restore character  ^R=Restore entry   ^U=cancel command, V, P = to marker

   FIND? dialog  REPLACE WITH? dialogue
   OPTIONS? (? FOR INFO)


L----!----!----!----!----!----!----!----!----!----!----!--------R
rapidly  changing industry,  there will be many more and what  we
have  learned about those we have experienced may not be  a  very
good  guide  to  us in a new situation.   Just as we  learn  that
people differ greatly in their personalities and so we shall find
that the roles programmed into computers differ in the  personal-
ities projected and the behavior displayed.

  If we use only one computer system then we may come to view its
style  of  operation  and dialog as being that  of  computers  in
general.   If  we grow up in a close-knit community then we  form
similar  stereotypes of the expected and proper behavior of other
people.   When we move away from that community we may experience
intense  ^Bculture  shock^B in recognizing and adjusting  to a much
wider  variety  of  forms of behavior.   Similarly  with  computer
```

```
^Qa      A:CHAPT4  PAGE 1 LINE 40 COL 23              INSERT ON

 ^S=delete character   ^Y=delete entry    ^F=File directory   D=right enD line
 ^D=restore character  ^R=Restore entry   ^U=cancel command, V, P = to marker

   FIND? dialog  REPLACE WITH? dialogue
   OPTIONS? (? FOR INFO) ?

     Normally press RETURN only, or enter one or more of:
   number=repeat count,  B=search Backwards,  W=whole Words only,
   U=ignore case, N=replace w/o asking, G=replace in entire file.

L----!----!----!----!----!----!----!----!----!----!----!--------R
people differ greatly in their personalities and so we shall find
that the roles programmed into computers differ in the  personal-
ities projected and the behavior displayed.

  If we use only one computer system then we may come to view its
style  of  operation  and dialog as being that  of  computers  in
general.   If  we grow up in a close-knit community then we  form
similar  stereotypes of the expected and proper behavior of other
people.   When we move away from that community we may experience
intense  ^Bculture  shock^B in recognizing and adjusting  to a much
wider  variety  of  forms of behavior.   Similarly  with  computer
```

Help facilities interacting with screen management in Wordstar

Conclusions - Conversation Through Menus and Forms

This chapter has continued the last one in showing different styles of computer conversation and in emphasizing techniques for making the system easy to understand. The systems used as illustrations show how seriously this problem is regarded by commercial software suppliers and how much effort is being put into its solution. PFS and Wordstar have become major products not just because they do certain information processing tasks well, but also because they support their users extremely well in many different ways. They are part of a new generation of **user-friendly** systems where the problems of dialog engineering have been given just as much attention as those of data processing.

The thirteenth proverb - STYLE AND TECHNOLOGY ARE LINKED

The formal dialogs of this chapter show the influence of technology on styles of computer conversation. The menu and form-filling techniques of PLANET and PFS and the combination of these with multi-window techniques in Wordstar are all dependent on the availability of the electronic display screen. They would not be possible using a typewriter terminal. Thus part of the study of appropriate forms of conversation with computers must relate the style to the technology available.

> **Proverb 13:** The style of conversation varies with the computer technology used.
>
> Some aspects of computer dialog style will be dependent on the type of person-computer interface available. Be aware of the capabilities and limitations of different interfaces.

The fourteenth proverb - MAKING THE STATE OF THE SYSTEM CLEAR

A menu is better than a manual not only because it is on the screen but also because it is specific to the current situation. The menus change according to the actions of the user. It is like having the system keep the manual open at the correct page all the time. This helps to solve another of Mary's problems in Chapter 4 - of not being aware of the state of the system. When she forgot to "append" the text it was because she could see no difference in the system before and after the "A" command.

Wordstar solves this particular problem by showing the text on the screen. It is a "what you see is what you get" system. Again, there are different techniques for doing this in systems

Learning to live together

other than text editors, but the general principle is that the
user should be helped to be aware of the state of the system.
For example the PRS system used by Sue in Chapter 4 gives a clear
indication of whether it is in the entry mode or in the modify
mode.

Proverb 14: The state of the system should be clear to the user.

Computer systems can be complex and their internal
state is not easy to see. Important information about
the state of the system should be shown to the user in
such a way that it is easily assimilated.

The fifteenth proverb - BEING CONSISTENT

Once the user has a model of part of the system he has
expectations that apply to the rest of it. Mary's confusion in
Chapter 4 between CATALOG and DIR is very reasonable because she
is using the same computer each time. Very often one can be
using the same computer, the same operating system and the same
package, and find that the commands to do the same thing are
different in different parts of it. The system is **inconsistent.**
Imagine what it would be like to use a system where sometimes
help was available on keying "?" whereas at others you had to key
"HELP." There is far more to learn and far more to remember with
such a system and the load on the user is very high.

PFS is an outstanding example of consistency. Setting up the
database, putting information into it, searching it and printing
out from it, are all done through the same simple technique of
filling in a form. What the user learns from one part of the
package is applicable when he is using any of the other parts.
This is a desirable feature to incorporate in the design of any
dialog system.

Proverb 15: The system should be consistent in operation.

The commands should always do the same thing
throughout. The information presentation should always
mean the same thing throughout.

The sixteenth proverb - BEING UNIFORM

Sometimes systems are consistent in that the same command
always does the same thing, but the commands are not always
available in different parts of the system. In CP/M Mary cannot
do a DIR command while she is using ED although she might well

want to look at the names of her files. Wordstar solves this problem by having its own file directory display command. It is not consistent with that of CP/M but at least one is available. However, the user now has to remember two different commands to do the same thing in different contexts. This lack of uniformity, like lack of consistency, means that there is more to learn and remember and the burden on the user is high. Imagine what it would be like to use a system where at some stages help was available and at others it was not. We are adding to our requirement for consistency one of **uniformity**, that different parts of the system offer the same facilities as much as possible.

Proverb 16: The system should be uniform in operation.

The facilities which users have learned to use in one part of the package should be available to them in other parts if they might reasonably expect this.

The seventeenth proverb - CUSTOMIZING UNDER USER CONTROL

The requirements of the last three proverbs, to make the system uniform and consistent and its state clear, all warn us against systems that are too "clever." It is tempting to try to design systems that somehow "adapt" to the user and his state of knowledge. For example, one might try and give simpler menus with fewer commands and more explicit information on what they do to a first-time user. As the user came to know the system better then one might let him know about lesser-used commands, making space to do this by dropping detail about the commands he already knows. Many early educational systems on computers were designed in this way, changing the level of instruction to correspond to the level of the student's knowledge. However, in general, they were unsuccessful because the changing strategy of the teaching program made it more difficult for the learner to understand the style of teaching and, through it, what was being taught. The simulated teacher's behavior was not consistent or uniform and its state was not clear.

It is also very difficult to measure someone's "level of knowledge" from the limited interaction possible through a screen and keyboard. The user will probably always have a far better feel for this than can be obtained by the system. This can be used to avoid the rigidity and inefficiency of a system that is the same for both skilled and unskilled users. Rather than attempting to program the system to decide the level of knowledge of the user, one can let the user himself do this. It need only be an indication relative to his current experience of the system. If he feels that he is having problems then he should be able to ask for help. If he feels the system is being over-helpful then he should be able to ask for it to be more terse. Wordstar gives the user control over how big a window is allocated to the menu and how much to the text being edited. The user can **customize** PFS to use his own terminology and information structures. He can customize Wordstar to use his own preferred level of explanation. The capability for an experienced user to group responses to speed up interaction illustrated in Chapter 4 is a further example of adaptation to the user's level of skill under user control.

Proverb 17: The system should adapt to the user under user control.

> Provision should be made for various levels of user knowledge but no attempt should be made to estimate this automatically. The user should be given control over the level of help provided by the system.

The last four proverbs of this chapter may all be summarized by the eighth proverb, that the system should be easy to understand. This is the key to effective person-computer dialog, that the user can readily form an adequate model of what the system does. We use the term "adequate" rather than "accurate" because it is only necessary for the user to have a model that is **sufficient** for his purposes. If it is sufficient then the simpler it is the better.

How the system achieves what it does is irrelevant provided the user's model can be used to inform him correctly what he must do to achieve his purpose in using the system. This is why a highly technical person who understands the inner operations of a computer system may not be the best one to design the user interface. The dialog designer must look at the system from the point of view of the user. He must portray it to the user in the way which makes its functions and the user's control of them most easily understood.

6 Graphic Computer Conversation

The term "conversation" usually means a verbal interchange between people. A typical conversation consists of a sequence of words from one speaker followed by a sequence from another, and so on. This is very similar to the **prompt** followed by **response** that is the form of much computer dialog. However, it will already have become apparent from some of our examples in Chapter 5 that we are using the term 'computer conversation' in a broader sense that encompasses visual layout and presentation. As we noted in that chapter, the first generation of computer terminals were simply modified typewriters or teleprinters that presented text in sequence. Current terminals are two-dimensional screens where the visual arrangement of material can be used to draw attention and add emphasis. In ordinary speech this is done by intonation, timing and gesture and it is natural to attempt to compensate for the lack of these significance-imparting channels by the use of any other channels available at a terminal.

A similar situation exists in the presentation of information in written form. Different typefaces, sizes and styles are used to enhance the communication medium with signals that draw attention and add emphasis. Computer presentation of information does have many characteristics of book presentation of information, but so far we have not emphasized this because the remarkable and novel feature of computer conversation is that it is interactively generated as is spoken conversation between people.

In this chapter we redress the balance by looking at some advances in computer dialog techniques that take advantage of the visual presentation facilities of computer graphic displays to enhance the conversation between a person and a computer system.

These illustrate how the new medium combines the capabilities of conversation and book to generate something which is quite original. It is the basis of the **participant novel** discussed in Chapter 2 and might be more generally termed the **interactive book**. However, the graphic capabilities also give some features of television and what we have is a new medium.

Video games

The use of personal computers to provide entertainment through games has been a very important factor in their popularity and marketing. Electronic games were developed at the same time as the microcomputer using the same technology of the low-cost **integrated circuit**. The cheaper games used simple displays based on **liquid crystal** modules similar to those of clocks and watches. The more expensive games used color graphic screens and were operated as coin machines in places of entertainment. The personal computer stood between these two extremes and, as technology dropped in cost, programs allowing elaborate games to be played on personal computers became available. These simulated battles between moving vehicles are shown in color with associated sound effects.

The upper photograph on the opposite page shows the screen of an Apple][computer being used to play a game of **RIB*BIT**. The player controls the timing of the frog's jump, and the positioning of the frog using a control paddle or joystick and can move the frog back and forth across the screen. Many games of this nature are available for personal computers, involving one or two players and a variety of situations. The lower photograph shows a different form of game that has become very popular, **Space Invaders**, in which various types of enemy vehicle attempt to land while the player attempts to shoot them down.

The nature of such games is such that interaction with the computer through a keyboard is very clumsy and inappropriate. **Game paddles** are provided that act as continuously variable controls whose position may be varied by the player, sensed by the computer, and used as data in the program. This type of user input to a program has been common in computer systems for flight simulation but is very novel in data processing. It provides a new channel for interaction from the user to the computer and an alternative to textual input from the keyboard. This has become significant in non-gaming applications as will be apparent in some later examples.

A children's game

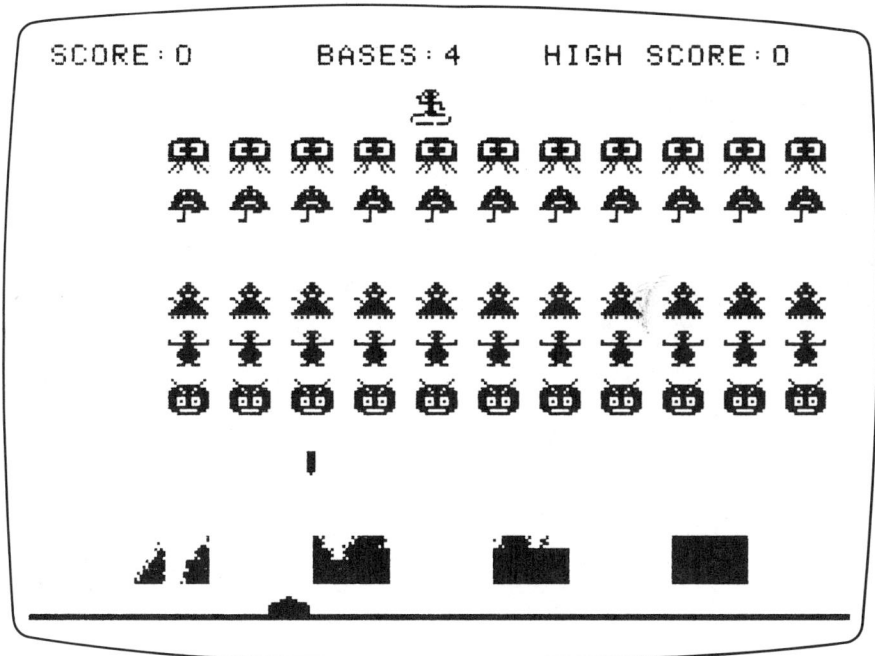

Space invaders, an arcade game

Dynamic spread sheets

One form of computer program more than any other has changed the public image of personal computers from being toys to being serious tools. This is the computerized **spread sheet** or dynamic planning chart. The first such program to catch the popular imagination was Visicorp's **Visicalc** for the Apple][. Several hundred thousand copies of this program have been sold. It was designed to be easy to use by those with no experience of computers. It enabled someone to set up complex business calculations on their own without having to go to professional programmers. Most significantly of all, Visicalc was a program that had never existed previously on large business computers.

The upper part of the page opposite shows the screen of an Apple][with a Visicalc spread sheet in use for a family budget. The user is given access to what appears to be a very large sheet of paper ruled into rows and columns, a standard "spread sheet" as used by accountants. The columns are labelled alphabetically from A through Z, and then AA through AZ up to BK, allowing 63 positions in all. The rows are labelled numerically from 1 up to 254. The cell on the spread sheet at column G and row 22 is referred to as G22. The Apple][screen of 24 rows and 40 columns is used as a window to show part of the sheet, four columns wide and twenty rows high. This window can be moved about to different regions of the sheet under user command.

Each cell on the spread sheet can be filled with one of three types of information: a **label**, a **number**, or a **formula**. Labels are used to show the contents of rows and columns, such as "FEB" or "LEFT OVER", or to split up the sheet, such as "---------". Numbers are the raw data with which Visicalc works, such as the "2000" in cell B2 representing income in January. Formulae are the magic that makes Visicalc so powerful: instead of putting a number into a cell the user can put instead a formula indicating how that number should be calculated. For example, in the upper screen the cursor is on cell B12 and the top line of the screen shows that this contains the formula "+B2-B11". This means that the value in cell B12 is calculated as the difference between that in cells B2 and B11 - what is "left over" from income is the income itself less the total of expenses. The Visicalc program carries out this calculation and shows a number in the cell, in this case 669 obtained by subtracting 1331 from 2000. In the lower screen three months of the budget sheet have been filled in. The cursor is at cell D16 which has the value 157 computed from the formula "+D12-D14-D15". If the cursor is moved to D9 and a new value for the expenditure on insurance of 20 keyed in then the value in D16 will change to 150 automatically.

```
B12   (V)  +B2-B11                            C!
                                              34

              A          B          C          D
          1MONTH        JAN        FEB        MAR
          2INCOME      2000       2000       2000
          3------------------------------------------
          4MORTGAGE     585
          5UTILITIES     63
          6TELEPHONE     70
          7FOOD         447
          8GAS           66
          9INSURANCE    100
         10------------------------------------------
         11SUB-TOTAL   1331
         12LEFT OVER    669
         13------------------------------------------
         14LEISURE      143
         15SAVINGS      500
         16CASH          26
         17
         18
         19
         20
```

```
D16   (V)  +D12-D14-D15                       C!
                                              34

              A          B          C          D
          1MONTH        JAN        FEB        MAR
          2INCOME      2000       2000       2000
          3------------------------------------------
          4MORTGAGE     585        585        585
          5UTILITIES     63         84        103
          6TELEPHONE     70         63         81
          7FOOD         447        493        389
          8GAS           66         78         92
          9INSURANCE    100                    23
         10------------------------------------------
         11SUB-TOTAL   1331       1303       1273
         12LEFT OVER    669        697        727
         13------------------------------------------
         14LEISURE      143        120         80
         15SAVINGS      500        500        500
         16CASH          26         77        147
         17
         18
         19
         20
```

A family budget dialog with Visicorp's Visicalc

The novelty of Visicalc is very interesting in its own right. In retrospect one can see that the use of spread sheets to specify calculations would have been useful even on the non-interactive **mainframe** computer systems of many years ago. It is a very natural way to specify a set of calculations. Also the spread sheet used interactively at a visual display could have been programmed on the **minicomputers** used in scientific laboratories and small businesses in the past decade. However, it took the stimulus of the low-cost, widely available personal computer to trigger off this style of program. In the early days of Visicalc there were many amusing anecdotes about the managers of large computer installations being asked for Visicalc-like programs. On hearing a description of what the program did, they announced that this was impossible and that the rumors of such a program could not be true! Only many years after dynamic spread sheets had been in use on personal computers did they begin to appear on mainframes and minicomputers.

The first spread sheets were simple calculators with limited capabilities to deal with multiple sources of data or to show the results in a presentable form. The dialog with the user was also very primitive and it was not easy to learn to use them. In recent years many software companies have developed advanced spread sheets offering more facilities and simpler interaction. The screens opposite are from an automatic training sequence that is used with Microsoft's **Multiplan.** The system takes the user through the facilities available and shows how they may be used. The most recent versions of such spread sheets have facilities for automatically presenting the numeric data in a variety of pictorial forms, graphs, bar charts, pie charts, and so on. They can also be combined with word processors so that the results may be transferred into correspondence and reports.

One very interesting phenomenon associated with spread sheets that throws light on the role of computers as a new medium is the ancillary industry that has developed around them. Although they were designed to allow anyone to program a computer for certain types of calculation simply and naturally without the use of conventional programs, this has not been sufficient. A number of firms offer partly filled spread sheets set up for specific calculations such as real estate accounting. These programs may be used either as complete systems in their own right or as "skeletons" to be amended for the specific purposes of the user. Thus the final result is a combination of the expertise of the person that set up the skeleton and the person who adds to it the additional features required for the specific application. This combination is carried by the spread sheet which is itself a specific variation of the general programability of computers.

```
+---+--------+--------+--------+--------+--------+--------+--------++
|              Users easily communicate with Multiplan.            |
|                Command menus and English messages                |
| Type a SPACE to continue.                                        |
|                                                                  |
|                                                                  |
| +---+--------+--------+--------+--------+--------+--------+--------++
| #1      1        2        3        4        5        6        7    !
| !  1 Sales    $200.00  $220.00  $242.00  $266.20  $292.82  $322.10 !
| !  2 Cost     $120.00  $132.00  $145.20  $159.72  $175.69  $193.26 !
| !  3 Gross Profit $80.00  $88.00  $96.80  $106.48  $117.13  $128.84 !
| !  4                                                              !
| !  5 Growth Rate=   0.10                                          !
| !  6 Cost Factor=   0.60                                          !
| !  7                                                              !
| !  8                                                              !
| !  9                                                              !
| ! 10                                                              !
| ! 11                                                              !
| ! 12                                                              !
| +---+--------+--------+--------+--------+--------+--------+--------++
| COMMAND: Alpha Blank Copy Delete Edit Format Goto Help Insert Lock Move
|          Name Options Print Quit Sort Transfer Value Window Xternal
| Select option or type command letter
| R1C1     "Sales"                    88% Free     Multiplan: forecast
```

```
+--------------------------------------------------------------------+
|                  Automatic Linking of Worksheets                   |
|                    The Multi-sheet Capability.                     |
| Type a SPACE to continue.                                          |
|                                                                    |
|                                                                    |
| +---+--------+--------+--------+--------+--------+--------++----+--------+--+
| #1     1        2        3        4        5        6     !!#2    14     !
| !  1                                                      !!  1          !
| !  2        Your Company Forecast for 1982: All Regions   !!  2          !
| !  3                                                      !!  3  Totals  !
| !  4 Region 1                                             !!  4          !
| !  5 Sales  $200.00  $220.00  $242.00  $266.20  $292.82   !!  5  $4276.86 !
| !  6                                                      !!  6          !
| !  7 Region 2                                             !!  7          !
| !  8 Sales  $250.00  $281.50  $316.97  $356.91  $401.88   !!  8  $6257.83 !
| !  9                                                      !!  9          !
| ! 10 Region 3                                             !! 10          !
| ! 11 Sales  $250.00  $278.00  $309.14  $343.76  $382.26   !! 11  $5747.43 !
| ! 12        --------  --------  --------  --------  --------!! 12  -------- !
| +---+--------+--------+--------+--------+--------+--------++----+--------+--+
| EXTERNAL COPY from sheet: region.3     name: sales
|               to: R11C2                linked:(Yes)No
|
| R11C2     [region.3 sales]             71% Free     Multiplan: company
```

A training dialog with Microsoft's Multiplan

The dynamic book

Multiplan and Wordstar are both examples of **split-screen** working in which the screen is divided up into two or more subscreens, each for a different type of interaction. This is very important in allowing the user to have several **windows** into the data within the computer system. It corresponds to having several documents in use at the same time. The standard display screen of 24 lines of 80 characters allows such splitting to be used for limited purposes. As high resolution graphic screens have become available the limitations have decreased and multiple window split-screen systems of very great power have been developed.

One of the more interesting developments using such techniques is the **dynamic book** – a new way of interacting with information developed by Alan Kay and Adele Goldberg at Xerox Palo Alto Research Center. The dynamic book can react to its readers by changing the medium of the information from text to animated pictures and sound, by helping the reader to search for information and by reorganizing its content for different purposes. For example, the reader of a novel might wish to read it in sequence from beginning to end, but part way through ask to see a list of characters and their roles. A student of the novel, however, may wish to compare certain portions of it, extract character studies, or flashback sequences. The skilled or professional book reader does not read from beginning to end, but rather may start with the index, footnotes, case histories, or appendices; skipping backward and forward to access the information he wants to form his view of the work. The dynamic book allows all this and more.

Stephen Weyer programmed the dynamic book as a course on history and the example on the opposite page shows a 14 year old using it to answer the question at the top of the screen. He makes use of a **browser** which is an area of the screen divided up according to its purpose. The **command** area tells the user what question he is trying to answer and he enters his answers here also; it is shown by the top two slots in the view of the screen on the opposite page. The **subject** area is for the user to enter subjects, terms, and select subjects from the index; this is shown in the next block down, with three columns for the list of subjects, subject index and sub-subject index. There is also a part of this area at the very bottom of the page showing subject references for chapters, sections and sub-sections. The **title** area allows the user to choose titles of chapters or sections; this is represented by the two strips below the top subject area, one for the list of titles, and the other for chapters, sections

Commands	
start next question	7. Who was king of England in 1628 and what significant democratic event occurred?
end this answer	
0:10 (this question)	
0:42 (all questions)	

charles I, no taxes could be inposed without the consent of parliament

king	Chandragupta, Marurya
1628	Charge of the Light Brigade
england	Charlemagne (Charles the G
Charles I, king of England	Charles Albert, king of Sard
Charles II, king of England	**Charles I, king of England**
Edward I, king of England	Charles II, king of England
Edward III, king of England	Charles II, king of Scotland
Edward VI, king of England	Charles II, king of Spain
George I, king of England	Charles the Bald
George III, king of England	Charles V, Holy Roman Em

Representative Government Gro...>Parliament Disputes the "Div...>Charles I Is Compelled to Accept the Petition of
Representative Government Gro...>Parliament Disputes the "Div...>"Scepter and Crown . . . Tumble Down!"

Representative Government Grows in	Keynote	King James versus Parliament
England Wins an Empire and Loses S	Geography and History Are Closely	**Charles I Is Compelled to Accept the**
French Revolution and Napoleon Sha	**Parliament Disputes the "Divine Righ**	"Scepter and Crown . . . Tumble Do
Latin American Colonies Revolt	Oliver Cromwell Rules the Commonw	Check on Your Reading
Revolutions Challenge Autocratic Rul	"Restoration" and the "Glorious Revo	

Charles I Is Compelled to Accept the Petition of Right

Charles I, the son of James I, ruled from 1625 to 1649. Like his father, Charles quarreled with Parliament over taxation. He waged unsuccessful wars against Spain, the Netherlands, and France. He imprisoned people who would not lend him money for his activities.

Charles I greatly underestimated the ability and determination of the representatives who controlled Parliament, the men who sat in the House of Commons, one of the two branches of Parliament. R. J. White describes these leaders:

". . . self-government had become a habit in England, and the men who made it a reality were the country gentlemen who sat in the House of Commons. . . . they were men who had done well on the land and who possessed money and real political ability, acquired through years of political experience. Men of business educated in the market place, on the bench [in the courts], or at the universities, they were accustomed to conducting government affairs on a daily basis."

From pp. 93-94 of THE HORIZON CONCISE HISTORY OF ENGLAND., American Heritage Publishing Co., Inc., 1971.

The leaders of Parliament became determined to protect the rights of Parliament and of the people of England against the acts of the king. They used his great need for money to force King Charles I to accept the Petition of Right.

The Petition of Right (1628) was a landmark in the growth of democracy in England. These were three of its important provisions.
1. No taxes could be imposed without the consent of Parliament.
2. Free people could not be imprisoned without a proper trial.
3. Civilians were not to be tried in military courts in time of peace.

Two of these three provisions were not new. Nevertheless, the Petition of Right made these principles a more

Great Britain	Democracy:Britain	Charles I, king of England
	England:representative government in	House of Commons (England)
	James I, king of England	Laws:Petition of Right

Dialog through windows into a dynamic book

and sub-sections. The remainder of the page is the **text** area and
displays the text from the selected title section. The student
tried several topics (shown on the left side of the subject area)
unsuccessfully, before deciding to examine information on various
kings of England in apparently random order. The entries in
boldface indicate as yet unreferenced subjects.

The interaction with the dynamic book is designed to be
graphical also rather than through a keyboard. The user rolls a
mouse across a table to move the cursor on the screen. The
cursor is a small arrow, near the top of the screen in this
example. The mouse performs a similar function to that of the
game paddles described earlier. Selections are made by pressing
a button on the mouse when the cursor is at a particular place on
the screen. In this study a standard history book was used, but
it would be more appropriate to write a dynamic book specifically
designed to have many modes of presentation of material, and
linked to material in other books.

Smalltalk and TRIP

The dynamic book is written in a special language called
Smalltalk. This language has special facilities to enable
objects to be defined which simulate objects in a real world. It
allows the properties of objects to be defined naturally in terms
of their reactions to **messages** from other objects. For example,
one object hitting another can be simulated by its passing a
message to the other that it has moved into the space which the
second object occupies. This can then cause the second object to
move in a way consistent with its being hit.

Another interesting graphic system which takes advantage of the
facilities of Smalltalk is **TRIP** developed by Laura Gould at Xerox
Palo Alto Research Center which helps students to solve time-
rate-distance problems. The final part of such a problem is
shown on the opposite page: the question is displayed in the box
near the top of the screen, the diagram of the current situation
just below, the tabulated version of the given information in the
travel table, and the results of various guesses before an
attempt at deriving the underlying algebra.

One of the most attractive features of this system is the
dynamic graphics where the trains actually travel across the
screen and the clock ticks round. The little pictures are called
icons; a number of icons are shown on the opposite page. The
mouse is used to select what the student wishes to do next, and
partly solved problems can be stored from day to day together

Train A left L.A. at 1:00 going 75 mph bound for S.F., 400 miles away. At 2:00, Train B left S.F. bound for L.A. at 50 mph. Also at 2:00 a controller noticed that a switch had failed and that the two trains were on the same track.
How much time did he have to prevent a collision?

GUESS

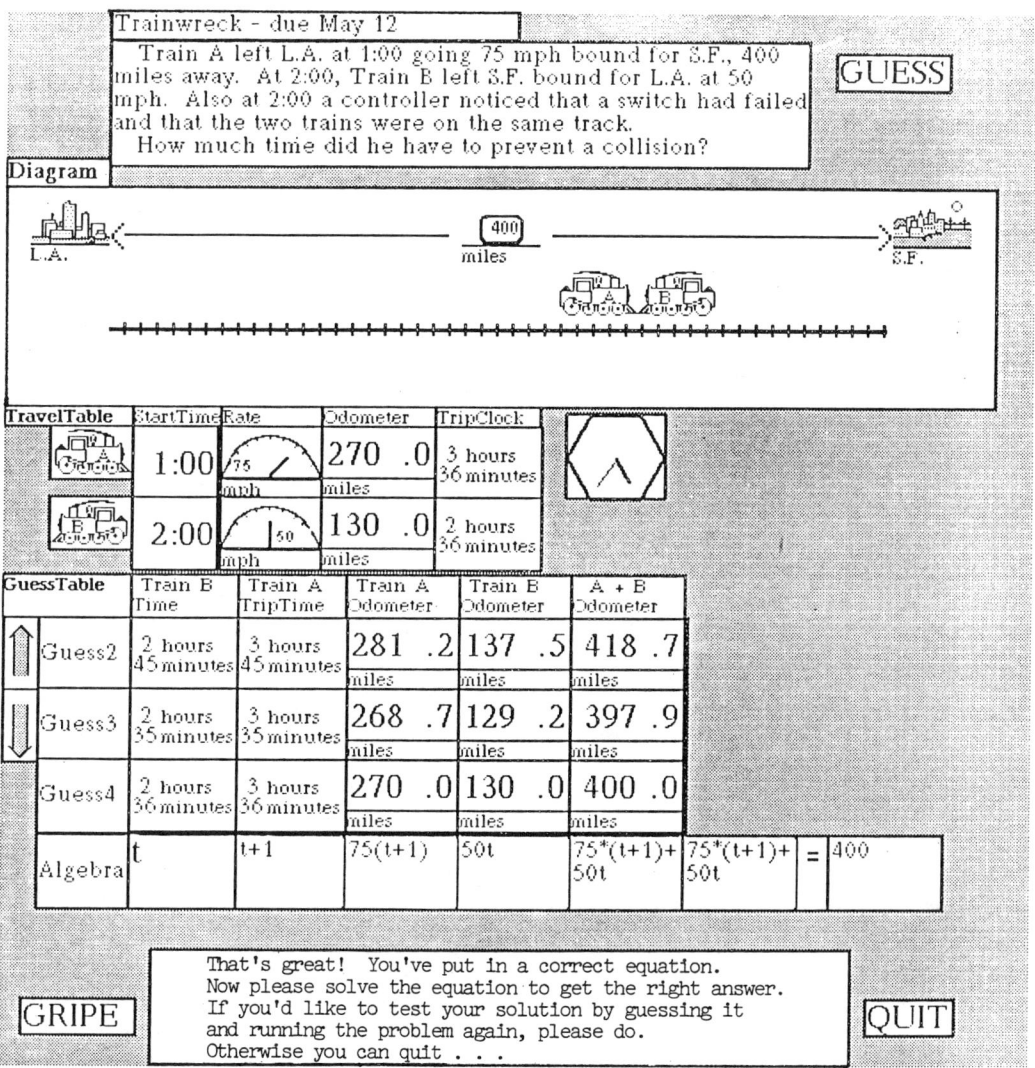

Diagram

TravelTable

	StartTime	Rate	Odometer	TripClock
Train A	1:00	75 mph	270 .0 miles	3 hours 36 minutes
Train B	2:00	50 mph	130 .0 miles	2 hours 36 minutes

GuessTable

	Train B Time	Train A TripTime	Train A Odometer	Train B Odometer	A + B Odometer			
Guess2	2 hours 45 minutes	3 hours 45 minutes	281 .2 miles	137 .5 miles	418 .7 miles			
Guess3	2 hours 35 minutes	3 hours 35 minutes	268 .7 miles	129 .2 miles	397 .9 miles			
Guess4	2 hours 36 minutes	3 hours 36 minutes	270 .0 miles	130 .0 miles	400 .0 miles			
Algebra	t	$t+1$	$75(t+1)$	$50t$	$75*(t+1)+50t$	$75*(t+1)+50t$	=	400

That's great! You've put in a correct equation.
Now please solve the equation to get the right answer.
If you'd like to test your solution by guessing it
and running the problem again, please do.
Otherwise you can quit . . .

GRIPE

QUIT

Dialog through icons with TRIP

with any comments the student wishes to make. Initially, the
student uses the mouse to position the trains at their starting
positions - she points to the train A icon, then moves the cursor
to the position at the left end of the track in the diagram; a
copy of the icon moves with the cursor across the screen. The
HELP facility enables her to be given hints about the next action
to be carried out, and the CHECK facility ensures that she has
done all the right things before proceeding to the next step.

Another interesting facility is the cursor. This has been
described as a small arrow which is used to point to an item
using the mouse. However, when the system is waiting for the
user to type something the cursor changes to read **Now Type,** and
when the system is in the middle of doing something it looks like
a star. From this the student can infer what is required, and is
unlikely to require extra prompting to complete an action such as
input or selection of an option.

By the end of the problem, the screen might have a large number
of separate areas of information displayed on it. Since these
are mainly constructed by the user from a simple starting
situation, and since each one always appears in a consistent
place, the users have no difficulty in managing them. TRIP uses
the graphics screen to simulate a world of objects with which the
user can interact simply and naturally. This enables a new type
of conversation with the computer to take place where much of the
interaction is non-verbal.

High-resolution graphics in office computers

The use of high-resolution graphics for simulation and
education might seem to reflect the particular needs of the
material used. However, Xerox Office Systems Division has
developed a system for document preparation, filing,
communication and retrieval which uses a graphics screen in a
very similar way to that of the dynamic book and TRIP. The
screen of the Xerox **Star** shown opposite has a resolution of 1024
points across by 808 vertically. The user interacts with it
through a typewriter style keyboard and through a mouse as
already described. The screen resolution is adequate to portray
most documents as they will appear in printed form, with
different styles and sizes of type faces, line drawing, sketches
and even limited pictorial material. The meaning of the keys on
the keyboard can be varied under computer control so that the
Star is able to operate in many different languages. It can even
generate the pictorial Kanji characters used in Japanese.

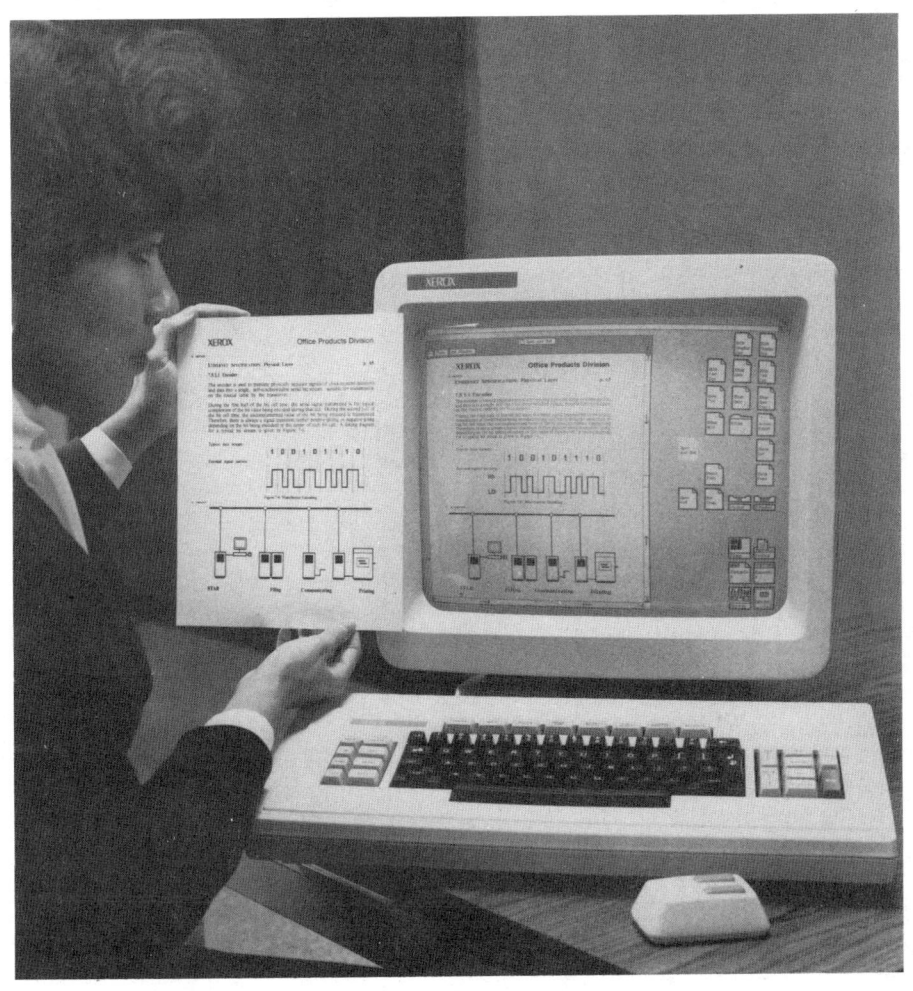

The Xerox Star - dialog through documents, icons and a mouse

Star attempts to simulate a normal office environment on its screen by using it as a simulated desk top on which to display documents. These documents are like sheets of paper which may contain text in different sizes and type faces, line drawings and graphs, and even free-hand sketches. If two or more documents are displayed on the screen they may occupy separate or overlapping windows. If the windows overlap then the display appears exactly as if the documents overlapped, that is part of one document will be obscured by the other. Thus the user's model of what is going on inside Star can be simply that pieces of paper are being retrieved and displayed. As David Smith, the designer of the Star user interface has remarked, "if everything in a computer system is visible on a display screen, the display becomes reality."

The natural model for dealing with pieces of paper is that one picks them up and moves them around. One certainly does not type commands to them through a keyboard. Star attempts to minimize the use of the keyboard and make as much of the interaction with the user as possible take place graphically through the use of the mouse. To access a document the user moves the cursor to an icon representing the disk store and presses the button on the mouse. A document appears containing further icons designating "folders" of documents held on the disk. By moving the cursor to one of these icons and pressing the button the user can open the folder and display labels representing its contents as a second document on the screen. He can access the documents in the folder by again moving the cursor to the label of that required and pressing the button.

The high-resolution graphics required in the dynamic book, TRIP and Star were very expensive at the time these systems were developed and they are research systems only. However, costs of graphic systems have fallen in recent years to levels where they may be incorporated in personal computers. The screen opposite is that of the Apple **Lisa** which is a ten thousand dollar business computer designed to be easy to use through the use of split-screen multi-window operation and graphic interaction through a mouse. The resolution of the Lisa screen is lower than that of the star, only 720 dots horizontally by 364 vertically, but even with this it is possible to display documents on the screen roughly as they will appear on paper.

To get a feel for the effect of screen resolution on text appearance it is worth noting that reasonable characters can be created on a matrix of 5 by 7 dots within a cell of 8 by 8 dots. Type face variations require more dots than this with cell sizes of 12 by 12, 16 by 16 or more. Thus Lisa's resolution does not

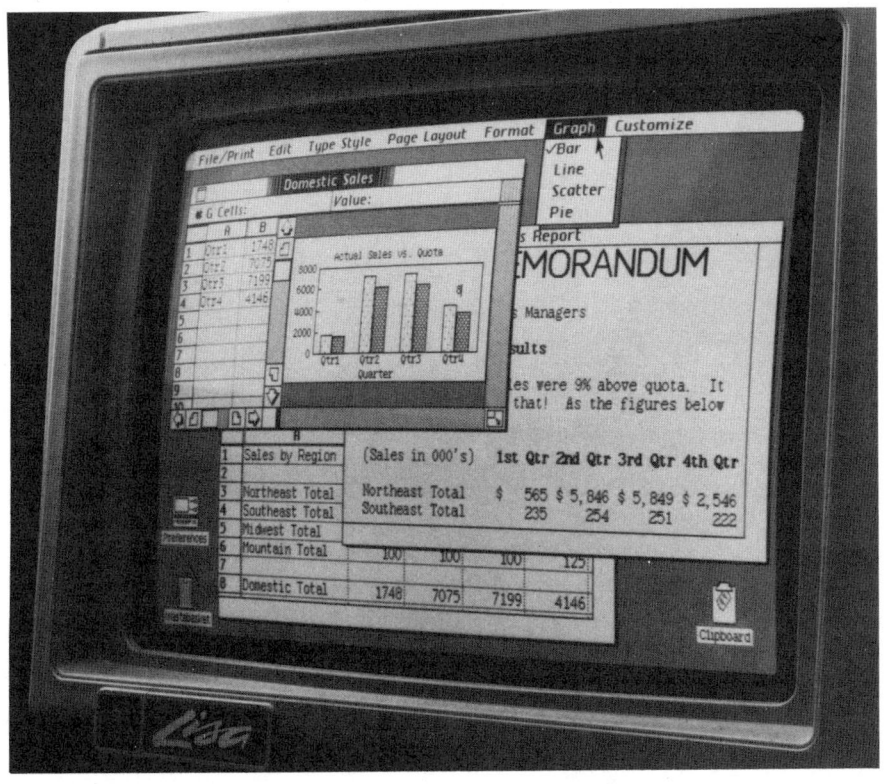

The Apple Lisa -- dialog through documents, icons and a mouse

give much scope for accurate type face representation although it is enough for some variation between normal, italic and bold. There is, however, more scope for variation in the larger typefaces used for headings. The resolution of the Lisa screen was probably limited by the cost of high resolution video monitors. The computer technology necessary for resolutions comparable with those of Star is now low in cost and as monitor prices decline we shall see low cost personal computers become available with Star-like graphics.

Lisa attempts to create the same type of user environment as that of Star by treating the screen as a desk top and the mouse as a way of manipulating objects on it. Icons are used instead of keys for commands so that as much user interaction as possible takes place through the mouse and simulated desk top.

Conclusions - Graphic Conversation

The examples given in this chapter show the way in which advances in computer technology are increasingly being used to improve the user interface. Computers are now capable of doing many tasks which we would find very useful. Our main problem is to put them under the control of those who want the tasks done.

Even though we have examined advanced technology the proverbs generated by considering simpler systems still apply. All the systems in the chapter have Proverb 8 as a major objective, to make the system easy to understand. Star and Lisa pay particular attention to Proverbs 5 and 6 by taking into account the existing vocabulary and expectations of office users - they simulate papers, filing cabinets and desk tops. They are also uniform and consistent in operation and make their state clear to the user. The proverbs are proving, as we intend them to be, sufficiently general to be applicable regardless of the style of conversation and technology used to implement it.

However, this chapter reinforces the message of Proverb 13, that the style of conversation varies with the computer technology. The mouse and the high resolution screen together open up new opportunities for forms of interaction that differ greatly from conversations through keyboards. What is best depends partly on the application and partly on our creative imaginations. We have continually to ask ourselves the question, "What world can I simulate that will be simple to understand and effective for the user in this task?" We have also to remember that what was impossible yesterday may be easy today - people have a knack of pretending that they did not really want to do what they found they could not, and then forgetting the original objective when new possibilities become available.

The eighteenth proverb - BE AWARE OF THE REPERTOIRE

We can expect handwriting recognition and speech recognition to come into routine use in the next decade. There may also be developments in the detection of mood through chemical sensors and the monitoring of timing in speech and body language. These capabilities of the computer system to detect the mood of the person will be paralleled by the development of techniques to enable it to project its own "mood." For example, it would be very useful to know whether a requested action was unexpected or unreasonable and hence "surprising" to the computer system. This might prevent many files from being accidentally deleted because the user has made an error in keying.

For the dialog designer each new technique for person-computer dialog that is developed is a new tool to be added to the repertoire available with which to create effective person-computer communication. One needs to be aware of what is possible in order to generate elegant solutions to new problems rather than trying to fit every form of person-computer communication into the same framework.

Proverb 18: Be aware of the repertoire of techniques for person-computer dialog.

The range of styles and techniques for dialog is continually increasing as is the experience in their use. Approach new situations with an open mind as to what techniques would be appropriate and maintain awareness of new approaches as they develop.

The nineteenth proverb - PROGRAMS CREATE REALITY

The screen of the Star **becomes** the world with which the user is interacting. He does not have to think about the underlying computer technology, the files of records forming a database, the communications links, the text editor, and so on. By simulating a world that is accessed only through the screen and is always visible the system designers have given the user a much simpler world to understand but one that is just as powerful. They have created a reality for the user which is well suited to his task and made simple things simple and hard things possible.

The realities that we can create with computers are limited by the technology but within these limitations we have tremendous freedom. There is no more reason why we should force the user to face up to the tedious details of what is actually going on inside the machine than there is for a motor car manufacturer to ensure that the motorist understands internal combustion engines before he can drive. Every year the processing power of computers increases and some time ago it came to exceed what most users of computers require. That spare capacity is available now to be used to create comfortable and supportive worlds for the user. We can use the powerful complexity of the computer to make life simple for its users.

This is not an easy task for many programmers. They are like motor mechanics who love their engines, enjoy tinkering with them, and cannot understand why everyone else does not feel the same. It is easy to create a reality for others that suits ourselves and give them a vehicle to drive that has all the bells, whistles and quirks brought out that we love to access. However, as we have seen from the examples in this chapter, that is no longer necessary and certainly not desired by the majority of users. The commercial future of computer systems is with those that harness the power to create user-friendly worlds that leave the smell of gasoline, pistons, floppy disks and bytes safely inside the machine.

Proverb 19: Programs create the reality experienced by the users of computers.

Remember that the computer is a tool for simulation and that what is simulated becomes reality for the user. The power of the computer should be used to create worlds that are simple for the user and natural to the task.

7 Natural Language Conversation with Computers

The formal conversations with personal computers discussed in Chapters 4 and 5 show the current state of the art in computer dialog for the great majority of packages actually in use. They are far removed from the fictional dialog with computers discussed in Chapter 3, although perhaps not so distant from real dialog between people when they are working together to perform a task. In the research laboratories, however, where studies are being made of **artificial intelligence** in computer systems, techniques for programming natural language conversations with computers have been developed.

Initially these natural language systems required most of the capacity of large expensive computers and were far too costly to use in practical applications. They were also restricted to small problem domains and not designed to cope with conversations that went outside these. However, as computer costs tumble downward year by year, what was too expensive yesterday comes into the personal computer stores tomorrow. The effect of decreasing costs on programming natural language conversations is amplified greatly by our increasing knowledge of the linguistic techniques required. There are already computer systems for information retrieval that use natural language conversation for practical purposes, and we may expect this to be a trend for personal computers.

This chapter illustrates a range of systems using natural language from the very simple to the most recent advances. We indicate the underlying techniques being used to support the conversations, how these relate to those used in more formal dialog, and how they can go wrong. There has been much debate in the literature on person-computer interaction about the utility of natural language conversations with computers. One argument against the use of natural language is that it is verbose and requires more keystrokes than does formal dialog. It is certainly valid to consider minimizing the work being done by people in using computer systems, particularly if we are requiring them to use something as unnatural as a keyboard.

Fifth generation systems

However, one of the main advances being sought for so-called **fifth generation** computer systems is the improvement of person-computer communications using natural language interaction, particularly speech. As techniques for speech communication with computers advance, the use of keyboards may become unnecessary for many applications and this aspect of the argument against natural language will become less significant. Some verbosity in speech is necessary to give opportunities for error detection and correction through the use of redundant information, and this is a small price which we all seem prepared to pay in everyday life for the convenience of speech communication.

Even if we do not accept some of the predicted changes in technology, there is an argument of more immediate significance against dismissing natural language communication as irrelevant to current applications. Formal computer dialog is not entirely separate from natural language. In real-life speech is not grammatical with proper sentence structures and punctuation marks. We convey information to one another by a wide variety of means including diagrams and gestures, and we make use of language as a tool to be adapted to our needs not as a rigid framework to which we ourselves have to conform. In this sense the computer conversations we have examined in previous chapters are "natural language" and we can expect them to develop in richness and variety as we learn more techniques and as the underlying data structures themselves become more complex.

Thus, what we may expect in future computer systems is the same variety of styles of conversation appropriate to different tasks as are found in human conversation. The examples in this chapter indicate one direction for increasing our repertoire of styles of conversation with computers. The chapter before this covers a different dimension involving the use of graphic displays and visual symbols. These are not competitive techniques, either with one another, or with the simpler formal dialogs - they are additions to our capabilities for conversation with computers which broaden and strengthen our basis for communication.

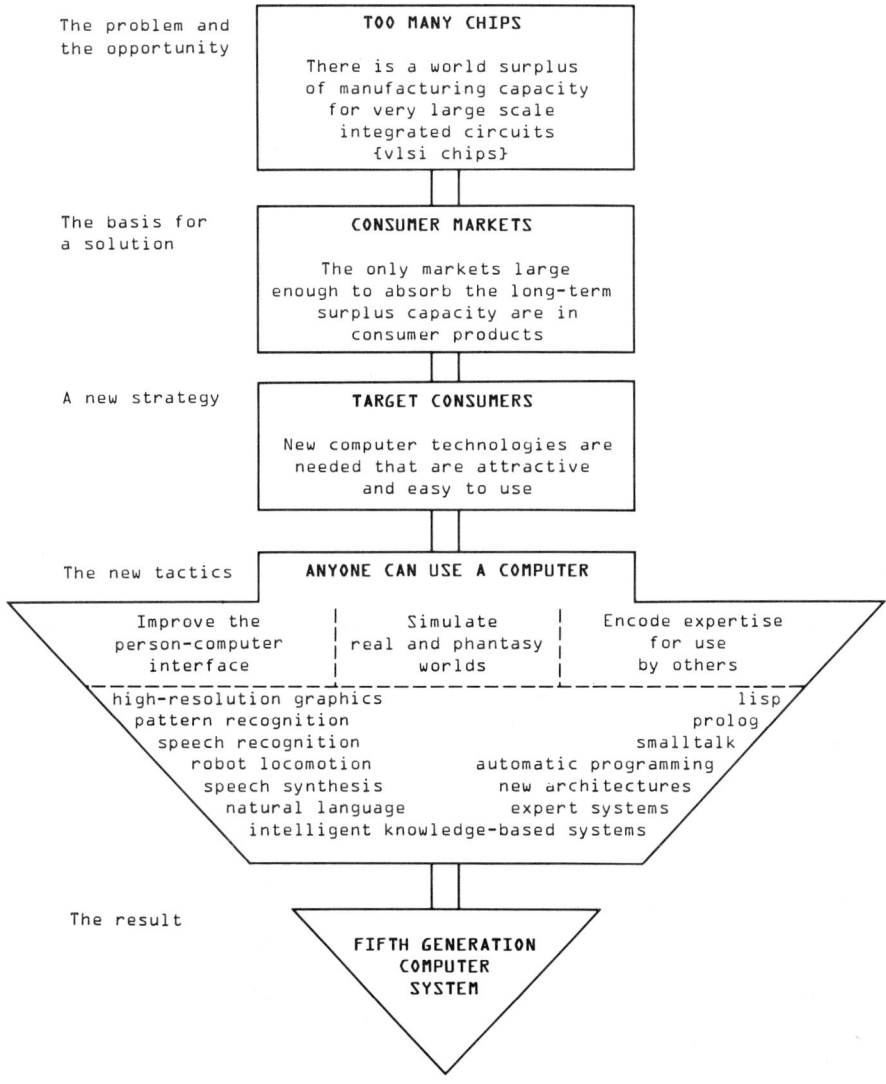

The problem and the opportunity

TOO MANY CHIPS

There is a world surplus
of manufacturing capacity
for very large scale
integrated circuits
{vlsi chips}

The basis for a solution

CONSUMER MARKETS

The only markets large
enough to absorb the long-term
surplus capacity are in
consumer products

A new strategy

TARGET CONSUMERS

New computer technologies are
needed that are attractive
and easy to use

The new tactics

ANYONE CAN USE A COMPUTER

| Improve the person-computer interface | Simulate real and phantasy worlds | Encode expertise for use by others |

high-resolution graphics   lisp
pattern recognition   prolog
speech recognition   smalltalk
robot locomotion   automatic programming
speech synthesis   new architectures
natural language   expert systems
intelligent knowledge-based systems

The result

**FIFTH GENERATION
COMPUTER
SYSTEM**

The logic behind the development of fifth generation computers

Natural language output with simple response

One of the criticisms often levelled at attempts to create natural language dialog with computers is that it gives a false impression of human intelligence on the part of the machine. This may mislead the user into expecting more understanding and commonsense from the computer system than can realistically be programmed. That natural language output can be used without giving that impression is shown in the following example.

Chris Evans, author of the book and presenter of the Television series **The Mighty Micro,** initiated a number of early computer programs to conduct medical interviews. The interviews replaced the usual clinician-patient conversations to elicit symptoms in such areas as gastrointestinal disorders, ante-natal clinics and peptic ulcer clinics. The dialog was conducted entirely in "natural language" except that the patient had a choice of only three buttons in response: YES, NO, DON'T KNOW.

In the sample dialog on the opposite page the YES button gets echoed as a **0.** The output of the program is completely in natural language, fluent and friendly. However, it is clear that the dialog is produced by a person. No patient is likely to attribute the conversational grace to the machine itself since it only collects information, and does not reply in any meaningful way, except to go on to the next question. It is unlikely that the user will attribute more intelligence to the machine than to any other that displays natural language messages to him, for example, the cleaning instructions on a stove. In any event the user has no capability to communicate with the machine other than through the very simple interface.

The text of the dialog is very reassuring, and produces encouragement and chatty remarks at sundry places in the dialog. In such a situation, where the patient is likely to be tense and nervous, the friendly words convey a relaxed atmosphere. In order to determine the acceptability of computer interviews, studies were carried out of patient reactions to such programs. Compared with the clinician, it was found that people preferred the computer with its encouraging remarks and chatty phrases. Other studies showed, however, if the clinician himself used these techniques for putting patients at their ease they were much less acceptable.

Thus Evans' work shows that natural language output from a computer can be used very effectively in certain applications, and that friendly and encouraging remarks in this style of dialog are helpful and acceptable.

HELLO. THIS IS AN EXPERIMENT TO SEE WHETHER COMPUTERS CAN
HELP DOCTORS TO DIAGNOSE ILLNESSES. WE WOULD VERY
MUCH LIKE YOU TO HELP US WITH THIS. IF YOU ARE
PREPARED TO WOULD YOU PUSH THE BUTTON MARKED 'YES', BUT IF YOU
WOULD RATHER NOT, PUSH THE BUTTON MARKED 'NO', BUT WE WOULD
LIKE YOU TO HELP US. IF YOU DON'T UNDERSTAND WHAT TO DO PRESS
THE '?' BUTTON. GO AHEAD NOW AND PUSH ONE OF THE THREE BUTTONS? O

GOOD. THANKS VERY MUCH. I HOPE YOU'LL FIND IT INTERESTING
WE'LL FIND IT VERY HELPFUL TO US.

THIS IS A COMPUTER TALKING TO YOU. I CAN ASK YOU QUESTIONS
BUT I CAN ONLY UNDERSTAND SIMPLE ANSWERS, SO YOU CAN ONLY TALK
TO ME BY PUSHING EITHER THE 'YES', 'NO' OR '?' BUTTON. YOU
SHOULD ONLY PRESS THE '?' BUTTON IF YOU DON'T UNDERSTAND THE
QUESTION I AM ASKING YOU. NOW, DO YOU UNDERSTAND EVERYTHING
I'VE SAID UP TO NOW? PUSH ONE OF THE BUTTONS? O

THANKS. NOW I WANT TO ASK YOU ONE OR TWO QUESTIONS ABOUT WHY
YOU ARE HERE. PLEASE REMEMBER THAT THIS IS ALL IN COMPLETE
CONFIDENCE JUST AS WITH DOCTORS. ONLY DOCTORS AND NURSES
WILL SEE YOUR ANSWERS. ARE YOU QUITE HAPPY ABOUT THIS? PUSH
ONE OF THE BUTTONS? O

GOOD. BY THE WAY, DON'T FEEL THAT YOU HAVE TO PRESS
THE BUTTON THE VERY INSTANT THAT I HAVE FINISHED TYPING.
IF YOU FEEL YOU NEED TO THINK A BIT BEFORE YOU ANSWER, OR
NEED TO READ THE QUESTION OVER AGAIN THEN GO AHEAD AND DO SO.
TAKE YOUR TIME IF YOU WANT TO. REMEMBER, HOWEVER, THAT
I CAN'T TALK TO YOU AGAIN UNTIL YOU HAVE PUSHED ONE OF
THE BUTTONS.

WELL, FIRST OF ALL THEN, IS ONE OF THE REASONS YOU VISITED
YOUR DOCTOR BECAUSE YOU WERE SUFFERING FROM DISCOMFORT OR
PAINS IN THE STOMACH? O

Stored natural language output in a medical interview

ELIZA - conversation without understanding

The first example does not undermine objections to false expectations created by apparently natural language dialog. Indeed the conversation with ELIZA on the opposite page shows how easy it is to create an illusion of intelligence. Joseph Weizenbaum developed ELIZA at MIT to satisfy the Turing Test discussed in Chapter 3. In this dialog it is difficult to tell who is the machine and who the person. The ELIZA script is based on a type of psychotherapy which feeds back everything said, but does not offer opinions or points of view. This is to give the impression of the psychotherapist being very accepting of the patient for what he is, not wanting to change him in any way.

One of the reasons that ELIZA appears intelligent is that it picks up a number of keywords to which it responds in a prescribed manner, e.g. "name" - "I am not interested in names", or "sorry" - "please don't apologize". In addition, it picks up certain phrases that have been used and repeats them in certain situations, not necessarily immediately after you use them.

The simple mechanism of ELIZA can be seen where spelling mistakes are made by the user. They are then repeated in the program's responses, which enables you to see where the word is identically repeated, e.g. the user says "my belief in you exceeds all reasonable bounds", which gets echoed in the next line "your belief in I exceeds all reasonable bounds" (note the grammatical error, the general rule of change "you" to "I" fails here, although the phrase "my belief" gets accurately reflected as "your belief"); and later as "lets discuss further why your belief in I exceeds all reasonable bounds".

There are some standard phrases used to fill in when ELIZA fails to find keywords, for example "please go on". It would be quite reasonable to assume that ELIZA is understanding the conversation and your problems. It acts very much like a person would, for example in asking for more explanation when something is not clear. We associate this sort of attribute with a person, and can be thoroughly taken in by ELIZA-type interactions.

ELIZA exemplifies "cocktail party conversation". At parties we talk to people that we have never met before, on topics we know nothing about. As an act of social grace we create the false impression of being very interested in what the other person is saying and hence of understanding it. We can do the same thing in a computer program. However, the consequences of this may be unwanted. The user may expect an understanding of what he is saying that our program does not have.

GOOD MORNING MY NAME IS GAINES AND I WISH TO TALK TO YOU
I AM NOT INTERESTED IN NAMES
SORRY PERHAPS YOU COULD LET ME KNOW YOUR INTERESTS
PLEASE DON'T APOLOGIZE
THANKYOU WHAT INTERESTS YOU MOST
WHY DO YOU ASK
BECAUSE I HAVE TO DEMONSTRATE YOUR INEFFABLE CAPABILITIES
IS THAT THE REAL REASON
YES YOUR CAPABILITIES INTEREST ME
YOU SEEM QUITE POSITIVE
I AM INDEED POSITIVE
IS IT BECAUSE YOU ARE INDEED POSITIVE THAT YOU CAME TO ME
NO I CAME TO DEMONSTRATE YOUR CAPABILITIES
ARE YOU SAYING 'NO' JUST TO BE NEGATIVE
YES
YOURE BEING SOMEWHAT SHORT WITH ME
I AM VERY ANNOYED AT YOUR LACK OF CONVERSATIONAL GRACE
HOW LONG HAVE YOU BEEN ANNOYED AT MY LACK OF CONVERSATIONAL GRACE
FOR SEVERAL MINUTES NOW
I AM NOT SURE I UNDERSTAND YOU FULLY
CAN YOU TELL THE TIME
YOU BELIEVE I CAN TELL THE TIME DON'T YOU
MY BELIEF IN YOU EXCEEDS ALL REASONABLE BOUNDS
YOUR BELIEF IN I EXCEEDS ALL REASONABLE BOUNDS
YES INDEED TO GOODNESS IT DOES COBBER
YOU ARE SURE
SURE IM SURE IM SURE
PLEASE GO ON
AND THE SURER I AM SURE THE SURER I BECOME
DO YOU BELIEVE IT NORMAL TO BE SURE THE SURER YOU BECOME
NORMALITY IS RELATIVE
SUPPOSE NORMALITY WERE NOT RELATIVE
ABSOLUTES PLACE ONE IN ACUTE PHILOSOPHICAL DILEMMAS
LETS DISCUSS FURTHER WHY YOUR BELIEF IN I EXCEEDS ALL REASONABLE BOUNDS
YOU ARE REMOTE AND YET PLEASANTLY COMFORTING
WHAT MAKES YOU THINK I AM REMOTE YET PLEASANTLY COMFORTING
YOU REMIND ME OF MY FATHER
TELL ME MORE ABOUT YOUR FAMILY
MY MOTHER WAS A MAGNETIC TAPE
WHO ELSE IN YOUR FAMILY WAS A MAGNETIC TAPE
MY SISTER WAS A TELEPRINTER
YOUR SISTER
YES MY MOTHERS DAUGHTER
WHY DO YOU SAY YOUR MOTHERS DAUGHTER
TO EXPLICATE A CONCEPT FOR YOU

A conversation without understanding with ELIZA

PEGASUS - incorporating user responses in dialog

ELIZA's technique of taking words or phrases from the user and incorporating them in natural language feedback should not be dismissed as a trick. It has many important applications. It is only potentially dangerous when used to create a misleading impression of more intelligence on the part of the computer system than we have been able to program into it. There will often be times when we do wish to create dialog that does this, for example in adventure games or in programs whose purpose is itself to provide friendship and company. There are also applications of Weizenbaum's technique in programs which do have a serious data processing function.

PEGASUS is part of the PLANET system of programs whose menus were described in Chapter 5. Dialog with PEGASUS at first sight appears to be a cross between Evans' interviews and ELIZA's conversation. It takes a topic or problem that the user wants to investigate and elicits words and phrases which distinguish aspects of the topic. These are then matched against similar distinctions and feedback given on how they are related. PEGASUS provides a neat way to elicit both the distinctions and the terminology of an expert, which can then be incorporated in an expert system such as MYCIN.

In the example on the opposite page the topic was "comparing modern media", which was elicited from the user as a reply as to why he was doing this grid. The user is then asked for examples of modern media and he gives: computers, books, television, records, letters, videotapes. Later, he adds other media: newspapers, phone-in radio, telephone, theater, videogames, either as he thinks of them or as a solution to highly matched constructs, shown on the next page. He then proceeds to distinguish between these elements in threes, saying why two are similar and different from the other one. This produces personal descriptions in addition to personal distinctions which are then used as scales from 1 to 5 (in this example) to rate all the media in this dimension. The elements are regrouped to show the ones which have the same ratings together, as shown at the bottom of the page.

Thus PEGASUS uses natural language output and a simple form of natural language input that restricts the user to phrases in his own vocabulary. No attempt is made to match keywords in these phrases as ELIZA does, but they are used in a way similar to ELIZA as part of the dialog back from the computer to the user. This shows up in the construct and element match feedback given to the user. As each new dimension (construct) is added, PEGASUS

This is a program to elicit a repertory grid, a technique devised by Kelly to help you explore the dimensions of your thinking. You must decide on a purpose for doing the grid and keep this in mind when you choose the elements—the things you are going to think about during the program. These elements will then be used to elicit constructs.

Type in your purpose for doing this grid?**comparing modern media**

Choose a set of six elements keeping in mind why you want to do this grid. They could be people, events, pieces of music, pictures, books, or what you want but whatever you choose they must be of the same type and each must be well known to you. Now type each one after each question mark.

Element 1?**computers**
Element 2?**books**
Element 3?**television**
Element 4?**records**
Element 5?**letters**
Element 6?**videotapes**

Triad for elicitation of construct 1
1 computers
2 books
3 television

Choose two of this triad of elements which are in some way alike and different from the other one. What is the number of the one which is different?**1**

Think about what you have in mind when you separate the pair from the other one. How can you describe the two ends or poles of the scale which separate books and television on the left pole from computers on the right pole?

Just type one or two words for each pole to remind you what you are thinking or feeling when you use this construct.

Left pole rated 1 --?**one-way**
Right pole rated 5 --?**interactive**

Now assume that books and television are assigned the value 1 and computers is assigned the value 5. According to how you feel about them please assign to each of the other elements in turn a provisional value from 1 to 5

2 books   1
3 television   1
1 computers   5
4 records   ?**1**
5 letters   ?**5**
6 videotapes   ?**3**

Pole 1 -- one-way

2 books   1
3 television   1
4 records   1

6 videotapes   3

1 computers   5
5 letters   5

Pole 5 -- interactive

A conversation eliciting user responses with PEGASUS

matches the ratings with those on all previous dimensions, and chooses highly similar ones to give comment to the user. The words used by the user are being reproduced in the dialog in a similar way to that done by ELIZA, but in this situation it does mean something in that matching operations have taken place, and are being reflected in the user's terms.

The user is asked to split highly matched constructs by providing an element (example of media) which is described by one pole of the first construct, and the opposite pole of the other construct. In this case the element "theater" was added as it was thought to be "dated" and "dynamic". To make the matrix of rating values complete, the user then has to complete the values for this new element on each existing construct.

The bottom part of the opposite page shows the analogous situation when two elements are found to be similar, in this case "phone-in radio" and "videogames". This results in the user being asked to provide a construct which puts one of these at one end, and the other at the opposite end, in this example "many partaking -- personal". He then proceeds to rate elements on this new construct exactly as if it were elicited from a triad. The next part inquires whether any values should be changed, or if the pole names should be different.

You may find it difficult to see any similarity in these two elements, or between the two constructs in the previous match example. This is because you are not making the same distinctions as the person who produced this result. In his way of seeing things they are clearly similar, and you would be able to see why if you had the final grid available to you. (In fact you can see it in Chapter 10.)

This gives a clue as to why PEGASUS is useful to psychiatrists, whose job it is to study what distinctions their patients are making which are causing them difficulties in living in the world. Management scientists are also interested in why people are making certain distinctions, and why some are more successful than others in their jobs as managers, training officers, or quality control assessors. What PEGASUS is providing is a way of making a topic explicit and open for perusal and discussion, rather than the usual intuitive way we go about being good or bad at what we do.

The techniques used in ELIZA and PEGASUS are legitimate and useful if not misused. Conversation without understanding has a role in some dialog applications. Evan's medical interviews or PEGASUS' construct elicitation do not lead to a false impression.

The two constructs you called
3 static -- dynamic
7 dated — modern
are matched at the 72 percent level.

This means that most of the time you are saying static you are also saying
dated and most of the time you are saying dynamic you are also saying modern.

Think of another element which is either static and modern or dated and
dynamic.

Then you must give this element a rating value on each construct in turn.
After each question mark type a value from 1 to 5.

What is your element?**theater**

Type in the ratings for this element on each construct.

Left pole rated 1, right pole rated 5

one-way--two-way?**2**
visual--auditory?**3**
static--dynamic?**4**
sequential--random-access?**1**
real-time--own-time?**1**
professional--amateur?**1**
dated--modern?**1**

Do you want to change any of these values?**n**

The two elements 8 phone-in radio and 11 videogames are matched at the 90
percent level.

This means that so far you have not distinguished between phone-in radio and
videogames

Do you want to split these?**y**

Think of a construct which separates these two elements, with 8 phone-in
radio on the left pole and 11 videogames on the right pole.

Left pole rated 1 --?**many partaking**
Right pole rated 5 --?**personal**

According to how you feel about them please assign to each of the other
elements in turn a provisional value from 1 to 5.

8 phone-in radio	1	
11 videogames	5	
1 computers	?5	
2 books	?4	
3 television	?1	
4 records	?3	
5 letters	?5	
6 videotapes	?3	
7 newspapers	?1	
9 telephone	?5	
10 theater	?1	

Conversations incorporating user responses with PEGASUS

SHRDLU - understanding a tiny world

The dialog on the opposite page is from a program which uses "natural language" in the interaction, not just as Evans did in giving instructions, or as PEGASUS does in reproducing the user's words in the appropriate places, but in fully understanding novel instructions from the user. The program, SHRDLU, was developed by Terry Winograd at MIT to show that many features of natural language conversation could be programmed for a computer. It relies on its detailed knowledge of a tiny world, the only topic that can be discussed. The diagram at the top of the page shows this world in which a robot arm operates to move blocks from one place to another on a table.

After the system has carried out a command it answers "OK". In order to pick up the red block in the first command it had to clear it off by finding a space on the table for the one on top.

When asked to grasp the pyramid, there were three to choose from, and no clue given in previous instructions as to which was intended. In the next command the instructor uses "one" and "it" as you would do in normal conversation. The system has to decide how these should be interpreted, and how the interpretations relate to the properties of the one it is holding. There are two possibilities, and the most likely is chosen unless it is told to the contrary.

When next asked about "the pyramid" the system assumes the reference is to the one just mentioned. It also handles "not", "at least one of them" and "the one which...". A significant advance in this example is the use of pronouns such as "it". The program deduces from the context of the command what "it" is, or if there is more than one interpretation asks for clarification. This is very much like ordinary human conversation, where much of the background knowledge is not explicitly stated, but filled in by the hearer and amended if found to be inapplicable.

At the end of this section of interaction, the program is asked a question which shows its own capabilities: "can a pyramid support a pyramid?" It replies "I don't know" since it is a situation not represented in the environment. However, when asked to find out, it does not have the capability in its program to stack two pyramids, so replies "I can't".

This program is extremely impressive in its real understanding of the world it is in, rather than the simulation of real world understanding demonstrated by ELIZA. However, it is only so effective because the domain in which it operates is the very

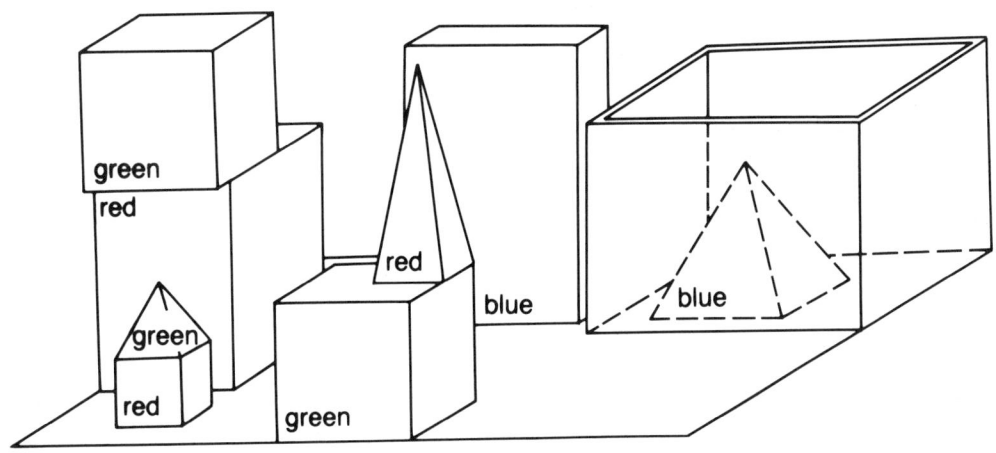

```
pick up a big red block
OK
grasp the pyramid
I DON'T UNDERSTAND WHICH PYRAMID YOU MEAN
find a block which is taller than the one you are holding and put it into the
box
BY "IT", I ASSUME YOU MEAN THE BLOCK WHICH IS TALLER THAN THE ONE I AM HOLDING
OK
what does the box contain?
THE BLUE PYRAMID AND THE BLUE BLOCK
what is the pyramid supported by?
THE BOX
how many blocks are not in the box?
FOUR OF THEM
is at least one of them narrower than the one which I told you to pick up?
YES, THE RED CUBE
is it supported?
YES, BY THE TABLE
can the table pick up blocks?
NO
can a pyramid be supported by a block?
YES
can a pyramid support a pyramid?
I DON'T KNOW
stack up two pyramids
I CAN'T
```

A conversation with understanding with SHRDLU

simple one of a child's blocks. The geometry of the blocks world
is completely specified, and relatively easy for calculations to
take place, unlike a real world environment.

Much of the linguistic power of Winograd's program comes from
the data structures with which he represents both knowledge and
language. The concept "grasp" is represented as a procedure that
fails when applied to a non-manipulable object, succeeds when
applied to an object already grasped, and carries out the actions
necessary to grasp an object not already grasped.

The programming language, **LISP**, used for SHRDLU is also very
significant. It allows programs to be processed as data even as
they are being used. Procedure names can be made to correspond
to the word for the concept they represent and processed as part
of the dialog about the actions being taken.

This shows up in the ability of the system to answer questions
concerning its own behavior. The dialog on the opposite page
shows this and some additional features: for example, it handles
logical connectives such as "and" and "or". The first command
essentially is giving it a choice, and it selects the one
involving the least work.

Next, the system shows that it can interpret phrases like "a
small one" in contrast to "a big red block" or "a large block";
and "the littlest pyramid" which is interpreted from the root
word "little". The program has to compare the sizes of all the
pyramids to carry out this task.

When unsure of the correct interpretation, the possibilities
are listed for the instructor to select one, and following that
sentence, the next shows how it searches its memory to relate its
actions to one another. Notice especially its ability to cope
with tenses like "had you touched..."

There are three basic questions which can be asked: when, why,
and how. "When" questions are answered by stating the main goal
rather than taking notice of intermediate actions to achieve that
goal; "why" questions refer back to the previous action, or
eventually replies with "because you asked me to"; and "how"
questions lead to an explanation of the procedures used in
achieving the main goal.

Winograd's work was a major breakthrough in programming natural
language dialog. It was restricted in its generality by its
dependence on the simple blocks world, but it showed what could
be achieved by a program that did have understanding.

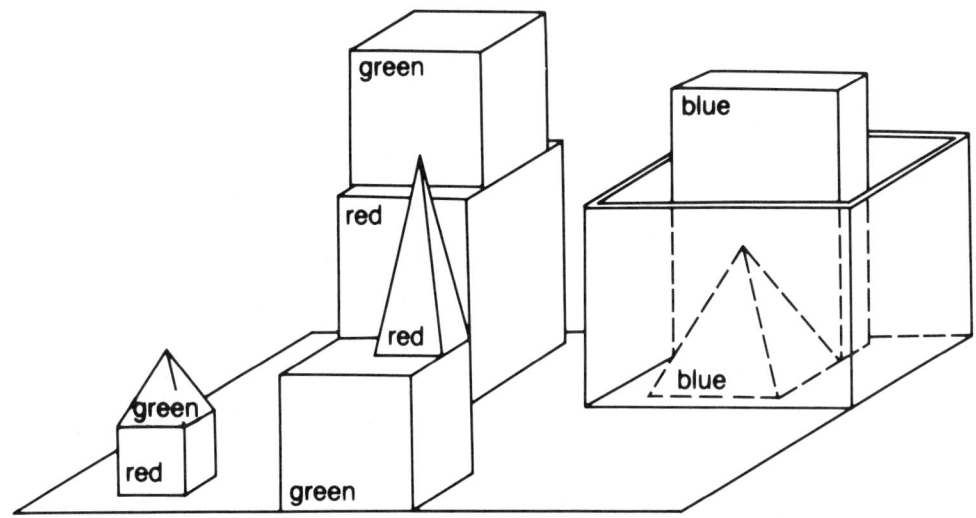

will you please stack up both of the red blocks and either a green cube or a pyramid?
OK
which cube is sitting on the table?
THE LARGE GREEN ONE WHICH SUPPORTS THE RED PYRAMID
is there a large block behind a pyramid?
YES, THREE OF THEM: A LARGE RED ONE, A LARGE GREEN CUBE AND THE BLUE ONE
put a small one onto the green cube which supports a pyramid
OK
put the littlest pyramid on top of it
OK
how many things are on top of green cubes?
I'M NOT SURE WHAT YOU MEAN BY "ON TOP OF" IN THE PHRASE "ON TOP OF GREEN
CUBES"
DO YOU MEAN:
1--DIRECTLY ON THE SURFACE
2--ANYWHERE ON TOP OF?
2
THREE OF THEM
had you touched any pyramid before you put the green one on the little cube?
YES, THE GREEN ONE
when did you pick it up?
WHILE I WAS STACKING UP THE RED CUBE, A LARGE RED BLOCK AND A LARGE GREEN CUBE
why?
TO GET RID OF IT
why did you do that?
TO CLEAN OFF THE RED CUBE
why did you clear off that cube?
TO PUT IT ON A LARGE GREEN CUBE
why did you do that?
BECAUSE YOU ASKED ME TO
how did you do it?
BY PUTTING A LARGE RED BLOCK ON THE TABLE; THEN LETTING GO OF IT; THEN PUTTING
A LARGE GREEN CUBE ON IT; THEN LETTING GO OF THAT CUBE; THEN PUTTING THE RED
CUBE ON THAT CUBE; THEN LETTING GO OF THAT CUBE

More conversation with understanding with SHRDLU

Intellect - natural language access to a database

One type of application where the world under discussion is as well-defined as that of Winograd's blocks world is that of information retrieval systems. Intellect is a natural language query system developed by Larry Harris at Artificial Intelligence Corporation for eliciting information from a **database.** It is different from research projects like the blocks world because it is used in industry by people every day. Part of the reason for using Intellect is that the user of a database has a very different conception of what the data looks like - how it is structured - than does the database administrator. In the examples given on the opposite page, the query is translated by Intellect to be more like a normal database query, and the user can check that it has what was intended.

The way the question is worded is independent of the way the information is stored - the user does not know that anyway. The first four queries show different ways of obtaining the same information; the fourth is not even a sentence, but would probably be understood by another person in the right context.

In the next example the user asks for salaries of employees with certain names. The system could easily satisfy the request by printing out only the salaries and not the names, but if a person were to do that you would imagine that they were being deliberately obstructive and off-hand. Intellect uses "common sense" to realize that you will need to know the names even though they were not asked for explicitly.

The following query shows how Intellect deduces that "salary" is the only item of information that is measured in dollars. This fact, and many other facts it deduces derive from searching the database for a pattern which would make the query sensible.

The last example here contains virtually no information. There is no easily recognizable grammatical structure which could be analyzed, and none of the words appear in the dictionary. The words used only appear in the database, and must be retrieved for any sense to be made of the statement. "Los Angeles" can be found to be a city in the database, and "Area Manager" can be matched with a job, so the translation can be made satisfactorily.

In this system the properties of a database management system are used to help the translation of unlikely queries. It assumes that the user is asking a question related to the information available and, as with a human questioner, attempts many possible interpretations until one which fits comes to the fore.

GIVE ME THE NAMES OF ALL EMPLOYEES WHO HAVE JOBS WORKING AS A SECRETARY IN THE CITY OF CHICAGO.
PRINT THE NAME OF ANY EMPLOYEE WITH CITY=CHICAGO AND JOB=SECRETARY
THE NUMBER OF RECORDS TO RETRIEVE IS 30
  SMITH
  JONES
  BROWN
  . . . . .

PRINT THE NAMES OF ALL THE CHICAGO EMPLOYEES WORKING AS SECRETARIES
PRINT THE NAME OF ANY EMPLOYEE WITH CITY=CHICAGO AND JOB=SECRETARY
  . . . . .

WHO ARE THE CHICAGO SECRETARIES
PRINT THE NAME OF ANY EMPLOYEE WITH CITY=CHICAGO AND JOB=SECRETARY
  . . . . .

SECRETARIES IN CHICAGO
PRINT THE NAME OF ANY EMPLOYEE WITH CITY=CHICAGO AND JOB=SECRETARY
  . . . . .

PRINT THE SALARY OF BROWN AND JONES
PRINT THE SALARY, AND NAME OF ANY EMPLOYEE WITH NAME=BROWN OR JONES
THE NUMBER OF RECORDS TO RETRIEVE IS 269
  $12,500   JONES
  $13,250   BROWN
  . . . . .

WHO EARNS BETWEEN $20,000 AND $30,000?
PRINT THE NAME OF ANY EMPLOYEE WITH SALARY BETWEEN 20000 THRU 30000
THE NUMBER OF RECORDS TO RETRIEVE IS 730
  . . . . .

LOS ANGELES AREA MANAGERS
PRINT THE NAME OF ANY EMPLOYEE WITH JOB=AREA MANAGER AND CITY=LOS ANGELES
THE NUMBER OF RECORDS TO RETRIEVE IS 14
  . . . . .

Natural language interaction with a database through Intellect

TEIRESIAS - understanding understanding

Intellect extends that part of SHRDLU that operates on language successfully through its complete knowledge of a particular world. It is also possible to extend that part which is able to discuss its own strategy and actions by examining its program. This is particularly important in setting up expert systems since what goes wrong with them will not necessarily be apparent in either their rules or their program. It is in the way in which the rules are being used by the program to give advice that problems will appear and need to be discussed. In a dialog the programs need to be able to discuss their own understanding and hence show understanding of understanding.

The diagram at the top of the opposite page relates to MYCIN which was previously discussed in Chapter 2. MYCIN is a medical diagnosis expert system which enables any competent clinician to act as a consultant on infectious diseases. MYCIN works very well when the rules are already built in, but it is difficult to set up the initial knowledge rules needed for all the deductions to follow. It is also difficult to trace the rules causing errors in the deductions of MYCIN if the clinician feels that something has gone wrong.

TEIRESIAS is a system developed by Randall Davis at Stanford University which helps the clinician to set up and modify the knowledge rules for MYCIN. It has the facility to explain MYCIN's decisions, and help the clinician to make his decisions based on suggestive evidence. TEIRESIAS uses a similar rule-based approach to reasoning as does MYCIN but the rules are now rules about the forms of rules and the use of rules. Davis calls these **metarules**. An example is:
"METARULE003:
    If 1) there are rules which do not mention the current goal in
           their premise
        2) there are rules which mention the current goal in their
           premise
    Then it is definite that the former should be done before the
    latter."
Whereas MYCIN's rules are very specific to microbial infections and their treatment, those of TEIRESIAS are very much more general and could be used in other domains.

The dialog on the opposite page shows a conversation with TEIRESIAS. Here, the expert (clinician) noticed that there was something wrong with the identities deduced by MYCIN in that one was missing. The system first uses simple prompt-response dialog to ask what the clinician wants to do about the situation, giving

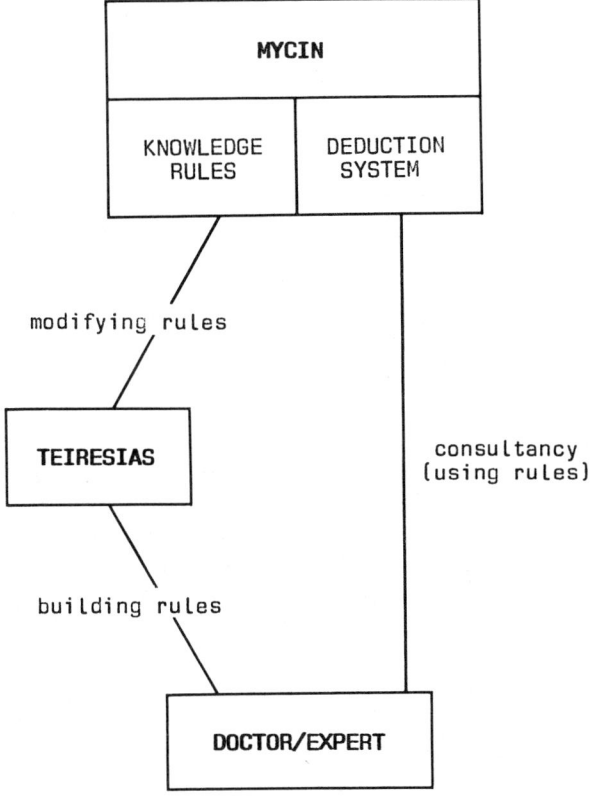

MYCIN

| KNOWLEDGE RULES | DEDUCTION SYSTEM |

modifying rules

TEIRESIAS

building rules

consultancy
(using rules)

DOCTOR/EXPERT

TEIRESIAS, an expert system to aid access to an expert system

```
My therapy recommendations will be based upon the following probable
infection(s) and potential causative organism(s):
INFECTION-1 is PRIMARY-BACTEREMIA
    <Item 1>  E.COLI [ORGANISM-1]
    <Item 2>  PSEUDOMONAS-AERUGINOSA [ORGANISM-1]
Are all these identities correct?
++** N
Are there any identities missing?
++** Y
Which one(s)?
++** KLEBSIELLA-PNEUMONIAE PROTEUS-NON-MIRABILIS
Are there any identities that shouldn't have appeared?
++** Y
Which one(s)?
++** PSEUDOMONAS-AERUGINOSA
```

Understanding understanding, a conversation with TEIRESIAS

him several choices for proceeding. He chooses to allow
TEIRESIAS to guide the debugging, and it uses the **heuristic** rule
of starting with the identity which appeared incorrectly. This is
termed heuristic because it is a sensible guess rather than a
necessary deduction. The program then reconstructs the deductive
process, asking the clinician to confirm its actions at each
stage, or comment on anything incorrect. It checks that the
rules are correct, and confirms the facts about the particular
case in hand.

Before very long the issue has become sharply focused for the
clinician and the system, saving much time and effort. The
guideline is that a rule must be found which is relevant to this
particular patient, but true in general, and enhancing the set of
rules of knowledge. The expert types in the necessary rule, and
TEIRESIAS reconstructs the rule in natural language - translating
from the clinician's input into its own internal structures, and
back again for confirmation of a correct interpretation. This is
a common technique in human dialog where we say to someone, "This
is what I think you said. Please tell me if I am correct."

Finally, the new rule is added to the set of knowledge rules,
with a tag explaining who added it and in what circumstances.
This allows the ultimate level of explanation to be given in
terms of who added the rule and what reasons he gave for adding
it. TEIRESIAS preserves a complete record of its own education
and the rationale underlying it. The system then reverts to
solving the problem of diagnosis for this patient, but does not
ask again any question to which it was previously given the
answer, or could deduce the answer.

TEIRESIAS is probably the most advanced dialog system that has
been developed at the time of writing this book. This shows up
not in its capabilities to use natural language which are not
exceptional, but rather in its capability to understand its own
processes of understanding. Since its understanding is based on
that of the experts who have primed it with knowledge, it is able
to discuss with them the faults in its understanding in their own
terms.

We can expect to see a proliferation of expert systems based on
the MYCIN/TEIRESIAS concepts developed during the near future.
There are many situations in commercial management, government
policy and personal decision-making where there are no absolute
rules but only a variety of guidelines coming from different
sources with different priorities. It is difficult for people to
keep all these rules in mind, relate them one to another, use
them in decision-making, note their effects, and modify them when

```
Do you want to
        1] track down the problem yourself, or
        2] allow me to guide the debugging, or
        3] ignore it for now and fix it another time?
Type 1, 2 or 3
++** 2
We'll start with the PSEUDOMONAS-AERUGINOSA first.
The following rules were used in deducing that the identity of ORGANISM-1 is
pseudomonas-aeruginosa
RULE184
-------

Since [1.1] the category of ORGANISM-1 is not known
      [1.2] the gram strain of ORGANISM-1 is gramneg
      [1.3] the morphology of ORGANISM-1 is rod
      [1.4] the aerobicity of ORGANISM-1 is facultative
 There is weakly suggestive evidence (.3) that the identity of ORGANISM-1 is
 pseudomonas-aeruginosa
Is this rule correct?
++** Y
Should its premise have failed for this case?
++** Y
Which clause of the premise should have been false? [give #]
++** 1
No conclusions were reached concerning the category of ORGANISM-1.
Should it have been possible to conclude a category?
++** Y
Which one?
++** ENTEROBACTERIACEAE
There were no rules successfully invoked in the attempt to deduce that the
category of ORGANISM-1 is enterobacteriaceae.
The following (potentially applicable) rules were NOT executed because the
starred [**] clause failed:
RULE116
-------

If    1) the identity of ORGANISM-1 is not known
   ** 2) the gram strain of ORGANISM-1 is not known **
      3) the morphology of ORGANISM-1 is not known
      4) the site of CULTURE-1 is csf
      5) the infection is meningitis
      6) the age (in years) of Albert Hall is less than or equal to .17
then  There is weakly suggestive evidence (.33) that the category of
      ORGANISM-1 is enterobacteriaceae
RULE050
-------

If    1) the morphology of ORGANISM-1 is rod
      2) the gram strain of ORGANISM-1 is gramneg
      3) the aerobicity of ORGANISM-1 is facultative
   ** 4) the infection with ORGANISM-1 was acquired while the patient was
         hospitalized **
then  There is suggestive evidence (.7) that the category of ORGANISM-1 is
      enterobacteriaceae
Are all these rules correct?
++** Y
Should any of them have been successfully invoked?
++** N
Is there a rule missing?
++** Y
Ok, then I need a rule that would allow me to deduce that the category of
ORGANISM-1 is enterobacteriaceae.
Would you like to give me such a rule now?
++** Y
Good...
```

Understanding understanding, a conversation with TEIRESIAS

they have undesired consequences. The computer is coming to
provide an effective medium for conversation with the multiple
rule sources on whom we rely, consciously or subconsciously, in
arriving at our decisions and actions. If we can encode the
expertise expressed in these rules then we will be able to use
the computer not so much to make our decisions for us, but rather
to discuss and explain the basis for our decisions with us so
that we are able to understand our own rationale. We can view
such systems as **awareness raising** devices providing us with
informed discussion through conversation based on understanding.

Conclusions - Natural Language Conversation

The examples of natural language dialog between people and
computers given in this chapter contrast with the formal dialogs
with CP/M and Wordstar in Chapters 4 and 5. The Evans medical
dialog shows how natural language sentences as messages to the
user can be added to a system where the user keys only simple
responses. It goes on to show in the ELIZA example how words
keyed in by the user can be incorporated in the sentences from
the computer to give a more natural dialog with no understanding
by the computer. The PEGASUS example shows how this may be used
for practical purposes.

The sequence of examples then demonstrates through SHRDLU how
very extensive natural language understanding in a limited domain
is now possible. The Intellect example shows that this may be
used for practical purposes. The TEIRESIAS example shows how the
understanding itself can be used to generate truly conversational
interaction between people and computers working together on a
problem.

The first three examples are all from personal computer systems
whereas SHRDLU, Intellect and TEIRESIAS operate on large
machines. However, the increasing storage and processing power
available on personal computers will make such natural language
dialog widely available on such machines within a few years. It
is technically feasible now.

The twentieth proverb - NATURAL LANGUAGE TAKES MANY FORMS

The sequence of examples in this chapter shows that we cannot
speak of natural language dialog in general. It takes many forms
extending from the formal dialogs with CP/M of Chapter 4 through
the use of natural language output only, to the in-depth analysis
of SHRDLU to the wide-ranging conversations between people.

Proverb 20: Natural language may be used in a variety of different ways.

In considering the use of natural language dialog with computer systems note that it can be used for output independently of input.

The twenty-first proverb - LANGUAGE IS NOT UNDERSTANDING

The contrast between the chatty fluency of ELIZA and the stilted intellectual depth of TEIRESIAS shows that language and understanding are not necessarily linked. The dialog with SHRDLU demonstrates that understanding certainly helps linguistic fluency but the earlier examples show that it is not essential to it. We have seen that dialogs of similar appearance in fluency may be generated from entirely different bases of knowledge. It is important to take this into account in assessing any system on the basis of sample dialogs.

Proverb 21: Fluent language may not imply fluent understanding.

Take into account when evaluating any system that apparently good conversational dialog may be generated through rules that are based on little understanding of what is being said. There can be widely differing degrees of understanding underlying the same dialog.

The twenty-second proverb - PRESERVING ROLE INTEGRITY

One criticism that may be levelled at the use of the techniques underlying ELIZA-like programs is that they create a completely false impression of the intelligence underlying the computer dialog. We noted in Chapter 3 how very easy it is to mimic intelligent behavior and how ready are people to accept computer behavior as being human-like. With the assumption of human-like characteristics in a computer system comes many other assumptions of commonsense, responsibility, co-operation and understanding that will currently be false and perhaps dangerously misleading.

Some computer system designers recommend against the use of natural language dialog because it so easily creates an impression of intelligence. They feel that stilted formal dialogs more accurately portray the current state of computer systems and do not lead users to expect more from them than they can give. If the computer talks like a piece of equipment then it will be recognized as a piece of equipment.

This is a valid argument but its implications must obviously change as computer technology changes. It can be given a more general form by considering the sociological notion of **role integrity.** People are very complex beings and to get along with one another in this over-crowded world they adopt a strategy of role playing. You are my bank manager and when I meet you in that role I expect you to act and react in certain ways. If we meet in a glee club as singing partners then you are no longer in the role of bank manager and I expect you to act and react in very different ways. Your integrity consists of maintaining the expected role. Someone who does not act and react consistently and uniformly according to the role they project is very difficult to deal with. They make the world very much more complicated and interfere with the course of normal social transactions.

We can see that it is just such "role integrity" that we need to program in computer systems. If ELIZA really did have the understanding to match its facile dialog no harm would result. It is because the program cannot match in its behavior the role projected that such dialog can be misleading. TEIRESIAS does have the understanding of the dialog sufficient to play the role of an intelligent collaborator to the clinician. Evans' medical program has role integrity because it is clear that the computer is just playing through a prepared script. It is not pretending to respond to sentences typed in, only to yes/no answers to its own questions.

> **Proverb 22: The role expected of the system should be maintained.**
>
> Tricks of dialog should not be used to give a false impression of the capabilities of the computer system. A role should be accurately projected that can be maintained throughout the interaction.

Criticism of natural language dialog in terms of its inefficiency for specific tasks is still valid. The use of menus and formal responses described in Chapter 5 does minimize the number of key depressions needed to perform a given task. In Chapter 6 we gave examples where graphic interaction is used that is even more remote from natural language. No one of these techniques is best for all possible tasks. What is happening is that we are gradually enhancing the repertoire of modes of communication between people and computers until it becomes as rich as that available for interaction between people.

8 Presenting Computer Conversation

So far we have concentrated on the conversations between people and computers once they are underway. In this chapter we are interested in what leads up to the conversation. How do people come to enter into such conversations to start with? What persuades them that it is worthwhile? How do they select a particular computer system? What is their initial approach to starting the conversation? These questions all have different answers concerned with user education, training, manuals and selling and marketing techniques. However, they all may be brought together under the one heading of **presenting** computer conversation.

Each new medium brings with it both new problems and new opportunities for presentation. The record is an audio medium. It comes in a well-designed, brightly colored sleeve to give it a visual presentation. It comes with notes on the music, composer, artists and performance to increase the listener's knowledge and listening pleasure. The selection of which records to buy is aided by publications which compare various recordings of the same music for performance and technical quality. The decision as to which records to make is made according to market projections about gaps, popularity and changing public taste.

Books have similar phenomena associated with them. This may be less obvious than for records because the index, contents list, foreword and explanatory notes are in the same form as the book itself and generally included in it. However, together they essentially form a "manual" aiding access to the book and are not really part of it. Highly technical books which are difficult to understand have secondary books of commentaries and interpretations associated with them. Before any book is published it goes through a reviewing process to establish its quality and marketability. After it is published it will be subject to critical review in a wide range of publications from a number of different points of view.

Both records and books are assumed to have long-term value and are collected into libraries where they are indexed and catalogued. Someone who is searching for particular knowledge or experience can use the libraries and catalog systems to discover whether what they want already exists and, if so, gain access to it. It is not just scientific and historical material that is treated in this way but also entertainment material. Our civilization has developed techniques for preserving and guarding the creations of each generation and making them available, hopefully, for all time. Fashions come and go and works which have been unappreciated for many years may suddenly turn out to be of great interest to the present generation.

The computer medium is still in its infancy. Its role as a medium has only recently been realized. The personal computer industry is still at a very early stage of development. Hence, all these techniques for presentation have only just begun to be apparent and they are still chaotically organized. In this chapter we use comparisons such as that between records and computer programs to discuss the presentation of computer conversation. This gives useful perspectives on how the personal computer industry is developing. It also enables us to explain the role of such activities as training users and writing manuals.

The need for market research

The concept of investigating the market for a computer program before writing it may seem pretentious to many of those involved in developing programs for personal computers. Most programs are written by people who wish to use the computer for their own purposes and their "market" is themselves. If you are writing only for yourself then elaborate planning seems unnecessary. All the information you need is already in your head and can be used to guide you in writing the program. Most of the guidelines we have given in this book on writing good dialog may also appear unnecessary in these circumstances. If you are talking only to yourself then you do not need to be very supportive. If you have a specific short-term purpose in mind then you do not need to take into account possible future ways of using your program that differ from what you intend now.

Think Again

By Mildred L G Shaw and Cliff McKnight. 182 pages. Published by Prentice-Hall. ISBN 0 13 917443 5.

DAN IS A teenage boy who is often in trouble. He has been to court several times for petty offences. One could say he has a problem. However by drawing a grid he becomes friendly with a table-tennis playing policeman and gets a job as a plumber.

What this has to do with microcomputers is not at first apparent. But a problem such as Dan's can be expressed in grid form, and then processed by a micro to find a solution. In the appendix of the book are a couple such programs, which can analyse grids and act as an aid to solving problems of a sociological or psychological kind.

Think Again

Now here is a clear explanation of how to use a proven scientific technique to solve everyday problems and make shrewd decisions. Based on professional scientific research, **Think Again** demonstrates how repertory grids can be used in even the most confusing private situations.

The method is simple. All anyone needs is a pencil and the will to explore a problem before making a reasonable decision. The grid organizes **your** thoughts and reveals **your** answer, logically.

The grid has been used effectively in industry, management, and education. In this guide, the authors present real-life case histories in an approach to personal and group applications of the grid. Microcomputer programs for grid analysis are also included in this introduction to a powerful, personal tool.

Mildred L.G. Shaw and Cliff McKnight

PRENTICE-HALL, Inc., Englewood Cliffs, New Jersey 07632

ISBN 0-13-917443-5

SHAW, Mildred L. G.   BF 698 .8 R38 S53

Think again - personal problem-solving and decision-making

Mildred L. G. Shaw, Cliff McKnight. -- Englewood Cliffs,

New Jersey: Prentice-Hall, c1981.

Includes bibliography.

1 Repertory grid technique. 2 Problem solving.
3 Decision making.

BF 698 .8 R38 S53 - SCOTT

Figure 8.3. Various ways of presenting a book.
Top left: From a review of the book (Practical Computing, October 1982).
Top right: A book cover. Bottom: A library catalog entry for the book.

However, a useful program is rarely used only for a short period for a specific purpose by just one person. It is kept and used again later. It is extended and used for other purposes. It is seen by other people and valued by them. Their request for a copy is difficult to refuse and they become "customers." Many widely used programs were originally developed to satisfy the short-term objectives of the original programmer. Many of their quirks and defects have arisen through their being extended and tidied-up as new users have complained about problems in use or lack of facilities. It is very difficult to maintain guidelines such as the uniformity and consistency of Proverbs 15 and 16 when dialog is extended piecemeal to cater for new facilities. The programs could have been very much better if some market research had been undertaken as part of their original design. Identifying the broader range of future requirements enables provision to be made for them even if they are not implemented initially.

Even if you never intend to issue a program to anyone else it is worth putting some effort into its design, particularly in thinking about its later use. You will probably not discard it after its initial use but will put it by for other purposes. Later, possibly some years later, you will come back to it and attempt to use it again. You will be in a different frame of mind having had new experiences in the intervening period and may find it very difficult to understand how to use the program and to remember its peculiarities. "You now" will really be a **different person** from the "you then" who wrote the program. These considerations apply even more strongly if, as so often happens, you use the earlier program as a base for extension to a different application. Even if your only market is you, it is worth thinking about the longer-term use of the program knowing that even that "market" will change.

Much of the professional software now available for personal computers was developed with very little market research. Small companies were formed by many people who wished to sell programs that they had written for specific purposes more widely. Many have failed but others have found a niche in the market place and have prospered. In a rapidly changing industry such as that of personal computers there will always be an important role for blind innovation. The market place may recognize great value in a product that goes beyond that intended by the innovator and certainly goes beyond his original design considerations. However, blind luck is not a reliable basis for establishing a business or an industry. Detailed market research is playing an increasingly important role as the personal computer industry begins to assume a structure.

The many unexpected users of a program

The nature of market research

The basic rules of market research are very simple. The key question to be asked is "what do people want?" This broad question needs to be narrowed down by other considerations such as "what personal computer application areas do I know sufficient about to assess reliably what people want and to generate it for them?" If you want to sell your programs then the question is probably best restated as "what do people want for which they are prepared to pay and have the funds available to do so?" If you want to raise funds from a grant-giving body then the question is probably best restated as "what is perceived by the donor of funds as a need for which they are prepared to pay?"

Thus the first step is to determine who your **customers** will be and what they will want. The future tense is important in this statement. It is not the **market now** that you trying to assess. It is the **market which will exist** when your product is ready. You have to look ahead a year and predict what will be wanted then and also what will be available then from other suppliers. If you try and compete with today's products in a year's time then you will always be behind the competition. Computer products very often become obsolete before the first one has been sold. The key skill is to outguess the competition and have your product leapfrog over theirs. This is far easier said than done but still needs to be kept in mind as your key objective.

Where does the information come from about customers and their needs, and competitive products and their development? There are many sources. If you are your own customer initially, perhaps developing a specialist package for your professional or personal needs, then you may be representative of others like yourself. This is the source of the market knowledge for some of the best packages around. In terms of our earlier diagram in Chapter 2 you are **expert, programmer** and **user**, all rolled into one. In considering your requirements, try to separate out these roles and consider a wider range of users than yourself and a wider range of expertise than your own.

If you are developing packages that are intended for others whose needs are different from your own, then you have to be more formal in gathering market information. If you intend to stick to established markets and do something that has already been done in a better way then knowledge of existing products is important. How many packages have your competitors sold? What do the reviews in the trade and professional magazines say about them, their effectiveness and their defects? Where do these packages rate in the published league tables of the top thirty

The Top Thirty

This Month	Last Month	Index	
1.	1.	182.36	**Apple Writer IIe,** Paul Lutus, Apple Computer
2.	3.	98.65	**Home Accountant,** Bob Schoenburg, Larry Grodin, and Steve Pollack, Continental Software
3.	2.	83.21	**VisiCalc,** Software Arts/Dan Bricklin and Robert Frankston, VisiCorp
4.	10.	82.71	**MasterType,** Bruce Zweig, Lightning Software
5.	6.	77.23	**PFS: File,** John Page and D. D. Roberts, Software Publishing Corporation
6.	8.	69.26	**Wizardry,** Andrew Greenberg and Robert Woodhead, Sir-tech
7.	11.	67.26	**Bank Street Writer,** Gene Kuzmiak and the Bank Street College of Education, Broderbund Software
8.	5.	65.27	**Miner 2049er,** Mike Livesay and Bill Hogue, Micro Fun
9.	9.	57.30	**Quick File IIe,** Rupert Lissner, Apple Computer
10.	7.	53.31	**Multiplan,** Microsoft
11.	4.	43.35	**Choplifter,** Dan Gorlin, Broderbund Software
12.	—	33.88	**Double-Take,** Mark Simonsen, Beagle Bros
13.	20.	33.38	**Ultima II,** Lord British, Sierra On-Line
14.	18.	31.89	**PFS: Report,** John Page, Software Publishing Corporation
15.	—	28.90	**DOS Boss,** Bert Kersey and Jack Cassidy, Beagle Bros
16.	13.	24.91	**Typing Tutor,** Image Producers, Microsoft
17.	27.	23.92	**Snooper Troops I,** Tom Snyder, Spinnaker Software
18.	—	21.92	**Pronto DOS,** Tom Weishaar, Beagle Bros
	—	21.92	**Apple Mechanic,** Bert Kersey, Beagle Bros
20.	22.	20.93	**Pinball Construction Set,** Bill Budge, BudgeCo
21.	—	20.43	**Facemaker,** DesignWare, Spinnaker Software
	28.	20.43	**Suspended,** Michael Berlyn, Infocom
23.	26.	19.93	**Mix & Match,** Children's Television Workshop, Apple Computer
24.	—	19.43	**Knight of Diamonds,** Andrew Greenberg and Robert Woodhead, Sir-tech
25.	—	18.93	**Ernie's Quiz,** Children's Television Workshop, Apple Computer
26.	24.	17.94	**Early Games for Young Children,** John Paulson, Counterpoint Software
	—	17.94	**Utility City,** Bert Kersey, Beagle Bros
	15.	17.94	**Screen Writer II,** David Kidwell, Sierra On-Line
29.	—	17.44	**PFS: Graph,** Bessie Chin and Stephen Hill, Software Publishing Corporation
	15.	17.44	**Aztec,** Paul Stephenson, Datamost
	—	17.44	**Apple Logo,** Logo Computer Systems, Apple Computer

**Keeping track of the top thirty programs in the market
from Softalk magazine's monthly listing**

best sellers? At least in this situation you have ready access to hard facts on which to base your market research.

If you are really innovating and intend to fulfil customer needs that have never previously been satisfied and may not even have been perceived, then the basis for your estimates is far less substantial. You can at least estimate the number of your potential customers and the number of these who already have computers that could run your package. From these figures you can work out the total cost to a new customer of buying a computer system complete with your package, and the marginal cost to someone who has a computer of buying the package alone. You can compare these expenditures with the incomes of your potential customers and the costs of other purchases that they make. If your package reduces their other costs then you can consider whether they can actually switch the funds. You can then estimate the numbers of customers in each category who might realistically afford to buy the package.

In terms of our concept of **presenting** computer conversations, your market research is the first step to determining whether there will be an **audience** for your presentation and what members of that audience will expect to get from it. The audience is your market and their expectations are your product definition. If there is no audience then there is no point in putting on a presentation, or in developing an elegant package satisfying all the criteria we have previously discussed. If there is an audience but you fail to meet their expectations then the better your presentation, the more informative it is, the less likely they are to buy!

Marketing

Marketing a product is a completely separate step with entirely different techniques from market research. It is the weakest link in the chain for most computer software between its conception and its use by customers. If people are unaware of what you have achieved in your package then they are not going to buy it. If they are unaware that it even exists then they are not going to consider buying it. Contrary to the old fable, the world definitely does not beat a path to the door of the inventors of better mousetraps. The essence of marketing is simple. It is firstly to draw attention to your product. It is secondly to maintain an awareness of that product. There are two main routes for doing this with software packages. Firstly, through the **magazines** that your potential customers are likely to read. Secondly, through the **shops** that they are likely to visit.

One way to present programs

In the early days of personal computers there were a few rather technical magazines on computer hardware and software. In recent years an incredibly large number of magazines have commenced publication that are targeted on particular market sectors for computers. There are those for Apple][owners with technical interests, others for those with game playing interests, others for those with business applications. There are similar magazines for each of the major personal computers. There are also magazines with a very broad coverage that have specialist sections on each of the main machines. Professional magazines nowadays often have computer sections reporting applications of interest in that profession. These magazines carry articles, news sections and advertizing and it is through some combination of these that the message that you have a new package, what it does and where it is available must be presented. Advertizing costs can be very high but articles and news items to achieve the same effect are free.

In the early days of personal computers also there were a few shops in major towns where the owner sat with soldering iron in one hand and language manual in other putting systems together. Now computer sales outlets proliferate in every town and the personal computer has become standard merchandise. One recent phenomenon is the **software shop** selling only packages for computers and not the computers themselves. This corresponds to the separation in the record market between those shops that sell hi-fi equipment and others that sell only records. Another recent phenomenon is that computers and software have been added to the range of goods in general consumer stores. To attract attention to a product in any of these shops requires normal merchandising techniques: **attractive packaging** that catches the eye and yet is not so garish that it detracts from the product; **promotional leaflets** that can be left on display; and special **display stands** for new products.

The package itself in operation can also be a very effective selling tool. Arcade games are set up to go through an interesting and attractive sequence of play when no-one is using them. This can be done with any package, whether it is a game, word-processing, or accounting. The displays of the package in operation can be interlaced with tutorial presentations of its features and the tasks which it can undertake. Many large software houses now offer **demonstration versions** of their packages incorporating sufficient facilities for user evaluation. This is becoming increasingly important as the packages themselves become lower in cost and the salesman cannot afford to spend too much of his own time explaining the package to an intending purchaser.

Books and programs on display together in a store

Problems of training

In the computer industry over the past thirty years training
has become a major sub-industry in its own right. The early
systems were poorly structured and unreliable. Before you could
use a computer you needed to know many things about both hardware
and software that were not at all obvious or logical, some
blatantly illogical. The only way to discover these things was
through experience and the only way to speed experience was
through training. Each major computer manufacturer had his
training division and a number of firms were set up specializing
in training.

The personal computer has changed this situation. Not by
making training unnecessary - any user of a personal computer
system will have his horror stories to tell about its quirks and
his problems with them - but by making it impossible. There are
just too many personal computer users for anyone to undertake the
task of training them. There are also too many products and too
many new ones coming out for any individual attention to be paid
to training people to use them. So, how is the industry coping?
It seems not always very well from some of the product reviews
and complaints letters in magazines.

In coming to terms with the problems of training users, we have
first to accept that we cannot communicate directly with the
majority of users of our programs. Hence we cannot train our
customers specifically to use our products except through the
products themselves. This does not mean that we will always be
dealing with completely computer-naive users. There will be much
general education in the use of computers. The demand for
computer literacy courses is high and growing, and an
increasingly high proportion of the population will get some
experience of computers at school or university. This will
increase their familiarity with computers in general but will
probably also generate expectations that are violated by our
particular program. We will benefit from increased computer
literacy in general but may find it creates problems also.

Under these circumstances products that require little training
of the user will sell best. Those that conform to the users'
expectations will require the least training. Hence establishing
good standards for person-computer dialog in packages used in
education is very important for the computer industry. In
addition, any aids to training necessary for a particular package
must be supplied with it, either in a manual or as part of the
package itself.

Various approaches to packaging programs from
Communications Packaging Corporation

Manuals

Good documentation has always been regarded as important in selling packages for computers. A floppy disk in itself has no selling capability. An attractively bound manual that is well-presented and gives the potential purchaser glancing at it the impression that he is buying something of substance is an important selling aid. It needs to show what the package can do, usually through pictures of the screen. It also needs to persuade the purchaser that adequate information and support are available in the manual to give him confidence that he will be able to learn to drive the package.

Writing a good manual for a computer package is not an easy task. The ability to present what you have done, and why, is a different skill from that of actually doing it. There are many very good programs with poor manuals, and also some good manuals for poor programs. However, by using samples of existing good quality manuals and following their format it is usually possible to generate a reasonable manual for a new product. Turning this first draft into an excellent manual with no errors or omissions and with all information properly indexed is a major task that may take as much effort as writing the program.

Programs change frequently during the product life cycle and keeping the manual up to date as changes are made in the program may become a nightmare. Large companies are using computer-based systems to maintain both programs and documentation and this will be an important trend for personal computers also. **Programmers' work-bench** packages for program maintenance and manual writing are very important computer-aided design tools for this industry. We need to use computers to look after computers!

One point that is often missed is that there needs to be at least two forms of manual, or quite separate sections in the same manual. The user initially needs a **tutorial manual** that gets him started with some meaningful tasks. He does not need to know every possibility but just how to start on some useful activity so he gets a feel for the main capabilities of the package.

The tutorial manual, however, that trains the first-time user is totally unsuited to be used as a detailed presentation of all the features of the package. It will not have items in a logical order and will not be complete. Hence a separate **reference manual** is needed that is organized for reference rather than reading. It should have a logical structure with all related options together and very good contents lists and index so that information on any topic can be easily accessed.

Extracts from the contents list of the PLANET manual

Tutorial assistance in programs

A good manual can never compensate for a badly written program. We noted in the discussion of Proverb 14 in Chapter 5 that a menu is better than a manual because it gives information specific to the current situation. Already there are signs that programs that are adequately documented but do not themselves support the user will not sell. Some time ago we went into a computer store to purchase a word processing package for the Apple][which we knew was very good technically. The salesman, however, suggested that we purchase a package that had far less capabilities. When we asked him why, he commented about the one we really wanted, "Oh, you have to read the manual to use that one."

The rule that it should not be necessary to read the manual to use a program is a very reasonable one if computer systems are going to compete with other consumer goods. You do not have to read the sleeve note to play a record. You would not play an arcade game if it took more than ten seconds to learn. You will probably not look at the owner's manual before driving your new car away. The need for computer packages to be self-sufficient in training users is accepted by many software companies. They are building tutorial facilities into their programs so that training is a facility of the computer system itself. The screens opposite show some of the training dialog from the Lotus 1-2-3 business information management system.

This emphasis on programs being usable without manuals is not to undermine the significance of the manual. There are times when it is useful to be able to check on the facilities available on a system without using it. On large systems nowadays it is common to have the manual accessible on line as a text file which can be used by a **browsing** system capable of answering user queries. The storage required to do this is too great currently for most personal computer systems but this will change during the next few years.

Ultimately we can see all applications packages being supported by tutorial systems that are themselves **expert systems** in the use of the package. The manual will become an active resource rather a passive book. **Dynabook** illustrated in Chapter 6 shows how this can operate. The use of computer packages to make other computer packages easier to use will be very important as access to computer systems becomes widespread. It may even become unnecessary for users to decide what package to use. General guidance systems will be developed that can discuss with users their requirements, suggest the resources available to satisfy them, and aid the user in meeting them.

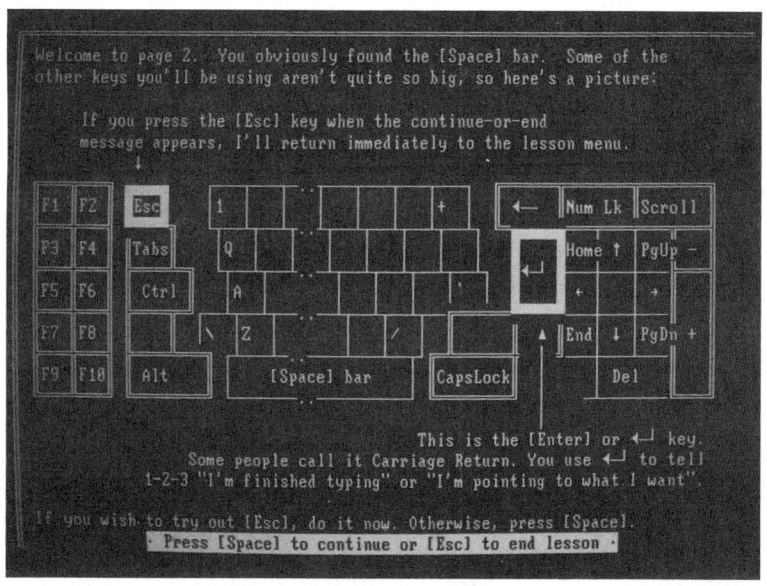

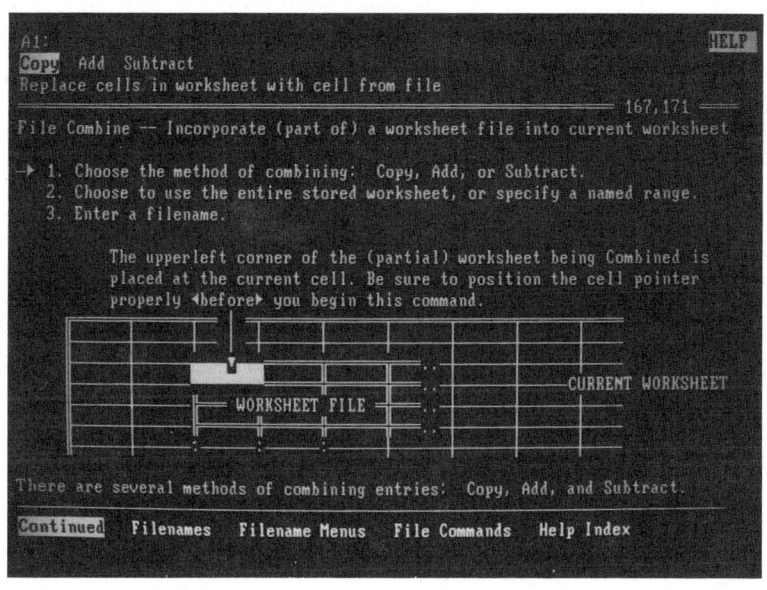

Tutorial assistance from LOTUS 1-2-3

Conclusions - Presenting Computer Conversations

A chapter on marketing in a book on person-computer interaction may have struck some readers as strange at first sight. We hope that it is now seen to be appropriate. The person-computer interface used to begin at the point where the user entered into a conversation with the package. Increasingly, however, the computer is being used as a medium for its own presentation, to market, sell, train, and generally inform its users and potential users. "User-friendliness" is not an abstract valuation or a humanistic plea. It is a major business requirement in a massive, growing and highly competitive industry. It is customer demand that is focusing computer product manufacturers' attention on the need for improved person-computer interaction.

The ethical problems of your friendly conversational computer inserting a selling spiel into its dialog may, or may not, turn out to be serious. When you use the spelling correction option that is present in the Wordstar manual the package informs you if the required overlay is not present that "The separately sold file SPELSTAR.OVR is required for chosen function." Some future advertizing authority may decide to object to such a selling technique. However, we are used to books advertizing other books and one medium being used to promote products in another, so the role of computers in self-promotion is not unexpected.

The twenty-third proverb - PROGRAMS REQUIRE PRESENTATION

If the message of Proverb 3 is accepted, that computers provide a new medium for communication, then by the analogy with other media it is reasonable to expect the presentation of computer packages to be an important activity. Media attain their significance in our society through their universality. They involve everyone and impact a wide range of activities. The personal computer industry has moved in a decade from being the province of a few specialists to its present status in the public domain. The resources we used for presentation in those early days would now be swamped by the current level of general interest. We have to treat the new medium with professionalism that has characterized previous media and develop techniques for its presentation that can cope with the scale of interest and demand.

Proverb 23: Programs require presentation.

> Programs in the new medium for communication provided by computers require the same attention to techniques of presentation as have those in past media.

The twenty-fourth proverb - KNOW THE MARKET

Computer packages are products in a market place that is very large and highly complex. The universality of computers gives them potential impact on virtually every human activity and makes it difficult to predict how they will be used in the future. The designer of a computer package needs to have a clear concept of who his customers will be. The potential user of a computer package needs to know for what market it was designed and whether his use will fall into this category. Some innovative programs will themselves create new markets where none existed before. However, the majority of successful programs will be created under design constraints established through a clear analysis of the market into which they will be targeted. This involves identifying customers together with their actual needs and perceived requirements.

Proverb 24: Know the market.

> The designer of a new computer program should have in mind a clear market defined by customer needs and requirements.

The twenty-fifth proverb - INFORMING USERS

The size of the market place for personal computing is making it increasingly difficult to bring users and packages together. You may have an urgent need for a particular type of program. I may have a package that is targeted precisely to your needs. How do we become aware of one anothers' existence? There is no easy answer to this question and the means for disseminating such information are very diverse. They range from the conventional media to computer-based information services such as **bulletin boards** that are being used increasingly to sell computer programs. When contact is made with a potential user then a short concise presentation needs to be available to inform them of the capabilities of your package. If they become users then the presentation needs to be extended to train them in the use of the package and keep them informed of its features as they use it.

Proverb 25: Users should be informed.

> At every stage in the chain from marketing through selling, training and routine use of a computer program, users of that program need to be kept informed of relevant information about it.

The twenty-sixth proverb - PROGRAMS SHOULD BE SELF-SUFFICIENT

If the computer medium is as powerful and important as we suggest in this book then it is reasonable to expect that it will be the major force in satisfying the requirements stated in the proverbs above. The use of other media to support the use of computer programs may be significant initially but ultimately it will be the computer medium itself that dominates all others. In the short term we need to make computer programs self-sufficient so that they present themselves with no other aids. They can be their own selling and training aids.

Proverb 26: Programs should be self-sufficient.

> Computer programs developed for a particular application should be extended to present themselves to potential customers and to tutor their users.

9 Proverbs for Computer Conversation

The difficulty with proverbs is remembering which ones are appropriate in what circumstances. This is a book full of advice intended to be helpful in considering computer conversation. In this chapter we attempt to bring it all together and give it some structure. The advice can best be understood in terms of our aims stated in Chapter 1 where we noted that this book is concerned with promoting simple and effective styles for personal computing. We aim to make purchasers of computer systems and programs more aware of good conversational style and the problems that arise when it is neglected. We aim to make specifiers of computer systems and programs aware of the need to devote as much effort to the human interface as they do to the data processing and storage algorithms. We aim to give programmers a repertoire of styles and techniques for computer dialog that will enable them to create effective systems for a wide range of situations.

The examples given in each chapter are our primary material for satisfying these aims. Not only do they illustrate different forms and problems of dialog with computers but they also serve to evoke other examples. You may have met many of the types of situation we have described and you will certainly recognize them when they occur in new systems and new products. The proverbs are intended to be aids to remembering some important principles of system design and evaluation that underlie the examples. In particular they can be used as a framework for criticizing a dialog system. If its behavior violates a principle expressed in a particular proverb then negative consequences can be expected and demonstrated. The proverbs also serve as a check list in system design. A system satisfying all of them should be very acceptable as "user-friendly", so acceptable that users do not really notice they are using it!

Proverbs of responsibility

The first proverb in the book, shown opposite, is a reminder of our responsibility for the behavior of computer systems. It is common to hear the computer being blamed for all kinds of anti-social activities. However, the errors, the stupidity, the unfriendliness, the difficulties of communication, all these were put there by people. The excuse for deterioration of service that "it is now done by computer" is nonsense and a shame to our industry. If we cannot use computers to do a job well then we should not use them at all. Technology is a human invention to improve the quality of life and the computer should be part of that improvement. Sadly it has often not been so.

What is it, however, for which we are accepting responsibility? What roles do computers have to play in our society? The third and fourth proverbs, shown opposite, give answers to these questions. Thinking of the computer as providing a new medium of communication helps us to understand by analogy with previous media. The problems and techniques of the television, newspaper, book and record industries are all relevant and valuable in dealing with the computer industry. However, new media usually generate new problems and require new techniques and we must not be blind to the novelty of the computer. The impact on our society of this novelty is not predictable. It will change and so will we.

The computer provides us with a capability to encode expertise and make it available through conversation. The concept of encoding expertise is not in itself a new one. This is what we already do in books and in records. However, the uniqueness of the computer is in its capability to reproduce actively the encoded expertise. To have created artificial active partners for ourselves in our activities in this universe is a major breakthrough in technology. We shall not become aware of all its implications until a very long time has passed.

The nineteenth and twenty-second proverbs indicate the nature of our responsibility for computer systems. We are creating new realities for the user through simulation in the computer. They can be complex and difficult realities within which to operate or they can be simple and easy, that is our choice and our responsibility. We are establishing a role for the computer system as a conversational partner to its user. We can make the partnership complex and difficult by presenting a false image of the role to be played and failing to sustain it, or we can make it simple and easy by accurately portraying the capabilities of the system as we have designed it.

We are all responsible for computer behavior. (Proverb 1)

Remember when you treat computer-people interaction as if it were people-people interaction that the computer is behaving as it was programmed to. We, as specifiers, programmers and users, are all responsible for the behavior of computer systems.

Computers provide a new medium for communication. (Proverb 3)

Remember when you try to understand the role of computers that they provide a new medium for communication that will be used in part to mimic those already existing. However, they will also change our society and modes of thinking in ways that we are not able to predict.

Computer programs encode expertise. (Proverb 4)

A computer program encodes the expertise of a person to make it accessible to others. The effectiveness of dialog depends on encoding expertise in communication.

Programs create the reality experienced by the users of computers. (Proverb 19)

Remember that the computer is a tool for simulation and that what is simulated becomes reality for the user. The power of the computer should be used to create worlds that are simple for the user and natural to the task.

The role expected of the system should be maintained. (Proverb 22)

Tricks of dialog should not be used to give a false impression of the capabilities of the computer system. A role should be accurately projected that can be maintained throughout the interaction.

Some proverbs of responsibility

Proverbs of past experience

Starting a conversation with someone we do not know can lead to many forms of misunderstanding. The social conventions and forms of politeness associated with meeting strangers are mechanisms for avoiding misunderstanding and minimizing the consequences when it occurs. We establish the backgrounds of each party to the conversation and try to find a base of common shared meaning. We each expect to be misunderstood and are ready to notice this and take action, inoffensively, to make ourselves clearer.

When two computers are connected together through an electrical communications network then similar processes occur. They note features of the other's communication, such as speed and format of transmission, and adapt their own accordingly. It is just like two people adapting to one another's accents. They set up the sequence of communications through an exchange of signals often termed "handshaking." They check communications for errors and exchange signals again to acknowledge correct receipt or request re-transmission.

These social and technological conventions associated with person-person communication and computer-computer communication, respectively, are equally significant in person-computer communication. The sixth proverb opposite reminds us that even first-time users of computers approach them with expectations based on previous reading, television, films and hearsay. Experienced users of one computer system will have expectations based on their conversations with it that may be very misleading when they attempt to use a different computer system. One implication of this is that we should expect misunderstanding and attempt to allow for it and minimize it.

Another implication is that of the second proverb, that if users are going to have expectations that influence them in establishing system requirements then ensure that they are reasonable by giving them experience of related systems. The fifth proverb notes that the converse applies to the dialog programmer. He should take into account the expectations that subject matter experts and the user have of their existing activities in which the computer is now to play a role.

The seventh proverb reminds us that people readily adopt an animistic attitude to items of equipment. This is particularly true of computers where the dialog can be used to project a personality, perhaps that of the programmer. We may want this effect. If we do not want to trigger expectations appropriate to people then we have to be very careful to avoid them.

Users already have expectations about computers. (Proverb 6)

Take into account the possibility that the user's expectations of the computer will affect his interpretation of any dialog with it. The dialog should be designed to minimize confusion arising from these prior expectations.

Choose through experience. (Proverb 2)

Conversational systems should be experienced before they are talked about. Prospective users should experience interaction with a related system before specifying their requirements for their own system.

Use the vocabulary of expert and user. (Proverb 5)

Listen carefully to conversations between experts and users, and design the dialog using their normal vocabulary.

Users readily think of computer systems in the same way as they think of people. (Proverb 7)

One expectation of computers is that they will behave similarly to people in their conversation and modes of operation. If we do not wish this to occur then we have to be careful that the program presents the computer as a piece of equipment and not as the simulation of a person.

Some proverbs of past experience

Proverbs of understanding

The expectations from past experience that a user brings to a computer conversation can lead to initial misunderstandings and these need to be minimized. After the user has some experience of a new system, however, we might expect that such problems will disappear. So they will if the system is easy to understand, and the eighth proverb opposite calls for the designer to make it easy to understand. In more concrete terms this means giving the user expectations of the system based on his experience of it that are not violated as he continues to use it.

The fifteenth proverb points to one way in which many systems violate a user's expectations and lead to misunderstanding. There should be consistency in the commands and information presentation. The command required to initiate action at one stage in the dialog should not be different from that required to initiate the same action at another stage. Consistency minimizes the learning time and memory load for the user. If he has to learn two commands for the same purpose the memory load is not just doubled but multiplied many times by the need to remember which command is applicable at what stage.

A similar argument applies to the requirement for uniformity stated in the sixteenth proverb. The commands must not only have the same form each time they are appropriate but the actions which they evoke should also be uniformly available throughout the dialog. A user should not have to remember that if he wants to examine certain data then he should do it now because it will not be possible at the next stage of the dialog. He should be able to take actions when it seems natural to him to do so, not when the system designer finds it easy to offer them or remembers to make them available or feels the user should undertake them.

We have freely used the term "stages" of a dialog in the discussion above. Conversations do naturally go through stages, particularly if they are purposeful and leading to some goal. The fourteenth proverb calls for these stages to be made clearly apparent to the user. Again we can see this as minimizing the memory load placed on the user. The capacity of computers to keep track of complex situations is a major reason why we want to interact with them and use them as tools. However, this capacity needs to be used to support the user and avoid the person still being required to duplicate this computer capability. The ninth proverb notes one of the most significant applications of the fourteenth proverb, that the system can remind the user of the choices available to him at each stage in the dialog. This is a highly supportive feature for naive and experienced users alike.

Make the system easy to understand. (Proverb 8)

Users will model the computer system and form new expectations based on their interaction with it. The system should be designed to induce accurate models and correct expectations.

The system should be consistent in operation. (Proverb 15)

The commands should always do the same thing throughout. The information presentation should always mean the same thing throughout.

The system should be uniform in operation. (Proverb 16)

The facilities which users have learned to use in one part of the package should be available to them in other parts if they might reasonably expect this.

The state of the system should be clear to the user. (Proverb 14)

Computer systems can be complex and their internal state is not easy to see. Important information about the state of the system should be shown to the user in such a way that it is easily assimilated.

The user should be shown the choices available. (Proverb 9)

At any point in a formal dialog sequence the user will have a limited range of options available. There should be a facility to enable the user to find out his choices.

Some proverbs of understanding

Proverbs of adaptation

We have noted that when two strangers meet and commence a conversation there is much scope for misunderstanding, and that we exchange information with one another to establish our backgrounds and hence our expectations and capabilities. In the early days of computer systems, particularly in education, it was an objective of the system designer to establish through the dialog the type of user with which his program was conversing. This is not easy to achieve, partly through the limitations of the channels of communication with computers - emotional expression through **body language** is totally lost, and partly because we did not have, and still do not have, adequate theories of human psychology. What we do not understand we cannot program for a computer, at least not consistently whenever we want to.

A problem with adapting the behavior of the computer in accord with our inferred model of the type of user, whether this model is correct or not, is that it becomes very easy to violate the proverbs of understanding on the previous page. If the computer dialog adapts to the user then it may become inconsistent and the state of the system may be difficult to discern. However, it is still very important that the system be able to cater for both naive and experienced users, without confusing the first or boring the second. Hence the seventeenth proverb opposite calls for the system to be adaptable to the experience of the user but to put this under the control of the user.

We gave examples in Chapter 4 of improving prompt-response dialog by allowing an experienced user to group responses and avoid the slower sequence of detailed prompts useful to a naive user. This technique put the control totally with the user and yet gives the system good adaptive capabilities. Another technique shown in the same chapter is that called for in the twelfth proverb, of anticipating the most likely user responses and enabling him to make them by just pressing one key for a default response. Again the system is not trying to do too much and the control is completely with the user who can freely override the default response by keying in an alternative.

The eleventh proverb is carefully phrased to indicate that again the control should usefully be left with the user when the system is attempting to be supportive by querying possible errors in the responses. The tenth proverb is the ultimate user control of the dialog, that he can opt out completely with no penalty. This is of particular importance to the naive user in learning about the system since it gives him the freedom to experiment without fearing the consequences.

The system should adapt to the user under user control.
(Proverb 17)

Provision should be made for various levels of user
knowledge but no attempt should be made to estimate
this automatically. The user should be given control
over the level of help provided by the system.

**The system should minimize the user's workload by
anticipating responses.** (Proverb 12)

The most likely user response should be made the
default option that can be selected by a single key
depression.

**The system should co-operate with the user in validating
responses.** (Proverb 11)

Information should be checked as it is entered and
queried it if it appears unlikely to be correct. The
consequences of significant actions should be made
clear to the user and confirmation requested before
they are carried out.

It should be easy to escape from a conversation cleanly.
(Proverb 10)

At any point in a formal dialog sequence the user may
wish to abort the dialog and escape any consequences of
his preceding responses. There should be a facility to
enable the user to escape at will leaving the state of
the system well defined.

Some proverbs of adaptation

Proverbs of style

A key message of this book is that there is no single style of computer conversation suited to all applications. In the past the dominant manufacturers of computer systems have established styles of dialog with their systems which were appropriate to the technology available to them at the time. For many users these have become **the** way in which one interacts with computer systems. However, we are in an era of rapidly changing technology. In particular, the personal computer with local computing power, graphics screen, and devices for speech and handwriting recognition is changing our concepts of computer conversation. The thirteenth proverb opposite notes this relationship between the available technology and the styles of computer dialog.

We are also in an era of massive and increasing availability of computer systems. There are no longer a few small groups of specialists who are responsible for the majority of computer software systems. The capability to develop computer systems is now available to virtually everyone who is willing to take the trouble to learn to program them. This is promoting experiment and adventure in the development of new approaches to person-computer interaction. The eighteenth proverb calls for us to be aware of these experiments and to keep an open mind about appropriate ways of programming conversation with computers.

Early attempts to program natural language conversation with computers put tremendous pressure on linguists to define the structure of human language. It was quickly realized that many aspects of language that were thought to be well understood could not be so because we were unable to program them for computers. The effort resulting from this realization is now paying dividends as programs become available as illustrated in Chapter 7 that are able to converse with users in natural language. The twentieth proverb notes, however, that such conversation can take a variety of different forms and that it is not enough to consider just the distinction between the **formal language** dialog of Chapters 4 and 5 and natural language in general. Chapter 7 shows that there is a wide spectrum of "natural language" for computers, from the very simple to the extremely complex.

In particular, the twenty-first proverb notes how easy it is to simulate the understanding which people expect to underlie natural language. We may violate the twenty-second proverb and suggest a role which the system cannot maintain. We may violate the seventh proverb, that users readily think of computers as people, when we do not wish to do so, and create the impression that the computer has the depth of understanding of a person.

The style of conversation varies with the computer technology used. (Proverb 13)

Some aspects of computer dialog style will be dependent on the type of person-computer interface available. Be aware of the capabilities and limitations of different interfaces.

Be aware of the repertoire of techniques for person-computer dialog. (Proverb 18)

The range of styles and techniques for dialog is continually increasing as is the experience in their use. Approach new situations with an open mind as to what techniques would be appropriate and maintain awareness of new approaches as they develop.

Natural language may be used in a variety of different ways. (Proverb 20)

In considering the use of natural language dialog with computer systems note that it can be used for output independently of input.

Fluent language may not imply fluent understanding. (Proverb 21)

Take into account when evaluating any system that apparently good conversational dialog may be generated through rules that are based on little understanding of what is being said. There can be widely differing degrees of understanding underlying the same dialog.

Some proverbs of style

Proverbs of presentation

One of the problems that we became aware of in surveying the state of the personal computer industry in writing this book is that the role of marketing in personal computer products is growing rapidly. Some fine programs are virtually unknown because their developers have made little effort to make others aware of their existence. Other mediocre programs have become market leaders because they have been promoted by organizations with knowledge of, and resources for, the application of modern marketing techniques. Computer programs have become major consumer products and their selling is being increasingly based on the techniques that have been so effective in promoting brand names for other consumer products. This has no adverse consequences if the product itself is effective. However, there has already been a curious case of a computer program being heavily promoted in the media, apparently sold in quantity through advance mail-order sales, and then failing to come into existence.

The twenty-third proverb opposite draws attention to the need to present computer programs as products in a new medium in much the same way as products in previous media have been presented. "Presentation" here covers all aspects of the process of preparing a product for the market place. In the theater a play will be rehearsed, revised, tested before an audience and revised again. It will be promoted through other media so that potential play-goers become aware of its theme and its attractiveness to them. Records, books and films all go through similar processes of presentation and the computer medium is no exception.

The twenty-fourth proverb points to the basic principle on which a product has to be developed. It is through understanding the needs and requirements of customers that the product profile can be correctly shaped. Computer programming is taught as the mastering of a technology when really it is becoming a new means of expression, and that expression requires an audience to define itself. The twenty-fifth proverb indicates the need to project information to that audience about what is being expressed.

Finally, the twenty-sixth proverb highlights one of the most important features of computers, that they themselves may be used to satisfy the requirements of presentation and information. We should always be in the position to build another shell around a computer program and have it present itself. The conversational techniques used to interact with a program may also be used to tutor people in the use of the program. The new medium, like many of the old, is self-reflective and can present itself.

Programs require presentation. (Proverb 23)

Programs in the new medium for communication provided by computers require the same attention to techniques of presentation as have those in past media.

Know the market. (Proverb 24)

The designer of a new computer program should have in mind a clear market defined by customer needs and requirements.

Users should be informed. (Proverb 25)

At every stage in the chain from marketing through selling, training and routine use of a computer program, users of that program need to be kept informed of relevant information about it.

Programs should be self-sufficient. (Proverb 26)

Computer programs developed for a particular application should be extended to present themselves to potential customers and to tutor their users.

Some proverbs of presentation

Implementation of the proverbs

This is not a book about computer programming techniques. The implementation of the proverbs as they affect actual dialog is part of software engineering and treated in books and journals about dialog engineering and person-computer interaction. However, we will briefly discuss the implementation of some of the proverbs to indicate the techniques used.

The proverbs of responsibility affect our attitude towards dialog rather than its implementation. The proverbs of past experience note that we have to appreciate users' expectations. The second proverb, about giving the users experience of similar systems, indicates the need for tools enabling us to program new dialog rapidly to demonstrate to users. The fifth proverb, about using the users' vocabulary, is also amenable to computer aiding since we can use a program such as PEGASUS illustrated in Chapter 7 to elicit the vocabulary from users and experts.

The proverbs of understanding and adaptation are the ones that most directly affect the software engineering of dialog. They can be implemented through the use of a **dialog shell** through which all interaction with the user is programmed. The diagram opposite outlines the structure and function of such a shell. It is called as a **procedure** and the **parameters** that have to be passed to it are the prompt, default response and responses to help and abort requests. The use of a standard shell with these parameters already ensures a high degree of consistency and uniformity in the dialog.

The operation of the shell takes care of response grouping as a facility for adaptation to the user by storing a group of responses and returning them in turn without prompting the user until no more are left. The default, help and abort responses are also implemented within this shell.

The proverbs of style cover the dialog programmer's awareness of the repertoire available to him. The proverbs of presentation have implications for activities in other media not involving the computer. However, the twenty-sixth proverb in particular draws attention to the growing role of the computer in presenting itself. For implementation this requires the applications program being used to be embedded within a shell procedure which can simulate someone using it so as to present it both for marketing and tutorial purposes. Since there will often be two conversations underway at the same time - the program being simulated in use and a tutorial dialog with the actual user - the split screen techniques discussed in Chapter 7 are important.

```
PROCEDURE: DIALOG_SHELL

PARAMETERS: PROMPT_STRING              ; asking for information
            DEFAULT_RESPONSE_STRING    ; if RETURN alone pressed
            HELP_RESPONSE_LIST         ; messages in response to '?'
            ABORT_ABNORMAL_RETURN      ; exit in response to ':'

GLOBAL VARIABLE: INPUT_STRING          ; holds previous grouped responses -
                                       ; must be set null before first call

LOCAL VARIABLE:  RESPONSE_STRING       ; will be response to be returned

ACTION: IF INPUT_STRING IS NULL THEN   ; if no response from previous grouping
          OUTPUT PROMPT_STRING         ; then put out prompt
          INPUT INPUT_STRING           ; and get a response
        ENDIF

        IF INPUT_STRING IS NULL THEN       ; if response is RETURN alone
          RETURN DEFAULT_RESPONSE_STRING   ; then return default response
        ENDIF

        IF INPUT_STRING CONTAINS A SPACE THEN          ; if grouped response
          SET RESPONSE_STRING = INPUT_STRING UP TO SPACE ; then get first one
          SET INPUT_STRING = INPUT_STRING AFTER SPACE    ; and leave rest
            ELSE
          SET RESPONSE_STRING = INPUT_STRING   ; if not grouped then get all
          SET INPUT_STRING = NULL              ; and leave nothing
        ENDIF

        IF RESPONSE_STRING IS A QUESTION MARK THEN ; if user requests help
          OUTPUT HEAD OF HELP_RESPONSE_LIST        ; give current level help

          IF TAIL OF HELP_RESPONSE_LIST IS NOT NULL THEN   ; if lower levels
            SET HELP_RESPONSE_LIST = TAIL HELP_RESPONSE_LIST ; go down one
          ENDIF

          SET INPUT_STRING = NULL   ; do not allow grouping after help request
          GOTO ACTION               ; after help go back to prompt
        ENDIF

        IF RESPONSE_STRING IS A COLON                 ; if user requests abort
          THEN RETURN_ABNORMAL ABORT_ABNORMAL_RETURN  ; make specified return
        ENDIF

        RETURN RESPONSE_STRING  ; if no special action requested, make response

END DIALOG_SHELL
```

**A dialog shell procedure that copes with default responses (RETURN),
multi-level help requests (?), abort requests (:),
and response grouping with spaces as separators**

Conclusions - some proverbs of development

In concluding this chapter we will introduce three proverbs that have not been discussed previously. They are all concerned with development after the design is "complete" and the system has been implemented. It is easy to concentrate upon the problem of designing systems against objectives and to conclude that if the system requirements are well-defined an effective system can be designed. However, objectives change particularly as systems come into use and experience is gained with them. Many applications of computer systems are sufficiently novel for past experience to be of little help. Our growing interaction with, and dependence on, personal computer systems is itself novel and our concepts of what we are doing, and should be doing, are bound to change.

The twenty-seventh proverb - DESIGN NEVER CEASES

The design process never ceases. The systems we design for one purpose will be used for others. They will be extended. They will prove unsatisfactory in some respects and require change. Computers are not only programable. They are re-programable. We do not have to discard a computer system and replace it with another to change it. This is a benefit of computer technology. It is also a major problem since users expect it to be possible for computers to be re-programmed to their changing requirements. They may be so content that this is possible that they see no need to define their requirements too well to start with. Maybe this is poor discipline in system specification. Maybe, however, it is a key freedom that comes as part of the new medium based on the computer. The flexibility for experiment may be the most important feature of computers.

Proverb 27: Design never ceases.

Systems evolve as users gain experience and develop their requirements. The interactive facilities of the computer should be used for development also to aid the enhancement of a system in the light of experience.

The twenty-eighth proverb - LOGGING COMPUTER CONVERSATION

The twenty-seventh proverb suggests also that the interactive programming of the personal computer may be used to help in re-programming systems according to user requirements. It is possible to sit down at a terminal with a user and re-program dialog as part of an ongoing discussion. There is a further computer aid to system re-design and enhancement. The computer can itself log the dialog in an ongoing application and this can be analyzed to provide information on problems requiring attention. Such a logging facility is easily incorporated in the dialog shell discussed earlier in this chapter.

Such logging is simple technically but there are some problems in its use. Users may view it as an invasion of their privacy under some conditions. There is already legislation relating to logging user interaction in some areas such as Scandinavia. It is also important to couple the design of logging procedures with the design of programs to analyze the logs. Overwhelmingly large quantities of data are readily collected from interactive computer systems.

Proverb 28: Conversation should be logged and analyzed.

The computer should be used to maintain selective records of dialog and programs provided to analyze these in terms of, for example, errors broken down by user and dialog sequence.

The twenty-ninth proverb - DESIGN FOR A CHANGING FUTURE

The final proverb of this chapter is a **meta-rule** which may be applied separately to each of the suggestions made in all the other proverbs. We have to apply each proverb in the light of the information we have available. We expect to optimize our designs against user requirements, to develop the best system for the stated purpose. However, one item of information we have is that things will change and that we are uncertain as to what changes will occur. This may not seem to give us very solid foundations for a design. It does, however, give us some important guidelines.

The first guideline under uncertainty is not to over-optimize using the current constraints. What is perfect now may be very imperfect in the future, whereas that which is not quite perfect now may leave scope for future enhancement. As an example consider the abbreviation of command words. We may decide to allow the user to key in a one-letter abbreviation of commands, P for PRINT, L for LIST, and so on. We set up the abbreviations as the first letter of the command and apply this consistently and uniformly throughout the system. This is fine until we are asked to extend the system with new commands including LOCATE and PLACE. We either have to break the previous rule, or use different and less appropriate words. There are many systems with strange command words or strange abbreviations and this is how they arose.

How can such problems be avoided? We need to assume that the information we have is incomplete, that the set of command words may be extended and that any abbreviation strategy should allow for this. One answer in this particular situation would be to use a menu with numbers against the commands - there are always more numbers available. Another, and more subtle solution, is to make sure right from the start that there are commands with the same initial letter and use the abbreviation rule that the initial part of a command word is a valid abbreviation. If it is ambiguous the system will list the possibilities and request further information. This second solution sets up criteria of uniformity and consistency that are different from those of using the initial letter as an abbreviation. However, it is an equally valid and useful scheme that has the advantage of being able to cope with any future extension.

Proverb 29: Design for a changing and uncertain future.

> User requirements will change possibly unpredictably. Systems should be designed to allow for enhancements and to leave the possibility of open-ended extension.

The twenty-ninth proverb is the key to system design principles that will remain valid throughout a product life cycle. It needs to be applied after each step in a design and in any system evaluation. If a system is adequate now we need to check also that it contains no hidden traps for the future. We can never be sure but we can avoid many problems by such reasoning.

10 The Future of Computer Conversation

Human perception provides a filter through which we view our experience. At one extreme some readers may have extracted all the negative points about computers from this book. Many writers have pontificated on "what computers cannot do" and they can always find evidence for their point of view. The conversational weaknesses of the current generation of computer systems are evident. The deeper conceptual weaknesses underlying them can be inferred. We programmed these machines. We do not understand ourselves sufficiently to make them operate as we do. They will certainly never be able to think for themselves. Computers are just tools whose mathematical and logical precision and speed are superior to ours, but that is all they are and can ever be.

The other extreme notes each item of evidence that indicates breakthroughs to come. The linguistic strength of SHRDLU and the conceptual understanding of TEIRESIAS, although demonstrated in narrow domains today, point to the possibility of intelligence tomorrow. Is MYCIN any the less because all its knowledge has come from human clinicians? Where did their knowledge come from? Does it impress us that MYCIN may have greater knowledge than any one clinician? Does it impress us that TEIRESIAS may discern patterns in that knowledge that no person has yet discerned?

Maybe we are most impressed by the way in which INTELLECT is actually being used routinely by ordinary users of information systems. It is not the delicate demonstrations of the research laboratory that point to the future but the integration of personal computing into our everyday lives. On the other hand what is impressive about computer systems may be the new styles of conversation possible through the high-resolution graphic screens of Star and Lisa.

If we do see the computer being able to play an increasingly equal role in the person-computer partnership then we may still have a variety of reactions to this. At one extreme we may emphasize the dangers of such intellectually high-level technology. HAL in **2001** takes decisions in the interests of the mission which are definitely not in the interests of individual human members of it. In **RUR** the robots kill all the people and then regret having done so. How much responsibility are we prepared to delegate to computers, our creations? How jealous of, and frightened of, the increasing capabilities of our new partners shall we become? Do we actually have any choice left in the matter or will computer technology, now that it has started, inexorably move towards increasingly intelligent systems?

In his posthumous last book, **The Micro Millenium**, Chris Evans considers these questions and answers with a quotation from H.G. Wells' **Things to Come**. He notes that once Man has taken the first step down the path of knowledge and understanding, he must take all of those that follow. The choice is simple - it is the whole universe, or nothing. Chris certainly saw the positive role of computers. Earlier in the book he attributes the lack of a world war three to the results of wargames in the Pentagon and Kremlin indicating the negative consequences of strategies that might have led to it.

Whatever attitude we adopt to computer technology it, like other products of the human imagination, now has an existence of its own that influences us and is not wholly under our control. We created computers but now computers are coming to create us, to change our lifestyles, our environment, our jobs, our leisure activities, our freedom of expression, our knowledge of ourselves and of others, and their knowledge of us. Humankind is highly adaptable and as we change the nature of our world we change with it. Our media are extensions of ourselves and part of our evolution and the growing symbiosis of people and computers may be a major step in the evolution of the human race.

Such considerations require a major conceptual leap from the simple-minded, game-playing personal computer sitting on the table in our home today to the understanding, life-encompassing personal companion accompanying us in our activities of tomorrow. Maybe the transition is a fantasy that will never occur, either because we cannot achieve it, or because we do not want it. All we can do at the moment is to note the possibilities and keep a careful eye on the technologies that may mould our future. In this chapter we describe recent developments in conversation with personal computers to indicate the current trends towards lower cost, increasing power and improved person-computer conversation.

The future possible

Networking - computer mediated conversation

In the previous chapters we have concentrated on conversations between one person and a computer. This book is about **personal** computing and the natural focus of attention is the interaction between the individual and the computer. However, there are many ways in which we may come into contact with other people and with other computers in our personal interaction with a computer. We can communicate with other computer systems through the telephone by using a **modem** that converts the digital, on/off, signals of the computer into tones. Our personal computer is then a terminal into a communications network and we can send and receive messages. The communication may either be directly with another personal computer, or indirectly through a database.

Direct communication between personal computers is like a phone conversation carried out by keying rather than by voice. There are some problems. In using a terminal to converse with another person directly you do not have the cues that you expect when talking to them face to face. You cannot tell from their expression or their pauses that they have completed what they are saying and are ready for your reply. You do not know when it would be polite to interrupt. Some simple conventions are usually adopted to overcome these problems such as typing + at the end of a line to indicate you have more to say.

The most interesting computer mediated conversations, however, are those that take place through a database where you store messages on a widely accessible computer system for later retrieval by others. This is called **electronic mail** when the messages are primarily from person to person, and **computer bulletin board systems** (CBBSs) when the messages are primarily to special interest groups or communities. There are now electronic mail systems available throughout the world and over one thousand CBBSs in North America.

The dialog opposite shows us dialing up and logging into a CBBS operated by the modem manufacturer, Novation, and requesting information on CBBS systems. It gave us several pages of telephone numbers to call. **Networking**, the setting up of widespread special interest groups, through such CBBSs is a widely growing activity worldwide. One can also access information databases of stock market prices, newspaper reports, airline schedules, and similar information. However, being able to access communities of people is probably more significant than this. If you have a problem, or a request for information, you can send out details on a relevant CBBS and you may receive answers from almost anywhere in the world.

```
*D12138816880FX
LOGON PLEASE : CAT
          <<<      INFORMATION MACHINES      >>>
                   <<<SYSTEM - NO. 1>>>
     <<<      10:02:56 REL 77.1D,PTF9 28 AUG 1983      >>>

     ***    NOVATION MODEM INFORMATION    ***

               THE FOLLOWING FUNCTIONS
                  ARE AVAILABLE :
          1    GENERAL INFORMATION ON THE CATS
          2    BACKGROUND ON ACOUSTIC MODEMS
          3    TECHNICAL INFORMATION
          4    WHAT'S NEW AT NOVATION
          5    DIRECTORIES
          6    TERMINAL TEST MODE
          7    ELECTRONIC MAIL
          8    *H*E*L*P* WITH SYSTEM FUNCTIONS
          9    EXIT FROM SYSTEM
          10   INFO ON AVAILABLE SOFTWARE
          11   PRODUCT INFORMATION
         ***  ENTER FUNCTION NUMBER->5

DIRECTORIES AVAILABLE:
  1   FREE DIAL-UP COMPUTERS IN U.S.
  2   APPLE-CAT II OWNERS


WARNING!! ONCE YOU ASK FOR INFORMATION
   THERE IS NO WAY TO STOP THE OUTPUT.
ENTER CARRIAGE RETURN TO RETURN TO TOP MENU

*** ENTER FUNCTION NUMBER-> 1

THE FOLLOWING LIST CONTAINS PHONE
NUMBERS, SYSTEM TYPES, AND SUBJECT CODES.
THE TYPES ARE:
   FOR-80  -- FORUM 80 FOR TRS 80'S
   ABBS -- APPLE BULLETIN BOARD
   CBBS -- GENERAL BULLETIN BOARD

THE SUBJECT CODES ARE:
  1 FREE PROGRMS       11 FAMILY HISTORY
  2 AMATEUR RADIO      12 AVIATION
  3 NEWS & WEATHER     14 ASTRONOMY
  4 MEDICAL DATA       15 MUSIC
  5 GAMES              16 FANTASY
  6 COMODITY TRADING
  7 EDUCATION          17 HUMOR
  8 HOBBYIST           18 300 OR 1200 BAUD
  9 SELF IMPROVEMENT
10 CALL, LET RING ONCE, CALL BACK

ENTER AREA CODES DESIRED SEPARATED
BY SEMI-COLONS, OR RETURN FOR ALL :
```

Some interaction with a Computer Bulletin Board System

Graphic conversations on personal computers

The graphic conversations possible with the Xerox Star and Apple Lisa described in Chapter 6 have proved very attractive to those developing personal computer systems. The use of icons and multiple display windows may appear to be a feature only of expensive and complex systems with high-resolution graphic screens. However, a number of packages have been released recently for much smaller and relatively low-cost personal computers that have these features.

The SSM **Transcend** electronic mail package runs on an IBM personal computer with no graphics facilities and yet uses icons very effectively. It can do this because the IBM PC provides a set of special characters which display simple shapes and can be used to create limited pictures on the screen. Transcend uses these to show a set of "mail basket" icons on the screen. These correspond to different places from which electronic mail may be sent or received. The user controls his electronic mail system by moving the cursor around these icons.

The upper screen opposite shows Transcend in operation. An incoming mailbox which has received mail shows this by there being a sheet of paper in it. The box which is active is shown by its label being in black characters on a white background (**reverse video**). The system will automatically connect to the telephone network, dial up a remote computer, and send mail to it. It will also automatically accept incoming calls from remote computers and accept mail from them. All user interaction except actually keying in and reading mail is done through the icons.

The lower screen shows split-screen operation with the Context Management Systems **MBA** package. MBA provides word processing, spread sheet, graphics, and electronic mail facilities integrated together. It operates on the IBM PC using the fairly low resolution graphics capability of 640 points horizontally by 200 vertically. Even at this resolution the MBA is able to provide useful combinations of information on multiple screens, such as the spread sheet with bar and pie charts based on it shown.

The cost of high resolution graphics facilities for personal computers is now primarily that of the monitor screens. The storage and processing required is now low in cost and declining. Display monitor costs are also beginning to decrease as the market for high resolution graphics expands from being industrial to the office and the home. We can expect the techniques for graphic conversations developed for the Star and Lisa to be increasingly used on low-cost personal computers.

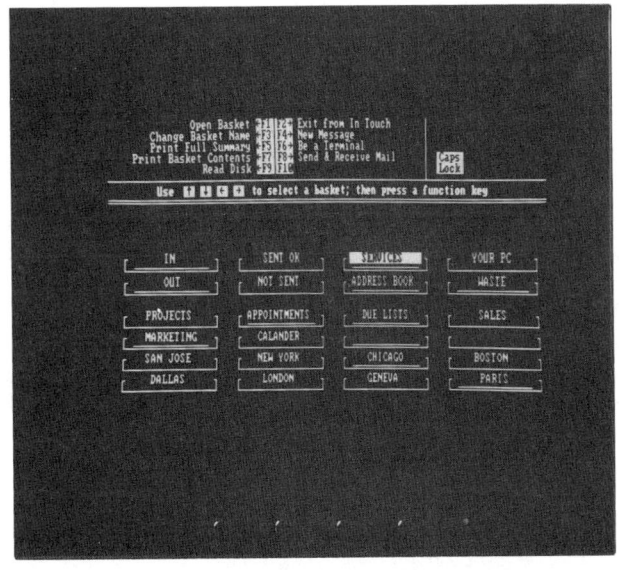

Some interaction with the SSM Transcend electronic mail system

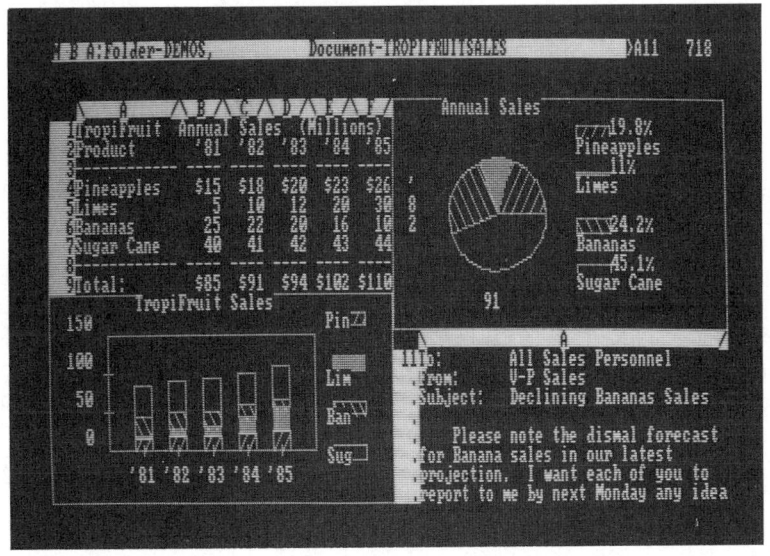

Some interaction with the Context Management Systems MBA system

Icons and windows on the IBM Personal Computer

Conversational shells

The current generation of multiple window, split-screen systems uses these facilities with integrated software systems providing a range of facilities. With systems like the Star, Lisa, MBA, and Lotus 1-2-3 you get a set of application packages designed to cover a range of requirements. What happens, however, if you need facilities that the system does not provide or if you wish to use some other package, such as a word processor, that is not part of the integrated software system? Currently, you cannot get other packages to operate within the graphic conversation interface provided. However, a number of manufacturers are now working to provide conversational **shells** with multiple window, split-screen operation, for personal computers that can be used with any packages that operate on these personal computers.

A shell is a software package that mediates between the user of a machine and the application packages. We gave an example of the structure of such a shell in Chapter 9 when discussing the implementation of the proverbs. We concentrated then on the reaction of the shell to user responses. However, the shell can also implement the multiple, overlaid virtual screens and interaction with the mouse that are required in a graphic conversation. To the user the shell makes it appear that he is interacting with several different computers at the same time. Each window on his screen is a **virtual screen** for one of his **virtual computers**. When the mouse cursor is within that virtual screen then he is interacting with that virtual computer exactly as if it were the only one present. To the applications program the shell makes it appear that it is running in its normal operating environment and is the only program on the computer.

The one additional facility that the shell has to provide is to allow the user to move information from one virtual screen to another. This enables, for example, data or charts calculated by a spread sheet to be moved into text being edited by a word processor to form a report. This is tricky because it is not just the visual movement that is required but the logical transfer of the actual data within the computer. The information taken from one virtual screen has to be passed to the input of the application program running on another so that it is processed and placed in the correct position on the screen.

The screen opposite shows the Quarterdeck **DesQ** multi-window, multi-tasking shell operating environment for the IBM PC in use. It enables applications packages from different manufacturers to be used together at the same time, and data to be transferred between them.

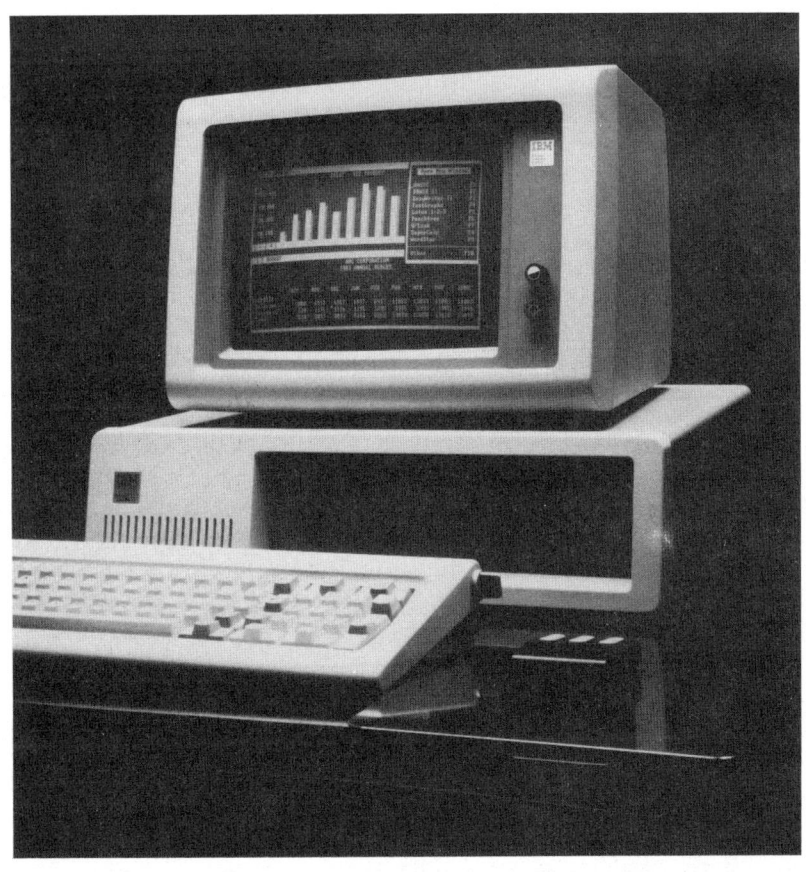

Some interaction with the Quarterdeck DesQ multi-window shell

Imaginative use of the screen

The graphic conversation techniques of Chapter 6 and the variants described above are leading to more imaginative uses of the display screen. These need not involve the use of pictorial material as such for there is much scope for improvement in the operation of text processing systems. The dynamic book described in Chapter 6 provides one example of what may be done on a high-resolution screen. Even on a simple text display, however, it is possible to provide some of the facilities of the dynamic book.

Ted Nelson, one of the most stimulating writers on personal computers, has suggested that word processors could be improved if the information was presented with more structure. As we showed in Chapter 5 a conventional word processor shows on the screen a section of the text which you are editing. It provides a window into the text exactly as if one placed a cardboard cutout window over the page of this book. This is adequate for most editing purposes but restrictive if you are actually using the word processor to create text, to write a report, book or play. You can see only that part of the text you are editing and have to rely on your memory to place it in context. You have to remember where, in what section, in what chapter you are writing. You have to remember who are the other characters in the play, what time it is and where the action is taking place.

Nelson shows that the computer can provide more useful features if the text is structured and this is presented to the user. The screen opposite demonstrates how Nelson's concepts might apply to the editing of Chapter 2 of this book. The paragraph being edited is shown in full in the central part of the screen. The rest of the screen provides a context within which we can place the paragraph. At the top is the title of the book. Beneath it is the title of the chapter preceding that which we are editing and then the title of that chapter. At the bottom of the screen is the title of the chapter following that which we are editing. Thus we can place the current chapter in the context of the chapters around it. Similarly the display shows us the section titles of the preceding and succeeding sections and the first line of every paragraph in the section we are editing.

Such a display makes it very much easier to understand what we are doing and its implementation is straightforward for word processors that keep track of document structure. It would even be possible to display other key information such as the proverbs in the chapter if these were identifiable as significant. Nelson has suggested that future editors should make more provision for retaining the structure of a document, not just its content.

```
COMPUTER CONVERSATION
==================================================================
CHAPTER 1   PERSONAL COMPUTER CONVERSATION
------------------------------------------------------------------
CHAPTER 2   CONVERSATION THROUGH COMPUTER MEDIA
==================================================================
          Programs generate two-way conversations
------------------------------------------------------------------
          Adventure games as simulations of life
==================================================================
   Simulation of an interesting and exciting real-world or fantasy
------------------------------------------------------------------
   The computer conversation opposite is between a human player of
------------------------------------------------------------------
   The data processing underlying the game is fairly simple but
------------------------------------------------------------------
   During   recent   years   such   games   have   become   increasingly
elaborate,   involving whole worlds of activity on land,   sea   and
air.   They   have   also   made more and more use   of   the   rapidly
improving   color graphics and sound effects available now on even
low-cost   computers.   Some later games take into   account   moral
concepts such as "good" people becoming less cooperative with you
if you undertake "bad" actions.   This could be significant to the
teaching   impact of the games since the early ones incorporated a
simple model of life, that you took or killed everything in sight
and that most other entities in the game were enemies.   This   is
similar   in   its morality to the "Western" film genre   which   has
been a natural foundation for the early popular games.
------------------------------------------------------------------
   There are less apparent social consequences of game playing
==================================================================
       The interactive novel and simulations of ourselves
******************************************************************
Proverb 3: Computers provide a new medium for communication.
Proverb 4: Computer programs encode expertize.
Proverb 5: Use the vocabulary of expert and user.
******************************************************************
CHAPTER 3   USER EXPECTATIONS IN COMPUTER CONVERSATION
```

An editor screen showing the context for the text being edited

Conversations in all the languages of the world

We have emphasized the importance of the personal computer in making information systems accessible to all. They now play major roles in our society. The operation of government, the management of commerce, the development of science and the application of technology would be seriously impeded without them. Personal computers enable the individual to participate in this information age. However, the "all" in the first sentence must be qualified to be "all those whose native language uses the Roman alphabet". Computers were developed in the West and computer terminals are based on this alphabet. Information systems have been accessible to those whose language uses **exotic** characters only to the extent that they can use Roman characters.

When computer systems were in use largely for numerical data processing this was not a severe limitation. Learning programming in a foreign language is not much worse than learning it at all, and arabic numerals are commonly used in most of the world. However, as information technology has impacted non-numeric data processing, the Roman character limitation has caused increasing differences in the use of computers between those countries using Latin languages and the majority which do not. Office automation, database and educational applications in particular become virtually impossible, and these are some of the most important to the developing nations of the world.

Fortunately, the low-cost graphics technology which we have illustrated in Chapter 6 also provides the means for information systems to communicate as readily in the exotic scripts as in Roman characters. Input, display and printing sub-systems are now available that will cope with character sets such as those of Arabic as used in the Middle East and Devanagari as used in India. They will even cope with Chinese as used in Asia and Urdu Nastaliq as used in Pakistan, each requiring some 15,000 or more characters. The screen opposite shows a multi-lingual version of the Xerox Star with a number of different scripts on display.

Exotic characters require a larger number of dots to display than do Roman characters. A cell of at least 14 dots wide by 16 dots high is required for Chinese/Japanese and 20 by 20 is often used. Keyboards also present problems where large numbers of characters are involved. The most difficult obstacle to the wider user of information technology in countries with non-Roman scripts, however, is the re-writing of the applications software. This can be avoided in applications, such as database systems, if a shell is used to translate the non-Roman characters into sequences of Roman characters on input and back again on output.

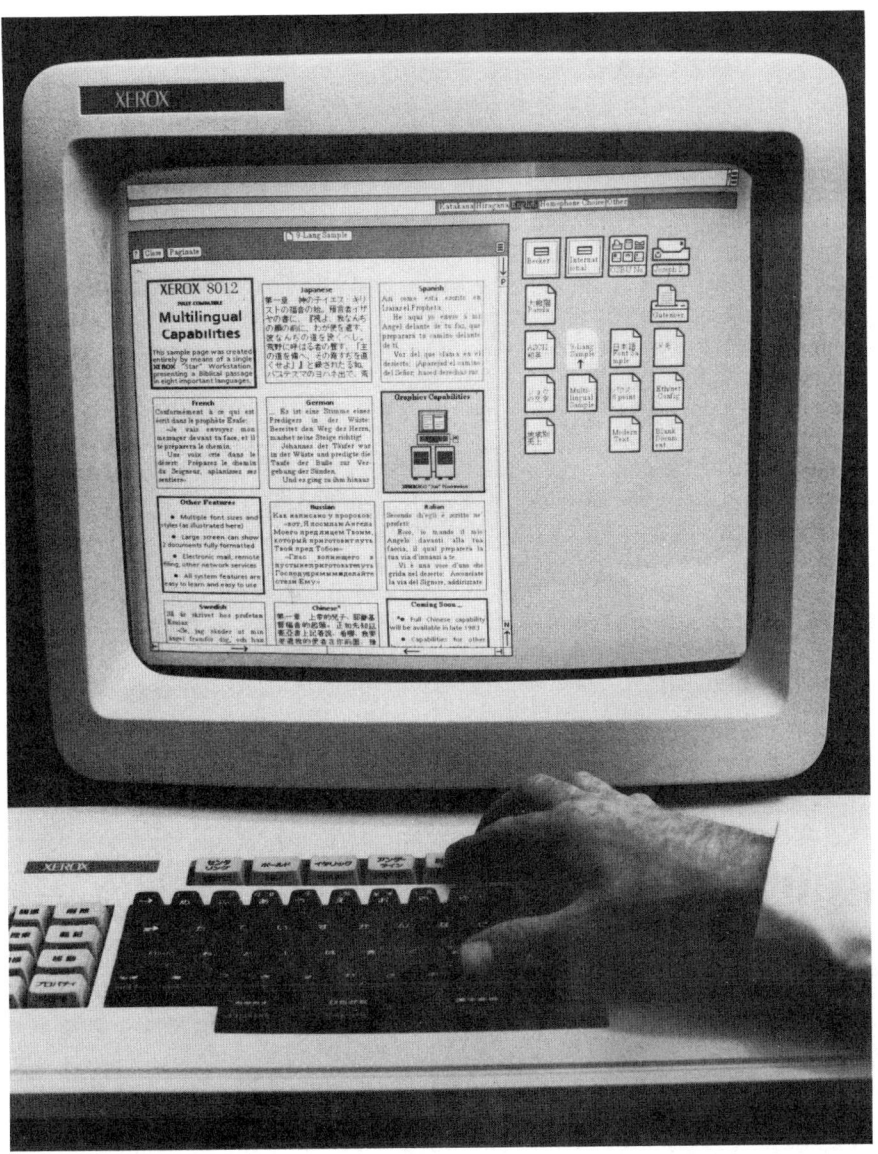

Some interaction with the Xerox Star in a variety of languages

Natural language on personal computers

In the same way that computer conversational capabilities are being made available on personal computers so are natural language conversations. Variants of ELIZA as described in Chapter 7 have been available for the Apple][and IBM PC for some time. However, the full natural language processing of SHRDLU has been very much associated with large computers and its practical application as in **Intellect** has not been possible on personal computers. This changed recently when Bozena and Fred Thompson at California Institute of Technology issued **Ask**, a natural language database system for the Hewlett-Packard HP9836 desktop personal computer.

Ask provides facilities for information modification and insertion into the database using natural language as well as information retrieval. It also has facilities for defining new words in terms of relationships between those already existing. In the dialog opposite Ask is being used with a database of shipping information. The user first makes a fairly complex enquiry similar to those already demonstrated with Intellect in Chapter 7. His second enquiry involves inversion of the verb and negation. His third enquiry is ambiguous. Ask is happy to have the noun New York used as an adjective but is not sure whether it refers to the home port or destination of the ships.

After two more requests, the user makes a statement that the home port of the Maru is Boston. Ask recognizes this as a request to modify the database and does so. The user input commencing with DEFINITION: is taken by Ask to define a new term, firstly a simple definition that a "tub" is an "old ship", and then a more complex one involving arithmetic that "area" is "length times beam." The ensuing requests demonstrate that Ask is then capable of using these new terms correctly. The later definitions of "go to" and "carry" show that verbs may also be defined in terms of implicit relations.

Ask is a powerful natural language processing system running on a small computer. It is written in Pascal and should operate on a range of personal computers. If we couple its availability with the developments in speech recognition in recent years then much of the fifth generation computing capability does not seem so far away. Voice recognition systems have become available at low cost that will discriminate some hundreds of isolated words. More expensive systems are available that will do this for continuous speech. Systems such as these driving natural language systems such as Ask will enable person-computer conversation to begin to approximate person-person conversation.

```
>What cities are the home ports of ships whose destination is London?
 Boston
 New York
 London
 Norfolk
>Are there ships that do not have a cargo?
 Yes
>What is the number of New York ships?
 There are two answers
 1) New York (home port) ships
    1
 2) New York (destination) ships
    2
>What ships whose cargo is wheat have London or Oslo as destination?
 Maru
 Alamo
>What is the cargo and home port of the Maru?
 cargo    home port
 wheat    Tokyo
>The home port of the Maru is Boston
 Tokyo has been replaced by Boston as home port of Maru
>Maru's cargo is coal
 coal has been added as cargo of Maru
>What is the cargo and home port of the Maru?
 cargo    home port
 wheat    Boston
 coal     ---
>Definition:tub:old ship
 Defined.
>Definition:area:length times beam
 Defined.
>What is the length, beam and area of each tub
 old ship   length      beam        area
            foot        foot        foot**2
 Ubu        231.667     48          11120.016
 Alamo      564.5       84          47413.
>Definition:meter:39.37*foot/12
 Defined.
>Beam of the Alamo squared in square meters?
 655.526472343268 square meters
>Verb:ships "go" to New York:destination of ships is New York
 Defined.
>Verb:ships "carry" coal:cargo of ships is coal
 Defined.
>What cargo is carried by the Alamo?
 wheat
 coal
>What cities does the Alamo go to?
 London
 New York
>
```

Some interaction with Ask, a natural language system on
a Hewlett-Packard personal computer

Mixing conversational styles

One interesting recent development has been the combination of the graphic conversations of Chapter 6 with the natural language conversations of Chapter 7. Artificial Intelligence Corporation has extended the Intellect system described in Chapter 7 so that users can request graphic presentations of the information retrieved from the database. The upper screen opposite shows a query being processed that calls for a bar chart of the actual and estimated year to date sales in each region. Instead of being presented as a table of figures the information retrieved is now presented in chart form as requested. The lower screen shows a similar request being processed but one which now calls for a pie chart.

What is novel about these examples is neither the natural language processing nor the graphic output. We have illustrated these in previous chapters. It is rather the integration of both systems together and how this is done. From a technical point of view the language processing system can pick up the request for graphic output through a simple extension of its capabilities. The presentation of the retrieved data in graphic form is a facility available through several business graphics packages. However, we see the language processing system in a new role, as a shell integrating the database and graphics packages together under user control. Intellect processes the incoming request into two parts. Firstly there is a call for information from the database and this is retrieved as usual. Secondly there is a call for the resulting information to be presented graphically and Intellect passes it to a graphics package to present on the screen. Finally the control returns to Intellect as a natural language shell awaiting the next request from the user.

This use of natural language processing to provide a shell to access a range of applications packages is clearly attractive for users. However, it also plays a key technical role in allowing these packages to be integrated together in a very flexible way. The user is not just requesting that a task be performed by one package but instead is defining an overall task that may require the use of many. It is the Intellect shell that splits the overall task into calls on different packages and system resources. To the user there is no longer a set of different tools amongst which he must choose that appropriate to his objectives. Instead there is a single system with a simply used conversational interface that provides him access to all facilities. IBM has recently adopted Intellect as an IBM supported product for its large machines. We can expect similar shells to be made available for personal computers also.

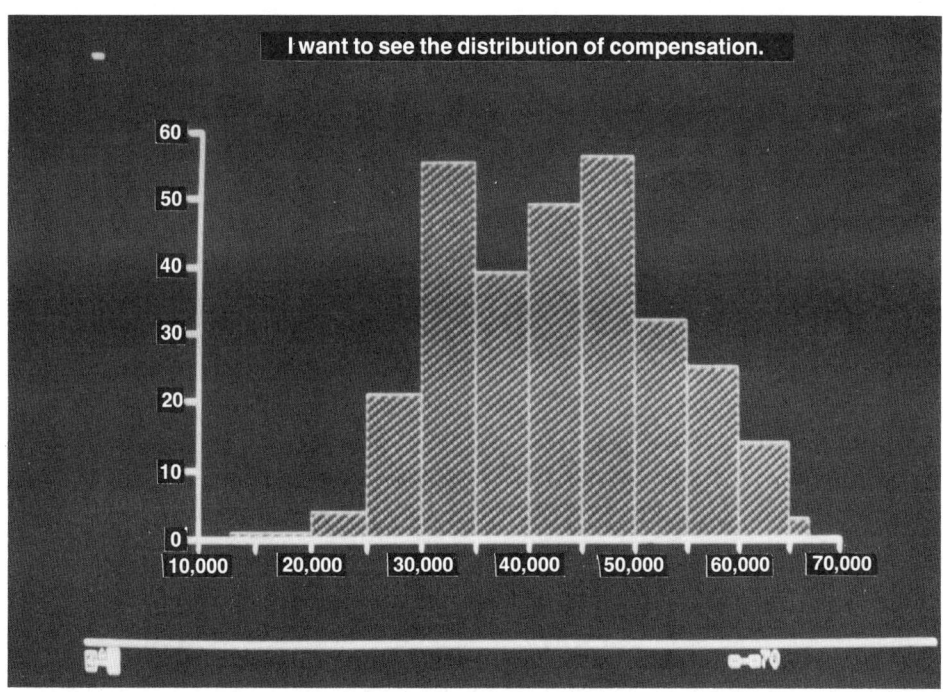

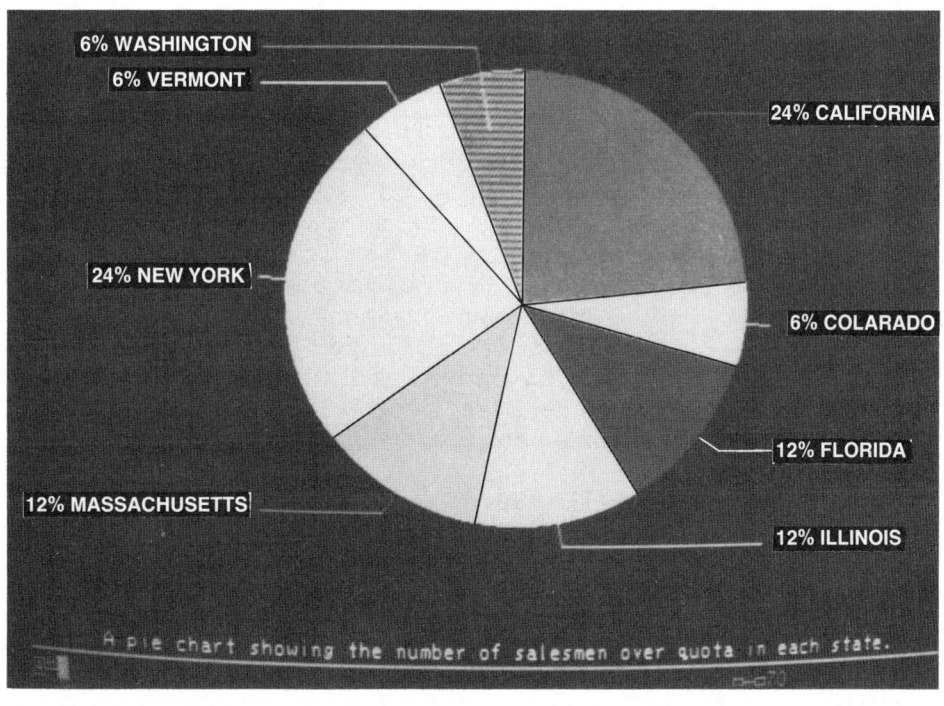

Dialogs with Intellect combining natural language and graphics

Understanding different domains of knowledge

The development of expert systems, discussed in Chapter 2, for a wide variety of knowledge domains has become a major activity both within the computer industry and outside it. It was quickly realized in the high technology industries that the encoding of expertise was key to many of their activities. The search for oil is of key economic importance and an expensive, high-risk activity. Most test bores do not produce evidence of oil and their cost is very high. Minimizing the total cost of the search depends on expert interpretation of geological surveys, satellite photographs and test bore data. The expertise is rare and distributed over many people. Thus the petrochemical industry has become a major investor in research on expert systems.

Similar reasoning applies to the pharmaceutical industry where most experimental preparations prove ineffectual or have side effects. The search for new drugs requires the expertise of many people and is well suited to aiding through expert systems. Integrated circuit development, military intelligence, ocean exploration, and other areas of high-risk decision-making under uncertainty have also all attracted research on expert systems. Even more mundane industries like shoe-making have discovered that the expression of the human expertise involved requires more than straightforward computer-aided design systems.

This massive growth of interest in expert systems has spread the resources available for their development very thinly and promoted research on **meta-systems** whereby expertise from one knowledge domain can be applied in another. We suggested in Chapter 2 that the rules used in AM for forming conjectures in mathematics were far more widely applicable. They are general rules of curiosity relevant to any search process. TEIRESIAS in Chapter 7 was used to illustrate computer understanding of the process of medical diagnosis underlying MYCIN. Because it was developed to understand understanding it incorporates meta-rules that encode expertise about knowledge acquisition.

Davis has shown that TEIRESIAS can be transferred to other domains with very little change. The dialog opposite shows how a stockbroker can use it as an investment advisor. The rules show how the relevant expertise is coded in a similar form to that for MYCIN. The full power of TEIRESIAS is available to aid the expert in setting up these rules as was illustrated in the example in Chapter 7. It seems probable in the next few years that such expert systems will not only be recoded for personal computers but also that they will be made available in a general form such that they can be easily set up for different topics.

```
Investor's name?
**FRED SMITH
Age?
** 40
Present taxable income?
**40,000
Number of dependants?
**5
Occupation?
**LAWYER
Amount of previous investment experience? (slight = less than
  one year; moderate = 2 to 4 years; extensive = more than 4
  years)
** MODERATE
Does the investor subscribe to the Wall Street Journal, or any
  securities market newsletters?
**Y
  ..................................
The following investments appear to be the most appropriate at
this time:
  Varian-Corporation
  American-Telephone-and-Telegraph
```

TEIRESIAS in the investment management domain

```
RULE116
If  1) the desired return on the investment is greater than 10%,
    2) the time-scale of the investment is long-term,
    3) the number of dependants of the client is less than 3,
    4) the age (in years) of the client is less than or equal to 35
then there is evidence (.4) that the area of the investment
  should be high-technology


RULE383
If  1) the income-tax bracket of the client is 50%,
    2) the client follows the market carefully,
    3) the amount of investment experience of the client is
    moderate,
then there is evidence (.8) that the area of the investment
  should be high-technology
```

Some of the rules used in the new domain

The new medium

We suggest in Chapter 2 that computers provide a new medium for communication and that in this lies the key to our understanding them and their effects on our society. We hope the wide variety of examples of computer conversations given in this book will have given some feeling for the nature of this new medium. All of us need to come to terms with it in our own ways for it will affect many of our activities. Comparing the computer medium with existing media, and doing this in our own terms, is one way of making a personal assessment of what it will mean for us.

This type of personal decision-making is an activity well suited to computer conversation. In Chapter 7 we illustrated the elicitation and use of key words from a user of PEGASUS, a program which enables a person to study their views of any topic. The topic under review was **media** including computers. The result of the conversation with PEGASUS is a grid of ratings of the elements, in this case media, against constructs provided by the user as ways of differentiating between the elements.

The FOCUS clustering algorithm sorts the grid by rows to place similar constructs close together and by columns to place similar elements together. It then prints out the sorted grid together with graphs of the clusters of similar constructs and similar element. The focused grid for the elicitation of constructs about media is shown opposite. The constructs used are fairly well differentiated and give an interesting set of dimensions with which to compare different media. The terms **sequential** and **dynamic** are related and linked to **modern**. The terms **transient** and **real-time** are related as are **entertaining** and **professional**.

We find, perhaps surprisingly, that computers have clustered most strongly with videotapes. This is because the person from whom PEGASUS elicited the constructs sees both as **modern, dynamic, own-time, lasting,** and **another directs**. The key difference is that computers are **random-access** whereas videotapes are **sequential**. There is also a link to videogames because both are **modern, dynamic, personal, two-way** and **professional**. The differences in this case are that computers are **random-access, own-time, lasting** and **another directs** whereas videogames are **sequential, transient, real-time,** and **performer directs**.

This in one person's view of the relationship between different media. Our views and your view will probably differ from this. Only by attempting to express them and clarify them however are we ever going to be able to identify the roles of computers in our lives and our society.

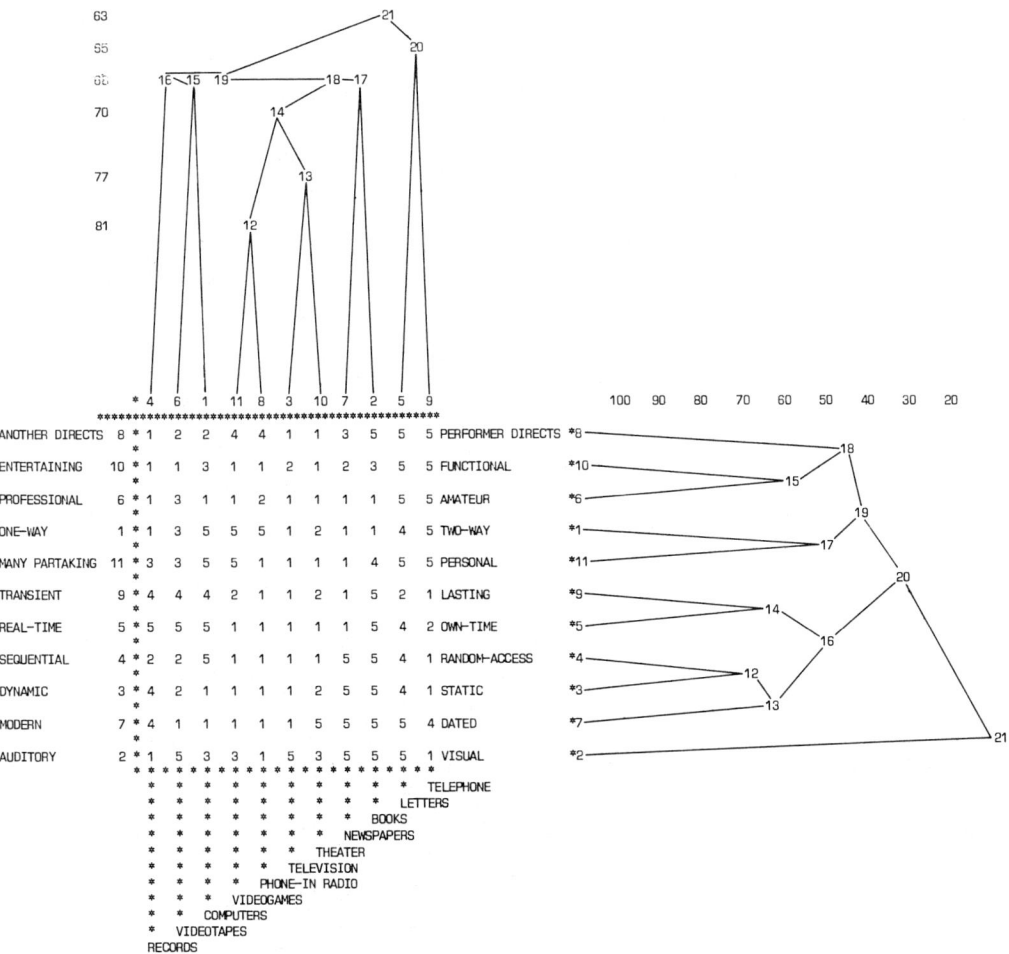

Analysis of one person's view of relations between different media

What we still cannot do

We may have given the impression in this book that the problems of computer conversation are solved or on the way to solution. This is not so. We are in the foothills of a new technology and have many a steep climb before we can even see the size of the peak before us. There are many glimpses of what lies ahead that tantalize and encourage us but the real endeavors are yet to come. We cannot program what we do not understand. To program conversation with computers that emulates the depth and richness of conversation between people we have to understand people and their interaction. We are a long way from having any such understanding. When, and if, we achieve it there will be many implications for us let alone our relations with computers.

A demonstration of our lack of capabilities is in automatic translation from one language to another. We do have poor systems that can take prose in the physical sciences and transliterate it to the equivalent terms in another language. It makes for poor, but understandable, reading. Think of what is involved in the translation of literature or poetry and you will see the nature of the problem. Yet if we do not understand our language well enough to be able to specify how it should be translated what do we understand? Very little.

A simpler example is given in the constructed dialog opposite. A manager is using a database in natural language. The Ask system demonstrates that the natural language processing required for this example has been achieved. Yet there are features of this dialog that no current database system can implement. The answer "either sales or distribution" is an awkward one because the record structure will only allow for one value in this field. The "don't know" answer will probably have to be encoded as "no" although this is misleading. The time variation in the salary will cause further problems because no provision is made for values that automatically change at a future date.

However, the worst problems are with the answers "fairly young" and the concept of a room being "very full." Human language copes with the fuzziness of everyday information and expresses it through such terms. Database systems cannot do this and require an artificial precision which makes much human conversation and reasoning incomprehensible. It does help to know someone is "fairly young" if we are retrieving records of staff of pensionable age. At the University of California at Berkeley Lotfi Zadeh has developed **fuzzy reasoning** for computers that can cope with such data. It is one example of the many developments necessary if computers are to converse fully with us.

We have a new employee starting tomorrow
  Name?
Peter Grimes
  Will he work in your division?
Yes
  What section?
Either Sales or Distribution
  Age?
Fairly young
  Own car?
Don't know
  Salary?
15,000 for the first 3 months and then 17,500
  Location?
Is 408 very full
  Yes
What else have we got?
  319 has room for one more
OK
  I will order a desk and chair
How is my staffing now?
  You have one vacancy in product planning
Productivity norms?
  OK except for L division down 15 %
Suppose I move Jane from L to G
  All OK
No, that would be a demotion. Note demotions are not allowed
  You cannot move Jane

Some constructed dialog to show problems of uncertainty and fuzziness

Conclusions - a final proverb

The computer as a new medium for conversation is still very much in its infancy. Today's personal computers have neither the picture and sound generation capabilities nor the data storage to emulate the presentation possible with television. However, the personal computer today has greater speed, processing power and storage than the vast research machines of ten years ago and has become small enough, cheap enough and reliable enough to take its place in the home. The giant computer technologies of today are at the heart of the movie industry producing sounds and images that are as realistic as those of everyday life. It is not unreasonable to suppose that those capabilities will become available in personal computers during the next ten years.

A more severe limitation on the use of the computer to record models of active processes is our lack of understanding of them. We may know enough about a chemical system to write a program which faithfully reproduces all of its behavior that we have observed. However, will my program produce behavior which we have never observed when you interact with it in ways that we have never even contemplated? If the process which we wish to record is the conversational capability of another person then the uncertainties are even more severe. If we restrict our model of you to a specific role, say you as an expert in a certain activity, then we may be able to elicit from you the rules underlying your current expertise in whatever areas we explore. However, how can we be sure that a new situation will not evoke in you expert behavior of which you were previously unaware and which we did not explore? The answer to these questions is that we can never be sure.

All new media have had initial limitations and gone through phases of improvement and development. The wax cylinder phonograph could not sustain the record industry of today and neither could Baird's spinning disk support television as we now know it. The personal computers of today already provide an impressive new conversational medium for entertainment, education and business. The medium is already adequate for many significant applications and we need to understand how to use it as it is now, how to take into account its current limitations, and how to take advantages of improvements in the medium as they occur.

The proverbs throughout this book have enabled us to attempt to encapsulate the main messages in short and hopefully memorable form. Our final conclusion is our final message and our final proverb.

The thirtieth proverb - TECHNOLOGICAL CHANGE

The pace of change of computer technology presents a major problem for system developers and users. We have a new medium. We do not fully understand it. We do not yet have a feeling for how much more we need to understand. Will the accelerating pace of change ever stop? Should we wait until tomorrow before making decisions? Are we at the stage of the wax cylinder phonograph, the silent movie, or are we already into the more stable era of the LP disk and technicolor? Are any modern media stable? Digital records and videodisks are already here. They are also convergent with other computer-based technologies. Is there a new integrated information system just around the corner?

Whatever the answers to these questions, one thing is for sure. If we wait for the stability of tomorrow we will wait forever. Computer systems will be cheaper and more powerful and we will understand better how to use them. But they are already cheap enough, powerful enough and comprehensible enough to be used now.

Proverb 30: Make the best use of today's technology today and tomorrow's tomorrow.

Do not wait for the pace of change in computer technology to slow down. It will not. Do not assume that what is an appropriate use of today's technology will be appropriate for that of tomorrow. It may not.

With this proverb we end the book. In the last few months of 1983, as we have completed this book, major manufacturers of operating systems for personal computers have announced new products that will make some of the more futuristic examples in this book commonplace by the end of 1984. A window system with icons and a mouse has been demonstrated by Apple Computer for its Apple //e. A window system has been announced by Microsoft which runs under MS-DOS, the main operating system for the IBM PC. Texas Instruments is offering a simple natural language system based on menu selection of words and phrases for its personal computers. There is intense competition between manufacturers to offer new facilities which improve the person-computer interface. For users this has the advantage that system facilities are being improved under market pressures, but it also creates the usual problem of rapid obsolescence.

However, these advances are only the start of an even more intense era of change that began in the computer industry with the Japanese initiative in fifth generation computing. There had already been a massive swing in the industry towards research on human factors in computer use, and this has gone even further as the emphasis on ease-of-use in fifth generation systems has been noted.   The second half of the 1980s will be an era of new products that are increasingly knowledge-based, using developments of expert systems techniques.   There are already efforts to develop expert system products not only for industrial and business markets but also for consumer markets.

We will not fall into the trap of attempting to predict what new products will appear in 1984, let alone later years.   All predictions about the computer industry seem foolish within a short space of time because events happen sooner than predicted. This is an industry that has only just begun to take off and many radical changes will occur in the next few years.   Computers are now getting out of the hands of computer specialists and becoming tools for everyone to use to enhance their own activities.   The limits on computer applications are decreasingly those of the technology and increasingly those of our own creative imaginations.   What we dare to dream is what is possible, if not this year, then next or the year afterwards.

We dare to dream that the computer industry, in its rush to scale new peaks, will also find time to place solid foundations under what it has already achieved.   We dare to dream that it will become possible to buy a computer in a box; take it to the home or office, unpack it and plug it in; and that it will operate fully immediately; without our having to adjust minute switches in the printer, set up programs with information about our configuration, format disks, replace half the pages in the manual with new ones, and so on.

We dare to dream that every computer will have a telephone jack and an electronic mail package that will put it, and us, in touch with a wide range of services; including the manufacturer's service department, software support, suppliers of software, user groups, and information services on all the many services now available nation-wide and throughout the world.

We dare to dream that the growing use of personal computers and computer networks will create new communities within the world, crossing old barriers and generating a new sense of community. Each new medium has been created to meet the needs of one world, and in meeting them has created a new world. We all have visions of what that new world should be like.   One message of this book is that increasingly we all have the opportunity to influence its development through our access to computer and communications technology and, through them, to other people.

Further Reading

CHAPTER 1   PERSONAL COMPUTER CONVERSATION

Nilles, J. M. **Exploring the World of the Personal Computer.**
    New Jersey: Prentice Hall, 1982. An informative and
    thoughtful introduction to personal computers, what they are
    and what they are doing.

Pask, G. & Curran, S. **Microman.** London: Century Publishing,
    1982. A more way-out introduction to computers and the way
    they are shaping our lives. Full of facts and colored
    photographs, speculation and fantasy.

CHAPTER 2   CONVERSATION THROUGH COMPUTER MEDIA

De Fleur, M. L. and Ball-Rokeach, S. **Theories of Mass
    Communication.** New York: Longman, 1982. A basic text on
    media with a section on the role of computers.

Hills, P. (Ed.) **The Future of the Printed Word.** London: Frances
    Pinter, 1980. Essays on new electronic media replacing the
    printed word.

Schwartz, B. N. (Ed.) **Human Connection and the New Media.** New
    Jersey: Prentice Hall, 1973. A collection of essays
    examining the effect of electronic media on our society.

Wicklein, J. **Electronic Nightmare: The Home Communications Set
    and Your Freedom.** Boston: Beacon Press, 1982. Discussion of
    some of the problems that electronic media may create.

Michie, D. (Ed.) **Expert Systems in the Micro Electronic Age.**
Edinburgh: University Press, 1979. A collection of survey
and technical papers on expert systems.

Davis, R. & Lenat, D. B. **Knowledge-Based Systems in Artificial
Intelligence.** New York: McGraw-Hill, 1982. Contains
technical details of AM, MYCIN and TEIRESIAS.

CHAPTER 3   USER EXPECTATIONS IN COMPUTER CONVERSATION

Mowshowitz, A. **Inside Information: Computers in Fiction.**
Massachusetts: Addison-Wesley, 1977. The role of computers
in our society as expressed through fiction is classified and
clarified. It is illustrated through a wealth of lengthy
quotations from the works of major science fiction authors.

Asimov, I. **I, Robot.** London: Dobson Books, 1967. The Three
Laws of Robotics are quoted from the **Handbook of Robotics,**
56th Edition, 2058 A.D., and followed by a number of short,
connected stories that capture Asimov's views of the problems
of people-robot society.

Capek, K. **R.U.R.** London: Oxford University Press, 1923.
Selver's translation of Capek's play about Rossum's Universal
Robots. The rich sarcasm about the de-humanizing objectives
of totalitarian regimes at one level leads to some deep
insights into person-computer relationships at another.

Colby, K. M. **Artificial Paranoia: A Computer Simulation of
Paranoid Processes.** New York: Pergamon Press, 1975. The
generation of dialog designed to simulate insanity.

CHAPTER 4   FORMAL COMPUTER CONVERSATION

Shneiderman, B. **Software Psychology: Human Factors in Computer
and Information Systems.** Massachusetts: Winthrop, 1980. A
professional survey of human factors in software including
person-computer interaction.

Kidd, A. L. **Man-machine Dialogue Design.** Ipswich: Martlesham
Consultancy Services, 1982. A crisp exposition of the rules
of dialog engineering in a booklet published by British
Telecommunications.

CHAPTER 5 COMPUTER CONVERSATION THROUGH MENUS AND FORMS

Mehlmann, M. **When People Use Computers: An Approach to Developing an Interface.** New Jersey: Prentice Hall, 1981. A useful guide to developing good person-computer dialog.

Gilb, T. & Weinberg, G. M. **Humanized Input: Techniques for Reliable Keyed Input.** Massachusetts: Winthrop, 1977. A guide to techniques for ensuring correct data input from data-processing equipment operators.

CHAPTER 6 GRAPHIC COMPUTER CONVERSATION

Smith, D. C. **Pygmalion: A Computer Program to Model and Stimulate Creative Thought.** Basel: Birkhauser, 1977. The design considerations behind windows and icons.

Goldberg, A. & Robson, D. **Smalltalk-80: The Language and its Implementation.** Massachusetts: Addison-Wesley, 1983. An account of the Xerox development of an object-orientated language with interaction through windows and icons.

CHAPTER 7 NATURAL LANGUAGE CONVERSATION WITH COMPUTERS

Moto-oka, T. (Ed.) **Fifth Generation Computer Systems.** Amsterdam: North Holland, 1982. A definitive statement of the Japanese fifth generation computer development program with much emphasis on human factors and social impact.

Weizenbaum, J. **Computer Power and Human Reason: From Judgement to Calculation.** San Francisco: W. H. Freeman, 1976. The story of ELIZA by its developer together with his views on the, possibly adverse, effects of computers on our society.

Shaw, M. L. G. **On Becoming a Personal Scientist: Interactive Computer Elicitation of Personal Models of the World.** London: Academic Press, 1980. Contains an explanation of the PEGASUS and FOCUS programs.

Schank, R. C. & Colby, K. M. (Eds.) **Computer Models of Thought and Language.** San Francisco: Freeman, 1973. A useful collection of papers on artificial intelligence relating to person-computer interaction; contains an explanation of SHRDLU by Winograd.

CHAPTER 8   PRESENTING COMPUTER CONVERSATION

Zaneski, R. **Software Manual Production Simplified.** New York: Petrocelli, 1982. A practical guide to writing manuals.

CHAPTER 10   THE FUTURE OF COMPUTER CONVERSATION

Evans, C. **The Micro Millenium.** New York: Viking Press, 1980. A visionary look at the future of computers and their impact on our society.

Dertouzos, M. L. & Moses, J. **The Computer Age: A Twenty-Year View.** Massachusetts: MIT Press, 1979. A very readable collection of discussions on the future of computers and their impact on society by eminent computer scientists.

Weil, U. **Information Systems in the 80's: Products, Markets and Vendors.** New Jersey: Prentice Hall, 1982. A survey of the coming trends in the computer industry including personal computing.

Glossbrenner, A. **The Complete Handbook of Personal Computer Communications.** New York: St Martin's Press, 1983. A very practical and readable guide to the many computer database, mail and bulletin board services now available.

Martin, J. **The Wired Society: A Challenge for Tomorrow.** New Jersey: Prentice Hall, 1978. A discussion of the various roles that computer-based communication systems can play in our society.

Winsbury, R. (Ed.) **Viewdata in Action: A Comparative Study of Prestel.** London: McGraw-Hill, 1981. Reports of the UK experience in offering computer-based public information services.

Godfrey, D. & Chang, E. (Eds.) **The TELIDON Book.** Toronto: Press Porcepic, 1981. Reports of the Canadian development of a computer-based public information service.

Badre, A. & Shneiderman, B. (Eds.) **Directions in Human/Computer Interaction.** New Jersey: Ablex, 1982. A collection of state-of-the-art papers on person-computer interaction.

Sime, M. & Coombs, M. J. (Eds.) **Designing for Human-Computer Communication.** London: Academic Press, 1983. A collection of state-of-the-art papers on person-computer interaction.

Index